# LIFE, LITERATURE, AND LINCOLN
## *A Tom Landess Reader*

# LIFE, LITERATURE, AND LINCOLN

*A Tom Landess Reader*

Chronicles Press
Rockford, Illinois
2015

*Special thanks are due to Dr. Thomas Fleming for making this publication possible, to Scott P. Richert for service way above and beyond the call of duty in seeing it through to press, to Aaron D. Wolf for an inspired cover, to Linda Moore for transcription of diverse and sometimes difficult materials, and to Kate D. Landess for help and encouragement. Also to Dr. William F. Campbell of The Philadelphia Society and Jed Donahue of the Intercollegiate Studies Institute for leading us to rare material.*
~ Clyde N. Wilson

*Professor Wilson searched far and wide—for long-defunct journals; through stacks of sometimes moldy, dusty, and coffee-stained manuscripts; and, on the internet, following trails of hints to the location of the treasure—to gather the selections for this book. He then did, as always, a superb job of putting it all together just right. Thank you for an arduous job beautifully, thoughtfully, and most kindly done for your late, dear friend.*
~ Mary Beth Landess

The following material appears courtesy of J.S. Sanders, a member of the Rowman & Littlefield Publishing Group (all rights reserved):

"The Introduction" to Caroline Gordon's *Green Centuries* (pp. 157-63)
"The Introduction" to Allen Tate's *Stonewall Jackson* (pp. 165-72)
"The Introduction" to Madison Jones's *The Innocent* (pp. 189-95)

"A Note on the Origin of Southern Ways" (pp. 15-25) first appeared in *Why the South Will Survive* (© The University of Georgia Press, 1981)

ISBN  978-1-943218-00-4

# CONTENTS

## LINCOLN

# LIFE, LITERATURE, AND LINCOLN
## *A Tom Landess Reader*

# Foreword

*Clyde Wilson*

Thomas H. Landess (1931-2012) was a consummate man of letters, something that is increasingly rare on both sides of the Atlantic. He had something interesting and valuable to say on many subjects and could say it well. He easily mastered multiple genres, both scholarly and popular—literary criticism, historical and cultural essays, high-end journalism, public lectures and speeches, and short fiction.

Another Southern man of letters, Thomas Nelson Page, once wrote that the main motive of a writer, besides making a living, was vanity—the desire to see one's name and words in print. If that is true, Tom Landess was the exception. He seemed to practice the craft of writing mostly to oblige friends and to forward good causes. He enjoyed the craft itself without any desire for personal glory. He used to say that he was the author of many books, a few of which were published under his own name.

Not only did he ghostwrite numerous books, perhaps most notably the memoirs of the Rev. Mr. Ralph David Abernathy, as well as speeches and statements for public officials, but for years he wrote anonymously and pseudonymously much of the content of the *Southern Partisan*. He engaged in that little-rewarded labor in the failed hope of establishing a true forum for the contemporary South. His writings are scattered, many of them occasional. Unlike most writers, Tom Landess did not save copies of his published work. On several occasions, after giving standing-ovation lectures (and his lectures usually received standing ovations), he discarded the notes even before heading for home. We have painfully reconstructed a few examples from surviving recordings.

To make this selection, then, has not been an easy task, but it has been done as assiduously as possible as a labor of love. We have included what we considered his most important pieces out of hundreds. Some of them have not been published before, and others, like his study of Lincoln's courtship rhetoric, were published more obscurely than their importance deserves. We may well have missed some good things, and we have omitted his work on Eudora Welty and Larry McMurtry, which is fairly accessible. We present only a few examples of his political commentary, prolific over many years.

Tom had a considerable gift for the short story also, as will be seen in a companion volume to come.

THE MERE FACTS OF TOM'S BIOGRAPHY do not account for his importance. As one eulogist wrote, he was "an unsung hero." Among other things, Tom Landess was one of the last surviving students of the Vanderbilt Fugitive-Agrarians and knew most of them quite well. Landess was Andrew Lytle's choice to succeed him as editor of *The Sewanee Review*, although academic politics yielded another choice. He wrote about the Agrarians perceptively and intimately and in ways nowhere else recorded.

Tom was the colleague, collaborator, and close friend of M.E. Bradford, whose importance in intellectual history grows more apparent with each passing year. They worked together on an unpublished book on Abraham Lincoln's rhetoric. Some of Tom's contributions to that work are included here, as well as his account of the Bradford/NEH debacle at the beginning of the Reagan administration, in which he was a firsthand participant. His account of that event is here for the permanent historical record.

Delightful flashes of humor pop up quite often in Landess's writings, as when he expresses surprise that Allen Tate was not set upon and murdered by the Boy Scouts for his disdain of FDR's Four Freedoms. Or when he remarks that a certain politician was "up to his chin in shallow water," and that a certain scholar's theory could not withstand the huff and puff of the Big Bad Wolf. Yet his pointing to the errors or misbehavior of others is usually gentle, as if to recognize that we are all sinners and are not entitled to judge others too harshly. That was a reflection of Tom's character and is undoubtedly why the extraordinary outpouring of statements from many different quarters at his passing frequently contained the term "gentleman." In other words, Tom Landess's writings reflect a mature Christian viewpoint of faith, hope, and charity. We are instructed to turn the other cheek to our assailants, but, as Tom wrote in his reply to the vile slanderers of Bradford, when our friend is the one struck in the face, it is a different matter.

Bradford once had occasion to describe the work of his friend Landess. He pointed to the remarkable variety of interests and expertise shown and suggested that the unifying theme is a critique of "abstractionist thinking." That is the implicit purpose, whether Landess is evaluating the work of an author or a critic, telling stories of the true effect of World War II on real people, or identifying the flesh-and-blood Lincoln as opposed to the imagined one. Landess's work is Southern and Christian. For him, and many others, the South was something concrete, while "American," as usually invoked in public discourse, is an abstraction. And as a Christian he was constantly aware that we live in a real universe with a divine Creator, Whom we presumptuously disregard at our peril. "Like God," he writes, "abstract truth is best understood when incarnate."

**IT IS A REAL PLEASURE** to be able to make available this selection from the pen of this outstanding man of letters in the old and true sense of the term. Many Southern writers of the past deserve that complimentary label, but Tom Landess was one of the last.

# LIFE

# A Note on the Origin of Southern Ways

A s Southerners we are so used to certain slanders that we no longer even bother to answer them. They are like old bruises turned yellow: The pain is so slight now and so familiar that it is almost a pleasure. Some of us still grow angry and write letters to the TV networks, but most of us smile and nod our heads, not so much in agreement with the charges as in acknowledgment that we are still listening. I think it is good of us not to have organized a Southern Anti-Defamation League. Such restraint is a testimony to our manners in an era of radical rudeness.

But there are some slanders that need answering in order to isolate our true vices as well as to affirm our virtues. No need to waste time curing sins of which we are not guilty; better to address ourselves to the real ones, which, God knows, are sometimes almost as bad as the Yankees tell us.

One of our faults, according to the Solemn Remonstrance of the Northern Elect, is a tendency to be "puritanical"; and whenever the question is raised of our religious life, the word *puritan* is likely to be used. In one sense only the charge is true. An elderly relative of mine was fond of saying that she did not go to church because there were too many sinners in attendance there. When we ventured to suggest that no one was guiltless, *she* became indignant. She, it seems, was no sinner, at least not according to her creed. After all, there were only three sins: smoking, drinking, and that other one, which she could neither name nor discuss without turning a deep shade of red. She had never committed the first two, and the third, which she had once been forced into as the result of a brief marriage, was 40 years behind her and had been no sin after all because she had never taken the slightest pleasure in it.

This kind of puritanism is still to be found in our region as part of the evangelical bent of the Southern church. But such an attitude is not solely characteristic of American puritanism; one finds it as a strong element in Ulster Scotch Presbyterianism, in Irish Catholicism, and in other world religions, non-Christian as well as Christian. Besides, even if this Southern tendency is an inheritance of the Pilgrim Fathers—and I seriously doubt such a theory—it is still no more than a doctrine wrenched away from the larger body of Puritan philosophy.

But Southern religion is considerably more complicated than our critics would like us to believe, and its essential nature cannot be dismissed by any phrase or sentence or paragraph. What that nature is I would not presume to say, but its importance to the way in which Southerners have behaved over the past 200 years of the Republic cannot be overemphasized. Indeed, I would suggest that what is regarded as quintessentially Southern grows in large measure out of a certain kind of regional orthodoxy which, in modern America, is a rare phenomenon, if not without parallel.

OUT OF A BELIEF IN RELIGIOUS PLURALISM most American Christians have been too prone to underestimate the importance of orthodoxy, too ready to dismiss heresy as harmless or irrelevant, as something which should be tolerated with casual good humor. For this reason Trinitarian heresies abound in modern America. An exclusive emphasis on God the Father— that is, on the Mind of God—has led one segment of modern Christendom to emphasize thought and discourse to the neglect of ethics and feeling. Such people tend to believe that when you've explained a problem intellectually you've solved it. And when the world fails to behave according to abstract precept, they either ignore such realities or else rationalize them with end-less revisions which further complicate the problem. Surely the Puritans and their spiritual heirs fall into this category.

An excessive focus on God the Son leads men off into another kind of heresy, one that places an undue stress on action apart from thought or feel-ing. The Second Person of the Trinity reveals God Incarnate acting out in history what the Father would be if He were us. Too exclusive a preoccu-pation with this aspect of God's nature leads men to say, "Give your life to Jesus. Never mind who He is." Or else, the results can be a benevolent ded-ication to destructive causes or a cold and efficient commitment to works of genuine charity.

An exclusive concern with God the Holy Spirit results often enough in an excessive emphasis on the emotional aspect of religious life and has led to revivalism, quasimysticism, and some of the more exotic forms of corpo-rate worship, which have no significant theological content and fail to alter the existence of those who participate in them, except, perhaps, to infect them with a twinge of sadness and frustration that such experiences cannot be sustained daily, hourly, in their ordinary lives.

Most aberrations in contemporary Christian thought and behavior grow out of one of these Trinitarian heresies, and as a nation we abound with them. In contrast to the rest of the country, however, Southerners have always been more Trinitarian in their religious outlook, which is to say they have been more orthodox. I am not suggesting that the South is a paradigm of modern Christendom. Our deepest thinkers have always been disturbed by our pluralism, which at best has been ineffectual and at worst divisive. The failure of the region to produce a single outstanding theologian, while boasting any number of literary artists and political thinkers, should give us some pause. Yet it would be erroneous to say that Southerners have no concern for theology or that they are less religious because they have produced no St. Thomas Aquinas.

We still retain enough of our emphasis on God the Father to unite in common cause against Modernism. More than any other Americans, we are suspicious of heterodoxy. If our theology is sparse and simplistic, it is by no means heretical. For example, Southern Baptists more than any other denomination in the country expect their clergy and laymen to affirm the ultimate truth of the gospels, including the historicity of the important miracles. There are times today when one suspects that no one on Manhattan believes in the Virgin Birth or understands the genuine importance of such a belief. If a Southern Baptist preacher has any doubts on the subject, he had best keep them to himself. And the same is true to some degree of clergymen from other denominations: It was a Southerner a few years ago who formally brought charges against fellow Episcopal Bishop James Pike.

Of course no one will deny a concern with the Holy Spirit in Southern evangelical churches. If sophisticated Christian congregations in the East and Midwest are rediscovering the importance of feeling in their corporate worship, Southerners have been aware of this dimension from the beginning and have never quite forgotten it. The tent-house evangelist has been both the scandal and the glory of Southern Protestantism from the beginning of regional self-consciousness. The so-called charismatic movement may well be novel and exotic to the congregations of Manhattan; it is ancient history to Tupelo, Mississippi, and Milledgeville, Georgia.

As for God the Son, He is continually stressed not only in the reaffirmation of the miracles of His Birth and Resurrection, but also in a Southern tendency to believe in His Personhood and to use His Name frequently in everyday conversations. Preachers speak of Him as if He were a close friend, someone known to every member of the congregation as the incarnation of the way they all should behave and never quite do.

Because of this familiar Presence (at times too easily familiar), Southerners have always paid some corporate attention to ethics, exemplary behavior as a mode of serving and worshiping God. Perhaps the best example of such an attitude is to be found in Robert E. Lee's famous statement, "Duty is the sublimest word in the English language." Such a sentiment is typical of low-church Episcopalianism as practiced in the Virginia of his time, and Lee himself, though the South's most paradigmatic 19th-century figure, was by no means exceptional in his religious attitudes. His sentiments are echoed in the letters of countless ordinary citizens as well as in those of public figures and are by no means narrowly sectarian.

Thus, a "good Christian" is someone who behaves well, and the phrase is still more likely to be used in the South than elsewhere in the nation. Indeed the attention to personal conduct that characterizes the South has considerably strengthened communal feeling over the years, though in ways that make many people uncomfortable. Typically, one is always under scrutiny in Southern towns and cities. Virtue is measured in terms of objective behavior as well as in properly orthodox sentiment, and vice is noted as well, though not in the same way that it was noted in 17th-century Salem. God the Son, after all, does not persecute witches.

This strong sense of the Second Person of the Trinity is the most important characteristic of the South's religious outlook. What, then, have been the political and cultural consequences of this religious attitude? In order to answer this question we might profitably examine those aspects of Southern life which are most characteristically Southern, the things about us that are both the pride and despair of our regional identity. Among these would surely be our identification with the land, our politics, and our literature.

SOUTHERNERS HAVE A SENSE OF PLACE in a way that sets them apart from other Americans. New Englanders, Easterners, even Midwesterners have always believed in abstract America, the land of the free and the home of the brave, with liberty and justice for all. Southerners have been more inclined to love her rocks and rills, her woods and templed hills, and more accurately, certain rocks and woods, the ones they see and move among and know are real. Abstractions, however pretty, are to most Southerners no more than vague and inaccurate rumors of the truth, a questionable report on the nature of God the Father.

As initial evidence of this difference I would offer the perennial reluctance of people in the South to celebrate the signing of the Declaration of Independence, a holiday which until fairly recent times has been characterized elsewhere in the nation by picnic oratory and editorial bombast. On the Fourth of July Southerners have tended to lie around and eat, or in a few urban areas to fire off a few rockets and Roman candles. It is unlikely that many of them believe in the sentiments expressed in the Declaration of Independence, not so much because they still harbor good feelings about slavery, but because they don't see any evidence of men being equal in the flesh-and-blood world.

Yes, it would be nice if they were, but they aren't. And yes, we ought to do what we can to make sure that less fortunate folks can have a better chance in life; but can such goals really be attained through changes in language? Better to pass the hat or gather a group of the church ladies or even—and here the ice gets pretty thin—give to the United Fund. Yankees, on the other hand, too often believe that all political and social ills can be cured by an amendment to the United States Constitution or a ruling by the Supreme Court. For Southerners, social justice is neither so easy nor so impersonal. At best it is something to be sought as a sense of duty in a world of imperfect people.

For this reason Southern elections are likely to be run less on issues and more on *ad hominem* arguments. For Southerners know that *argumentum ad hominem* is never a logical fallacy in an election campaign and that no one can be held strictly accountable for his campaign rhetoric, only for his character. Thus they will elect a man whose oratory is an embarrassment to them and whose intelligence seems questionable, provided they know him to be a man of personal integrity. For they still tend to regard politics as something to be carried on among people who know one another, however foolish such an idea may be in a nation of over 200 million people. It is God the Son who represents the family in the councils of the land. God the Father remains at home, brooding over the headlines in His newspaper, which tell of the perennial failures of mankind. He knows in His infinite wisdom that almost nothing can be done, but He sends the Son anyway, as a testimony to His good will and His agreeable nature.

The Son goes to the town council, or the state legislature, or the United States Senate knowing that He will be crucified. He is particularly well versed on crucifixions as the result of the War, which He knows was not Armageddon but one of the many just causes in history that are defeated by superior forces and confused logic.

When He wins a victory He knows that it is only limited and temporary, something the opposition will in time undo or mitigate to some significant degree, not because they are devils but because they are people, and people are finally unregenerate.

When He suffers defeat He may be disappointed, even angry; but what, after all, is one defeat among so many? The Great Victory is always made up of a string of defeats, the more the better. Or so He tells the Father in His letters home, which are preserved in the family album to instruct future generations in the fine art of losing like a gentleman.

When God the Son encounters graft or corruption He is better able to handle it than most. For example, a few years ago when scandal touched the White House, He was less angry with the President of the United States than was the rest of the nation because He expected less from the man in that office, given the true lessons of history. In fact, the Son looked with greater disfavor on the President's accusers, with their smug puritanical faces and their presumption of their own radical innocence. The Son believed in His heart of hearts that the accusers had done worse things than they were attributing to the President, that the President himself had undoubtedly done worse things than these. Far from believing in the President's innocence, the Son believed in the guilt of them all. During this period He, too, would have preferred that the President make a clean breast of it. He approves of public acknowledgments of sin as a means of purging the soul, but He does not believe that media priests in electronic booths are licensed to hear confessions. They are among the many false prophets who no longer even profess His Name when they are carrying on their crusades against social ills. If such people believe in sin at all, they believe in it as ideological transgression, and ideology is a heresy of those who believe only in the Father.

Indeed, Southerners have been relatively immune to the tyranny of ideas in an age characterized by the emergence of one ideology after another. Nazism and communism, the two dominant political schemata of the 20th century, have had some currency in the Northeast and even in the urban areas of the Midwest. In the South the Communist Party had no following, and during the 1930's, when the German American Bund was holding huge rallies in Madison Square Garden, there was not a single active chapter in a Southern state. Not one.

In some measure this reluctance to join the larger movements of the age results from the fact that Southerners do not believe they have to join anything in order to have a sense of belonging, to derive some personal satisfaction from an emotional identification with a larger group of their own kind. They belong, after all, to the family, which has the advantage over "the Folk," or "the Proletariat," or "the Party," in that the family is composed of flesh-and-blood people, whom you know well and who know you and who, because they are so complicated, defy ideological classification.

WHEN THE AGRARIANS WROTE *I'LL TAKE MY STAND* IN 1930, they shared the assumption that the region was an extension of the family and that in a sense everyone could know everyone else through connections and friends of friends. In the past 50 years the South as well as the nation has grown alarmingly in population; yet Southerners still have the feeling that they can meet strangers from other parts of the region and discover who they are in ten minutes of conversation. And during such encounters, even if they don't discover friends or acquaintances in common, they can know a great deal about strangers by recognizing signs that place them within certain branches of the larger family.

In such a world there is an ease, a grace, a comfort that other Americans neither understand nor share. There is a communal spirit that moves in the blood mysteriously, almost providentially to touch the heart and stir the memory. Any old lady in any small Southern town is your grandmother or great-aunt or distant cousin Maude—one of the three for sure.

Of course, such a recognition is not always pleasant and heartwarming; it can be a warning and an anathema. We recognize in one another the sins of the blood as well as the virtues. If we are all proud of our familial triumphs, we are likewise humble in the remembrance of our shared and inherited sins. In being members of the same tribe or clan we share with one another the secret of our own depravity, our certain knowledge of what it was that the Son died to save us from.

This knowledge, as many critics have recognized, is what has made Southern literature over the past 50 years the most significant in recent American history. Our writers have somehow set themselves apart from those of other regions by their capacity to deal with the enormous depravities that man is capable of, those special and imaginative sins that mark us all beyond self-redemption. I don't mean to suggest that Southern writers are exploiters of the sensational in the way that stringers for the *National Enquirer* are. In fact, they are subtle and delicate in their work, the way Mozart would be if he were writing the score for the Charles Manson murders.

They simply know where the soul really lives, the depths to which it sinks in self-revelry. Allen Tate has pointed out the irony inherent in the fact that Eastern critics once scoffed at William Faulkner's "A Rose for Emily" as utterly beyond credulity. Who could believe that an aged woman would sleep with the corpse of her dead lover for the last years of her life? Then, after the story's publication, authorities discovered just such a case—not in Mississippi, but in New York City. In fact, no such thing had ever been uncovered in Faulkner's home town of Oxford; but he had guessed at the potential depravity in the proud spurned hearts of old ladies. And both Tate and Faulkner have written subtly and movingly about lynchings, a sin which Eastern writers would like to view as somehow beyond the pale of their own community, despite the fact that more blacks were murdered by New York mobs in a few hours than were lynched in the entire history of most Southern states.

But Southern writers have placed the blame where it belongs, on the home folks—not because these writers hate their region, but because they understand its humanity, the innate wickedness which it shares with every other place on the planet Earth. In one sense the power of Southern fiction lies in the very fact that it is not about the South but merely takes place there. Thus it has a fine particularity that gives flesh and bone to its universal soul. In that respect it is analogous to the created order itself. We delight in its accidental variety and are spiritually moved by its substantial revelation of the Divine. As it is with great literature, so it is with people. Understanding this truth, who would believe that Faulkner in his greatest work is saying anything of importance about Mississippi or the South that he isn't saying about Philadelphia and the East? Just as in "A Rose for Emily" he is not merely rendering the pride and madness of certain old ladies, but ours as well. We all sleep with the corpses of our dead lovers. Faulkner knew that about us before he ever began to concoct his tale of horror.

TO BOIL THE MATTER DOWN TO AN ESSENTIAL PROPOSITION, the best of Southern literature is characterized by its ontological orthodoxy. For the most part Southern writers believe somehow, some way, in the Incarnation and in all that such a miraculous event implies. The flesh—the concrete particulars of time and place—are therefore important, good, and hence sacred. That's why few Southern stories of lynchings occur at no time and in no place, as in the case of "The Lottery" by Shirley Jackson, the rendition of an action which could not have occurred in Mississippi. In that story, as you may recall, without anyone really knowing why, members of a village conduct an annual lottery in order to choose one among them to be stoned to death by the rest. In the final scene a woman is duly chosen, whereupon those of her own family, including her small child, with relative unconcern join the rest in the ritual execution.

But, as I said, none of this occurs in Mississippi. In the first place, if such a practice were to persist in, say, Yazoo City, any number of old maid aunts would be able to tell you *precisely* why it was done. Their facts might be in error, but they would have an explanation. And in the second place, no one in that part of the country would participate in organized cruelties that cut so easily across family lines. Other kinds of cruelties might be (indeed, are) perfectly acceptable in Mississippi; but where the South is still the South, the family remains its most important institution.

As a matter of fact, it is the family that has given Southern writers their true subject matter, for where else do you learn about the remarkable virtuosity of sin except from your own flesh and blood? Such conduct as Miss Emily's, were it to occur in Mississippi (and, come to think of it, maybe it did), would be a family scandal, to be hidden at all costs from the eyes of outsiders and then whispered about at reunions for the next hundred years. Sooner or later such tales find their way into print, with names and addresses altered in order to protect the writer from the wrath of his kinsmen, who, despite his protests, never quite trust his loyalty again.

Yet, what else is he to do? He must write about the things he knows, and what he knows best is the family, which includes the distant as well as the near, the dead as well as the living. When he writes, he is involved in a communal act, for all the aunts and cousins who accuse him of treason have been his accomplices in repeating the old gossip—and they know it, which is why they are so hard on him. Perhaps in response to their disapproving stares William Faulkner once said: "If a writer has to rob his mother, he will not hesitate; 'Ode on a Grecian Urn' is worth any number of old ladies."

Of course he didn't really mean it: With a few exceptions old ladies come off well in his fiction. But something of his attitude is essential to the good poet or novelist: He must be willing to tell all, whatever the costs to his region, his public preoccupations, his personal pride.

And Southern writers tell all because, with their familial consciousness, they know all and know it so well that they do not easily fall victim to ideological distortion. For example, the family never completely exonerates its errant members just because they are economically deprived. To do so would be to remove from all the kinship their dignity as free human beings and creatures of God. But neither is the sinner cast out completely. Rather, he is claimed the way the executed black is claimed at the end of *Go Down, Moses*, not because he is redeemably good but because he is redeemably bad and in some way an extension of the family itself, a little bit of every member, black and white, executed in some impersonal Northern death house as partial atonement for us all.

And Allen Tate, at the end of his poem "The Swimmers," also claims for the community the dead black who has been lynched by local night-riders, claims him not only as a victim of corporate malice but as kinsman to every man, black or white, who suffers the pain and indignity of being human.

Indeed, the tendency to *claim kinship* is primarily what distinguishes Southern poetry and fiction from the more ideological strains of modern literature. Shirley Jackson, Theodore Dreiser, Sinclair Lewis, and others tend to *disclaim* some or most of their characters, to define themselves (and by implication their readers) as different, superior, "saved" in some limited secular sense from the aberrations of the aliens who inhabit their fictional world like pasteboard demons. On the other hand, Southern writers have claimed for themselves, their families, and their region the largest household of flesh-and-blood monsters in all of modern literature: idiots, rapists, murderers, sodomites, fanatics, sadists, hypocrites, lynchers, child molesters, maimers, necrophiliacs—virtually every human depravity known to the police dockets or to Krafft-Ebing. And they're all ours, they invariably suggest, and more to the point, *they are all us.*

The source of such familial recognition is surely the Christocentric vision of the world, imperfect, ill understood, but something still vaguely akin to Christianity. For though Southern writers are often theologically confused or ostensibly heterodox, or even skeptical, they all seem bound together by a kind of "orthodoxy of the blood" which makes them less susceptible to the temptation of falsifying the fallen world. It is not, after all, a mere abstraction to talk about the brotherhood of man under the Fatherhood of God if you acknowledge in such a statement that there is more than a little of Cain in every brother. Any other meaning is the worst kind of theological or literary sentimentality.

FINALLY, THEN, it is the concrete world with its transcendent implications that Southerners believe in and bear witness to in their daily lives. In politics, in social arrangements, even in their literature there is always the implicit presence of God the Son, both as the crucified Jesus and as Christ the King.

The crucified Jesus is most obvious in the continuing defeats that have beset the region, whether economic, social, or political. We have had a fine instinct for disaster since the days when we believed we could overcome modernity on the field of battle. More than the War itself, Reconstruction taught us the essential lesson of life, the one that everyone eventually learns. But as a community we absorbed that lesson more quickly and thoroughly than the rest of the nation, and when we are not too defensive or greedy, it gives our lives the touch of grace we need in order to endure the perpetual mockery of the Gross National Product, the persistence of hatred, the implacability of nature.

Christ the King, who embodies all we aspire to be as a people, provides us with a better paradigm than the Average American or the Economic Man. Not that we often heed the model. Flannery O'Connor has suggested that no longer can any segment of the nation be termed "Christ-centered," and she was surely correct. But she believed that the South, unlike the rest of the nation, was still "Christ-haunted," and therein lay the capacity of Southerners to recognize the present abnormality of everybody in the world, including themselves. Such a capacity is often enough a curse rather than a blessing. It makes us stupid, improvident, and hopelessly reactionary, a people whose perverse past is so full of contradictions that the rest of the nation cannot abide us without undertaking significant alterations in the nature of our being.

In the past few decades the image of God the Son has diminished to some degree, and God the Father has begun to assert Himself in a new Southern self-consciousness and a new attention to our history and its philosophical implications. Hegel has suggested that when philosophy paints its gray in gray a shape of life has grown old, that at this stage in history it cannot be rejuvenated but only understood. Such may be the case with the continuing dialogue on the meaning of the South. The gray owl of Minerva may indeed have spread its wings at twilight.

But then Hegel did not believe in resurrections, only in the upward spiral of history with progress, the cold immutable God of the universe. On the other hand, we still have some expectation of the grace of God and the descent of the Holy Spirit on our dream of community. To be sure, a few of us believe He will come down from New York, Chicago, and Detroit, His pockets full of money in search of better air and non-unionized labor. But the number of believers in this kind of millennium has been drastically reduced in the past 20 years. Most of us now regard such an advent as the coming of the Angel of Death, and we are beginning to consider what can be done to avoid such a fate.

As for the rest of us, we figure we will get along until that other millennium, the one that occurs beyond time when all our sins will be revealed for what they are—the accidental flaws of mortality which are sloughed off in the resurrection of the body. We believe in that resurrection because we believe in the body itself, not as the ultimate revelation of our existence but as the place where truth begins to have meaning. In that respect we are still peculiarly though not perfectly Christian, which probably makes us unique among Americans. And it is in that uniqueness that we find our patience, our uneasy pride, and our enduring sense of belonging to one another in the mysterious and substantial Body of Christ.

# Approaches to *I'll Take My Stand*

*I'LL TAKE MY STAND*, the so-called Agrarian symposium, is one of those works that people in the academy talk about and write about without ever having read. They can lecture on the subject with world-weary authority until you ask them about particular essays or cite specific passages; then they stop short, and their eyes glaze over—but ever so briefly. It's been years since they read the book, they quickly explain, relegating it to the toy box in the attic. I suspect that if everyone with a Ph.D. were given truth serum and then asked to make a public confession of the books they haven't read, no one would show up at the professional meetings this year.

Thus opinion on *I'll Take My Stand* comes from an oral tradition rooted in ignorance and from a handful of critical studies, most of which are unreliable for one reason or another. Too many are ideologically tainted and either denounce the symposium in simplistic horror or else praise it for the wrong reasons. Among the former I would place *The Burden of Time* by John Lincoln Stewart and *Tillers of a Myth* by Alexander Karanikas. These full-length exposés, published in the 1960's, are no more than long articles of opinion with footnotes to gain academic respectability. Neither author bothers to examine in detail the texts of the 12 essays, choosing instead to "summarize" the positions of the Agrarians and then vigorously to attack that summary. Would that we could all deal with our enemies in such a manner: No battles would ever be lost, no wounds ever sustained. And these Armageddons all funded by university presses like Princeton and Wisconsin.

On the other hand, those who praise the Agrarians can sometimes be almost as misleading. Beware the commentator who tells his readers that *I'll Take My Stand* is no more than "image," "myth," "metaphor," or "pastoral"— a way of talking about some deeper and less explicit truth. I suspect that someone like Louis D. Rubin, Jr., who wrote an excellent Introduction to the paperback reissue, would just as soon avoid being caught in the act of taking the work literally and so claims that what he is offering to his public is best read as "an extended metaphor, of which the image of the agrarian community is the figure, standing for and embodying something else."

This approach is reminiscent of biblical scholars who would want us to believe that there is more to be gained from the Gospels by reading them not as history but as if Jesus were simply a literary trope for the good life. It was terribly important to the Gospel writers and to the faithful that the Resurrection was an event in time and place; it was terribly important to the Agrarians and to their admirers that Southern and American rural life actually existed, that—like Aristotle in his *Politics*—they were describing something they saw rather than, like Plato, defining a Republic that existed *in potentia* or perhaps only in the world of Ideas.

IN HER UNPUBLISHED DISSERTATION Virginia Rock terms *I'll Take My Stand* "utopian," which is another way of saying, as does Rubin, that the Agrarian image of the South is to be taken seriously only as it suggests some larger and hazier abstraction. The original Utopia was no real place where people might hope one day to live. Thomas More invented it to cast light on the failures of his own social order. Subsequent utopias were also imaginary, though some were devised as self-fulfilling prophecies.

The Agrarians were not utopians. For the most part they were not even idealists in the popular sense of that word. Their attitude was a familiar one in Southern history. They admired country life as opposed to city life; and country life in the South in 1930 was no impossible dream, any more than it was in 1705 when Robert Beverley expressed a preference for it in *The History and Present State of Virginia*.

No. If anyone was utopian in 1930, it was the chief opponents of the Agrarians, the apostles of the so-called New South, who dreamed dreams of the future and described a society, as yet uncreated, that was as bright with promise as the Emerald City of Oz. While the Agrarians were willing to stick with what was already in existence, the world of their adversaries was always *in potentia*, just around the corner, over the next hill. Industrialism, capitalism, urbanization would inevitably usher in an era of unparalleled prosperity. And that in turn, of course, would bring happiness to all.

When the Agrarians looked at the future, they were not starry-eyed but apprehensive, even pessimistic. Nothing was inevitable to them. Everything turned on human choice and on God's inscrutable grace. They neither predicted prosperity for a continuing rural society nor looked for unmitigated happiness. The past had produced hard times; so would the future, though things would not be nearly so bad if the spokesmen for industrialism did not have their way. But if they did, said the Agrarians, civilization would go into a decline. The cities would spawn terrible social problems. Traditional religious attitudes would decay. People would lose their good manners. And nature would be desecrated in the process.

Today the liberal grandsons of the New South advocates complain about the exploitation of workers by greedy mill owners, the rise of Republicanism in the region, and the plight of blacks in the urban ghettos. They no longer criticize *I'll Take My Stand*, because they no longer have a strong position from which to launch such an attack. So they are silent on the subject, or else they tell us that the volume was a metaphor. In so doing they obfuscate the obvious truth that what the Agrarians predicted about the urbanization of the South has come to pass, and almost to the last detail.

IN CONTRAST TO THESE CRITICS, therefore, let me offer a different approach to the Agrarian symposium, given the lapse of half a century and the most substantive changes in the nation's relatively brief history. In the first place I would suggest that readers try to understand that *I'll Take My Stand* was only a radically eccentric book within the brief period in which it was written, that in the larger sweep of Southern (and European) history it simply restates an old orthodoxy which would have been immediately recognizable to Virgil, Burke, Jefferson, John Randolph, and John Taylor, to name but a few. The ideology of industrialism, which had its birth in secularized Puritanism and was nurtured in the Gilded Age, has all but run its course in our lifetime. Chambers of commerce throughout the nation still meet to discuss the ways and means of attracting industry to their town, but their options are narrowing. Few people fail to recognize the dangers inherent in such a policy, if pursued without restraint; and all the Agrarians ever advocated was restraint.

This observation leads me to a second point: that *I'll Take My Stand* should be seen as an essentially moderate statement of the older values, despite an occasional immoderate tone that asserts itself in two or three of the individual essays. In this regard, it is necessary to realize that there are certain problems inherent in the structure of the volume, difficulties that have already managed to confound more than one scholar. It is a matter of fact that the Agrarians were not a closely knit group of colleagues who worked out a manifesto in concert, signed it, and then kept a copy on their desks while they wrote their separate contributions. The "Statement of Principles" at the beginning of the book is more like a party platform than the Thirty-Nine Articles of Religion.

Therefore, it simply will not do to read this introductory segment and then close the book; but the "Statement," written by John Crowe Ransom, has a great deal to recommend it. The essays that follow both specify and emphasize not only points that Ransom has stated generally but aspects and implications of rural life that go beyond the preliminary statement, which is precise but general in its approach. In a way the essays are to Ransom's prefatory remarks as flesh-and-blood human beings are to a dictionary definition of humanity. The former by their existence alone justify the latter.

With this reservation in mind, the Introduction may be read with considerable enlightenment as a keynote to the moderate nature of the symposium as a whole. It was, after all, approved *ex post facto* by all the contributors as a statement to which they might subscribe; and its tentative probing of the "metaphysics," "epistemology," and "theology" of the Agrarians should prove interesting to any reader, whether hostile or sympathetic, provided he is not too steeped in Puritan logic.

Properly read, "A Statement of Principles" cannot be labeled as "ideological," "Luddite," or "neo-Confederate." In some ways it is opposed to all of the above in its precise dissection of the complexities of American politics *circa* 1930.

Ransom begins by reaffirming the integrity of each individual essay: "and so no single author is responsible for any view outside his own article. It was through the good fortune of some deeper agreement that the book was expected to achieve its unity." These sentences are important. For one thing, they make the word "Agrarianism" a relatively vague abstraction (only occasionally is it used in the volume). Then, too, Ransom here suggests the contributors' inherent respect for the discreteness of individual experience, while at the same time believing that even without the rational imposition of order, cultural truth will out—naturally and obviously. They may have been mistaken about this point, but their faith must be noted and respected as indicative of the degree to which *I'll Take My Stand* is nonideological. The work is, according to the implications of this passage, the *a posteriori* examination of a way of life, not the *a priori* definition of a paradigm to which the existent world must be corrected.

After explaining the limited function of his "Statement," Ransom makes several additional concessions to the real world that later critics of the symposium often want to ignore, if only because such qualifications block easy refutation of the whole. Ransom writes: "An agrarian society is hardly one that has no use at all for industries, for professional vocations, for scholars and artists, and for the life of cities. Technically, perhaps, an agrarian society is one in which agriculture is the leading vocation."

So much for the charge that the Agrarians were Luddites, that they wanted to return to the past or abolish the technological advantages of the present. Indeed, in the separate essays, these points are made again and again, sometimes explicitly, sometimes implicitly.

As for the Agrarians being nothing more than local apologists or neo-Confederates, Ransom also answers that charge in his "Statement," indeed so specifically and unequivocally that one would have thought he could not be misunderstood:

> Proper living is a matter of intelligence and the will, does not de-
> pend on the local climate or geography, and is capable of a defini-
> tion which is general and not Southern at all. Southerners have
> a filial duty to discharge in their own section. But their cause is
> precarious and they must seek alliances with sympathetic com-
> munities everywhere. The members of the present group would
> be happy to count themselves as members of a national agrarian
> movement.

Again, we must remember that all the essayists subscribed to this initial
statement of principles; so the sentiments expressed therein should be taken
seriously as they shed light on the individual contributions to the symposium. Of course all are not uniformly intelligent or significant, though most
are, from the vantage point of the present, surprisingly moderate in tone.

IN ORDER TO ILLUSTRATE these generalizations I would like to examine
briefly the essays of the four Fugitive-Agrarians, not because they are necessarily the best contributions or even the most suitable to my purposes, but
because they are the ones most frequently subject to commentary by critics
and scholars and hence the most familiar.

Ransom's contribution, "Reconstructed but Unregenerate," is a case in
point. In it he concedes the good intentions of many industrialists, rejects the
idea that the South was ever an aristocracy, and admits that "the old Southern life was of course not so fine as some of the traditionalists like to believe."
He also says that "the South must make contact again with the Union. And
in adapting itself to the actual state of the Union, the Southern tradition will
have to consent to a certain industrialization of its own . . . The South must
be industrialized—but to a certain extent only, in moderation."

A cry for moderation! What could strike the contemporary reader with
greater authority? And yet the critics of the Agrarians were forever saying,
"Moderation in defense of tradition is no virtue; extremism in pursuit of
progress is no vice." In some ways Ransom sounds today like a polite liberal
in a T.V. drama who, seated among his archconservative business associates,
ventures to suggest that they might wish to slow down their irresponsible
development of forests and greenbelts in order to preserve the environment.

If all of this sounds too sensible Ransom closes his essay with a call to
political arms that rings a little hollow across the years, but only, perhaps,
because the options he suggests have long since vanished in the wake of

new political and social developments. One thing is certain, however: At the time he wrote this essay, John Crowe Ransom did not conceive of himself as speaking in metaphor.

**NOR DID DONALD DAVIDSON** in "A Mirror for Artists," the second essay in the symposium. Davidson, whose reputation as a poet is less secure than those of the other Fugitive-Agrarians, may have been a better polemicist than Ransom, Warren, or Tate—despite the fact that his political and social views were, in later years, sometimes less realistic. His symposium essay shows a promise of his later rhetorical skill and defines a stance which he was to maintain to the end of his life. Essentially he takes the position that the artist and the businessman are by their very natures at cross purposes, that technology, no matter how highly developed, will not produce the kind of society conducive to great art.

He cites historical examples to demonstrate that alienation of the artist from society began with the Industrial Revolution, and he argues against the proposition that with greater leisure in a technological society will come greater creativity by predicting, with some authority, the debasement of popular taste and the rise of dilettantism.

Most of what he says by way of criticizing the industrial regime is familiar and widely accepted dogma in The Republic of Letters, hardly controversial at all when divorced from a discussion of the South.

His defense of the agrarian order is a little less convincing, though by no means extravagant or immoderate. He is willing to grant that the South has yet to produce great art; but he is hopeful that artists will seek out agrarian regions in the future, and in this respect, like Ransom, his ultimate concerns are national in scope: "For many reasons the Southern tradition deserves rehabilitation, but not among them is the reason that it would thus enable Southern artists to be strictly Southern artists. If the Southern tradition were an industrial tradition, it would deserve to be cast out rather than cherished."

**TURNING TO ALLEN TATE**, his "Remarks on Southern Religion" is one of the essays I would prefer to avoid in a discussion of moderation in *I'll Take My Stand*. The swaggering tone of Tate's rhetoric undercuts all but the most heroic attempts to place his thoughts into proper perspective. It is a tone, I would note, that derives in part from G.K. Chesterton and in larger measure from the intemperate pronouncements of Pound and the early Eliot.

Tate's position, however, is no more than a brief for religious attitudes that will satisfy the whole of man's nature, rather than merely his pragmatic or rational aspect. Such, he argues, was the older European view, and such, he insists, would be the ultimate salvation of the South. In expressing these opinions Tate is really speaking as a cultural historian rather than as a Christian apologist. He believed through most of his productive years that a coherent religious myth was an essential ordering principle in any viable culture, and he finds no more than the vestiges of such a myth in the Southern scene of his own day. Indeed his essay is almost as critical of the region as it is supportive, though he has no use at all for the "American" alternative.

He closes by saying that the method for Southerners to use in reanimating their religious vision "is political, active, and, in the nature of the case, violent and revolutionary." Taken out of context (as it often has been by hostile critics), this statement seems to promote a second firing on Fort Sumter. But Tate is not talking about such nonsense, for he has already said at the beginning of his essay that "any discussion of religion is a piece of violence." His "violent and revolutionary activity," then, is to be intellectual and polemical rather than military, and his weaponry in his own essay is arch and inflammatory rhetoric. Later he would rethink this strategy and turn instead to a more moderate subversion.

ROBERT PENN WARREN'S ESSAY, "The Briar Patch," has inspired commentary in recent years, not only because of his achievements as a poet and fiction writer, but also because in *I'll Take My Stand* he addressed himself to the question of the black community and its role in a Southern agrarian order. Warren himself says, "My essay in *I'll Take My Stand* was about the Negro in the South, and it was a defense of segregation. I haven't read that piece, as far as I can remember, since 1930, and I'm not sure exactly how things are put there."

As a matter of fact, "The Briar Patch" is not unlike Warren's later statements on the subject, which have been characterized by a calm and rigorous attention to the complexities of the situation. In the first place, the essay is not a defense of segregation any more than *The Magic Mountain* is a defense of tuberculosis, and Warren was ill advised in making such a statement. By his own admission he had not read the piece in almost 30 years; and after all, segregation in 1930 was a fact of life, part of the given in American society, both North and South, as Warren himself notes in the same interview. The Agrarians did not waste time defending anything that was not under attack. Sufficient to the day was the evil thereof.

What Warren does do in his essay is to show that, given the nature of the fallen world, most Southern blacks would do better in the year 1930 if they prepared for a career in agriculture rather than industry or the professions. He does so with considerable regret and with the clear understanding that he believes the same principle applies to whites in similar circumstances and that a higher economic destiny for blacks is the ideal toward which everyone must aspire. He criticizes both the Northerner who felt that the abolition of slavery would solve all racial problems and the Southerner "whose prejudice would keep the Negroes forever as a dead and inarticulate mass in the commonwealth . . . " And in a strong anti-aristocratic statement he says: "It will be a happy day for the South when no court discriminates in its dealings between the negro and the white man, just as it will be a happy day for the nation when no court discriminates between the rich man and the poor man: and the first may be a more practicable ideal than the second."

What he does that offends many of his critics is to show with a cold and impartial historical accuracy the degree to which Northern industrialists have exploited the black and reduced him to economic peonage. Of industrialism in the South, he says that it can aid the cause of blacks "if it grows under discipline."

All in all, Warren's essay is among the most balanced and intelligent in the symposium. It takes into account the conditions extant in Southern society at that particular moment and attempts to exercise the virtue of prudence in addressing the plight of blacks, which he neither underestimates nor sentimentalizes. If Warren himself has still not reread his essay [in 1981], I hope he does so. He will find it far less embarrassing than his critics have led him to believe.

THE REST OF THE ESSAYS in the volume are in the spirit of these four; in some cases they are more measured in tone, and in some less so. What they all share in common, however, is a coherent vision of a society that is yet in existence, whose virtues, if they have been mitigated at all, are still recoverable because they are still embodied in the palpable world of experience. No one in *I'll Take My Stand* wants to go back to an earlier time; no one even wants to remain stationary. They all wish to proceed with caution, knowing the degree to which modern ideology, whether capitalist or communist, can pipe the young off into a terrible land beyond the present imagination.

I must caution those of you who are unfamiliar with the controversy surrounding this work that few critics regard it as the soul of moderation. I suspect that the degree to which they do not can be explained by the fact that the political and social order under discussion is the American South and that no one can quite approach that subject with the fine impartiality necessary for objective analysis. When Massachusetts freed its slaves it was free of them forever. The South has yet to be emancipated, despite a proclamation as eloquent and true as *I'll Take My Stand*.

But the year of Jubilo may not be too far away. There are some signs to that effect in more recent commentaries which have begun to explore the essential sophistication of the work and its subtler complexities. Up North there are rumblings, even in the academies of old New England; and before too very long an army of scholars may be dispatched to strike off our chains.

I take all of this as sure and certain evidence that some people have at last begun to read the book.

# Two Types of Neo-Agrarians

Recently [in 2003] Vanderbilt named the university's 25 greatest gifts to the world. One of them was the homosexual psychiatrist who appeared masked before the 1972 meeting of the American Psychiatric Association and told the assembled members how tough it was to live in the closet. Neither *I'll Take My Stand* nor the Agrarians made the list. Clearly the group was deemed too reactionary, too conservative for Vanderbilt's social-climbing chancellor, Gordon Gee, whose chief mission, aside from raising money, was to improve the university's yearly ranking by that highly esoteric journal *U.S. News & World Report*.

Gee and Vanderbilt obviously haven't read the Agrarian symposium nor do they understand its place in the current debate over such front-page issues as urban blight and the environment. They might be surprised to learn that *Mother Jones* regularly advertises *I'll Take My Stand* on its website. Libertarian Virginia Postrel, on her website Dynamist.com, denounces the "green" tendencies of the Agrarians: "Intellectually, the roots of many conservative reactionaries lie in the anti-modern writings of traditionalists such as Russell Kirk and the Southern Agrarians of the 1920s and 1930s, who anticipated many green arguments against the open-ended future." Indeed, the critique of industrial society in *I'll Take My Stand* is, in some respects, astonishingly similar to the arguments found in *The Communist Manifesto*.

Perhaps the Vanderbilt regime would be more sympathetic if they knew that the Agrarians did not regard their point of view as exclusively "Southern." As John Ransom wrote in an initial "Statement of Principles" to which all 12 subscribed: "The communities and private persons sharing the agrarian tastes are to be found widely within the Union . . . The members of the present group would be happy to be counted as members of a national agrarian movement."

Since its publication in 1930, *I'll Take My Stand* has never been out of print, and each succeeding generation produces new disciples, albeit with a slightly different take on the original document. In recent years, some have seen in the Agrarian critique of industrial America a precursor of Al Gore's books and the Unabomber's tracts. And in fact neo-Agrarians were, from the beginning, concerned with what industrialism was doing to the land, the water, and the sky. They were also concerned with other matters even

37

more important.

As an example of how this "failed political philosophy" could continue to exert such an influence on reasonably intelligent people, let me offer two examples of the kind of people who became influenced to some degree by *I'll Take My Stand* in general, and Donald Davidson in particular. The two I offer are my roommate, Edwin "Buddy" Godsey, and myself—two students of Donald Davidson.

I always had a difficult time talking to Mr. Davidson. When I took his creative-writing course, he would invite me to meet him in his office "to discuss these works and other matters." When I got there we talked about nothing. I had no sense of what he wanted to hear, and he had no small talk, not when it came to poetry and fiction. On the other hand, my college roommate, Buddy Godsey, would come back from a two-hour visit with Mr. Davidson pumped up, ready to write an epic or a novel. They would have talked about hunting, about the differences between East Tennessee and West Tennessee, about the TVA, about poetry, which Buddy was trying to write. The two understood each other because they inhabited the same world, though Davidson had lived in it longer and seen more of it fall to pieces.

BUDDY WAS THE NATURAL AGRARIAN, who understood what the Agrarians were saying before he ever read or heard the words. I was bewildered by the depth of his wisdom, and still am in awe of his rapport with Mr. Davidson, who was like Yahweh to me—remote and terrifying.

Buddy had grown up on a medium-sized farm in Bristol. Half of the town was in Tennessee, half in Virginia. He was a mountain boy and spoke with a mountain accent—the hard *r*'s, the drawn-out diphthongs, the twang. He pronounced *Tennessee* with a strong emphasis on the first syllable. His parents were older—his mother already in her 60's, his father way up on his 70's. His father believed in beating the devil out of his two sons, and he routinely inflicted severe pain on Buddy—so much so that once when they were working out in the field, Wiley, the hired man, told Mr. Godsey, "Will, if you hit that boy one more time, I'll kill you."

Instead of breaking him, the harsh discipline made him tough—mentally and emotionally as well as physically. He contracted diabetes as a small child and was plagued by the disease for the rest of his life. But when he and I roomed together the only evidence I ever saw that he was a diabetic was a syringe in the refrigerator. I never saw him use it, and he never complained. So he was no spoiled kid; no sentimentalist, long on sympathy and short on good sense; no easy prey for the left, its croker sack stuffed with *ad misericordiam* arguments.

Also, his respect for nature and its gifts sprang from no abstract sense of brotherhood with possums and poison ivy. Nor did it derive initially from Mr. Davidson or from *I'll Take My Stand*. Had Agrarianism been an ideology, like contemporary environmentalism, or had Mr. Davidson been a poseur like Al Gore, Buddy would probably have bought stock in a paper mill or a strip mine. He spent much of his youth hunting and fishing in the mountains and valleys of East Tennessee, and appreciated more than most what civilization had left for him—in that part of the state, vaulting hills, mountains, streams, and at least one good river. Houses were as yet unbuilt, except for a few stone structures protruding from the mountainside.

I suspect, though I can't prove it, that most of Al Gore's myrmidons come from the cities, where the battle had been lost a century earlier, when enlightened "developers" like John Jacob Astor began to pave the sidewalks so that New Yorkers could trip the Light Fantastic with Mamie O'Rourke. No one had to alarm Buddy with the wild speculation that Nashville would be underwater in a few generations if America didn't abolish the internal-combustion engine. He had read Rachel Carson, and he contributed regularly to the Sierra Club, when most people had never heard of it and when it was still a group without a radical political agenda.

In his small way, he merely wanted to preserve the world of particulars that existed for him and for everyone else in that part of the earth—doves, quail, and deer—brought down with buckshot, falling with grace in a dying arc. And trout taken from a mountain stream so cold it froze your toes inside socks and boots. Those spoils of the good earth—and the oaks, maples, pines, and brush that sustained them—were worth the dollars he contributed and the brilliant poems he wrote on the subject.

When my wife and I bought a house in the country with 22 acres of farmland attached, Buddy suggested that we plant a large garden, one that covered a couple of acres. He knew what he was doing. Had done it before. So he was the plantation owner, and I was the sharecropper. He told me what to plant and how to hoe; and I did what he told me—the two of us working side by side in the afternoons, after we had taught our classes at Converse College and met our office hours. We planted rows and rows of corn (three different varieties), field peas and black-eyed peas, tomatoes, cucumbers, squash, watermelons, cantaloupes, grapevines, and okra.

The corn sprouts were the first to appear, along with some weeds, and I couldn't tell the difference; so Buddy had to drive 40 miles round trip to show me which ones to execute and which ones to spare. By the middle of summer, we were looking at some heartening successes and some frustrating failures. The squash bloomed, then died—and no squash to eat. (We figured we had planted all females or all males.) By the time the watermelons ripened, they had rotted on their undersides. Some ears of corn had turned a malignant green inside; and the grapevines didn't produce a single grape, much less enough to make a bottle of wine.

But our successes were spectacular, at least to me. My wife and Buddy had grown up on farms. I had never eaten corn or tomatoes or cucumbers right out of the field. They are entirely different vegetables from the ones by the same name that you buy at Piggly Wiggly, shipped in from Mexico or Guatemala, with stickers that say "vine ripened." (No one who buys groceries exclusively at a chain store has the right to believe in the idea of progress.)

We had an Indian summer that year, and though the corn stalks, stripped of their ears, turned brown and bowed their heads toward the coming winter, the tomatoes and okra continued to flower and bear. I remember standing in late November on the front porch, shivering, watching a cold autumn wind whip the yellow-green okra flowers, looking a little like forlorn tulips. A few days later they were all gone.

Next year, we didn't plant a garden. Buddy and I and two or three others—in protest against what we regarded as the mistreatment of a colleague—resigned our positions at Converse. I was able to keep the house for another year by teaching at nearby Furman University. Buddy took a job at the University of North Carolina at Charlotte.

He and his wife, Julia, bought 90 acres of land in the country, which included a small lake. He intended to raise his boys in an unpaved plot of earth where the seasons were still distinguishable and where you didn't hear the screech of tires at 3:00 A.M. or smell the poisonous air of the city in dead winter. Greater Charlotte had just proclaimed itself an area of over a million people. Buddy wanted to get his family away from all that, and he seemed to have found the ideal spot—not Walden (a hiding place for a weird little mama's boy), but a way of holding urban America at arm's length. Only an hour and a half away, we visited them several times during the summer, and watched their two boys doing cannonballs off the dock into the lake.

In February, I came home from Furman in the late afternoon, the sky already dark. My wife gave me the grim news: Joe—the younger of the two boys and my godson—had fallen through the ice that covered the lake. Buddy had broken his way through in an effort to save Joe. Both had drowned. By the time we arrived, with Julia and the two surviving children huddled glassy-eyed by a fire, police and divers were already down by the lake, flashlights and lanterns casting shadows across the cold, snow-bound earth. In an hour or so, Julia's brother Frank arrived from Tennessee; and by then Mary Beth and Julia had packed what needed to be taken. Just before

Frank, Julia, and the family left, a policeman came up to the house to say that both bodies had been recovered.

As we drove back to South Carolina, I recalled a conversation I'd had with Buddy a few years earlier. We had talked about dying, and agreed that wasting away with cancer or Lou Gehrig's disease would be the worst. As for quick deaths, I said I most feared falling from a great height. He said for him it would be drowning.

MY OWN CONCERN FOR THE ENVIRONMENT came, not from a youth lived in the country, but from Mr. Davidson and *I'll Take My Stand*. I grew up in Sarasota, Florida, where, until after World War II, the county maintained a fine balance between agriculture and tourism. The farmers—who lived out in the very rural county—raised cattle, tomatoes, and celery for cash crops, ate their homegrown vegetables, and butchered their own hogs and an occasional cow. They would come to town on Saturdays to do the week's shopping and to visit with one another along Main Street, while their kids ran up and down the sidewalk, shooting at each other with ten-cent cap guns.

We lived in town, where my father was a dentist and where the cash crop was Yankees, so I paid little attention to what the farmers did. Indeed, the fact that Florida was then the second-largest cattle-producing state seemed more an embarrassment than a virtue. At 12 I read *Time* and the *New Yorker* and wondered why a just and merciful God had allowed me to grow up in such a backward region. After two years at a New England prep school, God suddenly seemed more benevolent than I'd previously suspected. When I graduated from Vanderbilt, I was a second-generation Agrarian.

I suppose that's why years later I became involved in the politics of Irving, Texas, a city of some 100,000 people, as unlike Sarasota and other rural Southern counties as Los Angeles or, for that matter, Mars. However different it may have been, Irving—like most small and middle-sized American communities today—was governed by real-estate developers and their allies, the building industry. At that time, these greedmongers were constructing apartment houses so fast that if you didn't watch the lot next door every minute of every day, you'd wake up one morning to see a six-story high-rise with several hundred cars in the parking lot. And if you continued to live there for 20 years, you'd see the building fall to pieces—so slowly, so imperceptibly that you'd be unaware of the moment when it ceased to be a residence and became an eyesore, eventually to be condemned by the building inspector, torn down, and replaced by a second generation of the same family. At the time I heard that apartment owners could shelter all their earnings by depreciating their buildings over a very few years, then trading apartments with each other and starting all over again.

Meanwhile schools overflowed with brawling brats. Unrepaired city streets were as cratered as the moon. The landscape disappeared daily, eaten alive by chainsaws—trees by the hundreds in a part of Texas not overly endowed with greenery. And roadrunners, scissortails, rabbits, possums, and foxes. The hawks hung on tenaciously. I remember seeing one red-tail plunge in between two city warehouses, sink its claws into a scurrying rat, haul it wriggling and squealing to the top of a telephone pole, and methodically bite its spine in two. In the middle of a campaign, I identified with the hawk.

I managed some 15 city-council campaigns over a four-year period, and we lost all but one. (A hawk with that kind of killing record would have starved to death.) Why did we lose to a handful of well-financed, well-organized business interests? I can't help but remember Andrew Lytle's explanation of why the Agrarians failed: "We couldn't convince people that the world they knew was under attack, much less in danger of disappearing. Now it's all gone." In a sense, the same was true of Irving, whose eyes were always turned westward toward Dallas, a city that had no apparent desire to be a community. A friend who worked in those campaigns told me recently that all the signs in downtown Irving are now in Spanish. If true, it doesn't surprise me.

I don't regret the time lost to these campaigns—literally thousands of hours, for which I was paid nothing. In the first place, down where I come from we're used to losing. In fact, we rather like it. There's nothing worse than winning completely and finally, the way Sherman won. It's like owning every piece of property on the Monopoly board. I've seen winners offer losers huge sums of play money just to stay in the game. Then, too, even though you lose a bitter fight, you enjoy the satisfaction of having inflicted pain, of disrupting the lives of complacent winners, of costing some fat cat significant sums of his ill-gotten gains.

Right now it looks as if the ideological environmentalists are winning. Hordes of scientists—who can be just as partisan as precinct captains—have received their orders and are marching in lockstep toward apocalypse. The polar bears will die of heatstroke. The oceans will wash across Detroit, Topeka, and Boulder. The Rockies will crumble. Gibraltar will tumble.

As you may have noticed, this time apocalypse is set for a somewhat more distant future than the apocalypse Robert Ehrlich established when he wrote *The Population Bomb* and predicted that, by 1972, food would be so scarce in the United States that people would be fighting each other in the streets of New York for the limited amount available. The government is now issuing frantic bulletins, warning Americans about obesity.

**FROM THE BEGINNING**, Buddy Godsey and I were two different kinds of second-generation Agrarians. He was a natural, born and bred. It was in his blood and bone before he ever got to grade school, much less to Vanderbilt. Without prompting, he always knew precisely who he was. Though his kind are being killed off systematically in a postmodern world of Hollywood fantasy and Washington ideology, millions still survive, enough to keep social planners and domestic-policy advisors tossing and turning nightly on their orthopedic mattresses.

As for me, I'm a neo-Agrarian by education. There are some of us left as well, mostly old and gray and full of sleep, but a few young and formidable, their minds honed to the sharpness of an executioner's axe.

# It's Hard Times, Cotton Mill Girls: Manufacturing, Gone With the Wind

**H**ISTORIANS TEND to make the same argument: The South lost the Civil War because its economy was agrarian rather than industrial, with too few munitions factories to supply Confederate troops with weapons and too few textile mills to clothe them. According to these same historians, the post-bellum sharecropper system proved to be an economic disaster, in part because it was grounded in agriculture. Only when the South turned to industry in the late 19th century did she begin to live for the first time. Color flooded into her cheeks. She was able to get her hair done and buy a couple of new dress-es. Looking at herself in the mirror, she asked, "Why didn't I do this before?" The textile industry in the Carolinas is routinely cited as the best example.

Such historical accounts illustrate the degree to which the ideology of industrialism has wormed its way into the soul of the nation, as if South-ern farms were never prosperous or even self-sufficient and all antebellum women went around wearing ragged dresses made from flour sacks, their hair perpetually in tangles.

At the beginning, the rise of the textile industry in the South primarily enriched Northerners. Eventually, Southerners scraped up enough capital to get into the game—or else, like Confederate Capt. John Montgomery of Spartanburg, secured the backing of New England investors.

The Northerners did not come South to save the conquered region from hoeing and plowing in the hot Southern sun. They came for the same reason 21st-century manufacturers have begun moving their operations to Mexi-co and other Third World countries: cheap land, cheap labor, and few legal restrictions. The South had no child-labor laws in the 19th century, and New England mill owners preferred to hire children because they were more sub-missive, cheaper, and less likely to strike.

Sarah Norcliffe Cleghorne, a New England Quaker, wrote a memorable quatrain on this subject.

> The golf links lie so near the mill
> That almost every day
> The laboring children can look out
> And see the men at play.

By the 1830's, the trade-union movement had begun to take hold in the Northeast; and, from the beginning, unions criticized child-labor practices (though not necessarily out of humanitarian concern). In 1836, Massachusetts outraged local mill owners by passing the first child-labor law, which required children under 15 working in factories to attend school at least three months out of the year. In 1842, the state crossed the line between responsible government and zealotry by restricting the workday of children to ten hours.

Small wonder that, after the War Between the States, New Englanders saw in such states as South Carolina an oasis of half-starved children and few restrictive laws. With these optimum conditions, the textile industry blossomed in the Piedmont. In 1880, there were 14 mills in South Carolina. By 1920, there were 184, employing over 55,000 workers. And by 1925, the state boasted more mills than Massachusetts or any other state.

In order to lure folks down from the mountains, mill owners built entire villages for workers, the rent for each unit determined by the number of rooms. Lined up in rows on both sides of the street, the wood-frame houses were identical: Each was identically tiny, painted an identical off-white, its clapboard siding the color of unginned cotton. Each had an identical front porch almost too narrow to accommodate a metal glider comfortably, and the identical front lawns were so small they could easily be mowed in five minutes. Though mill houses were not in the backyards of owners, they were hauntingly reminiscent of slave quarters. If these workers were not postbellum slaves, they were the Mexicans of the late 19th century.

IN THE SOUTH, the mills once again favored the hiring of children. In the late 1930's, Fannie Miles told a WPA interviewer about her first day at work in a textile mill:

> I was just nine years old when we moved to a cotton mill in Darlington, South Carolina, and I started to work in the mill. I was in a world of strangers. I didn't know a soul. The first morning I was to start work, I remember coming downstairs feelin' strange and lonesome-like. My grandfather, who had a long, white beard, grabbed me in his arms and put two one-dollar bills in my hand. He said, "Take these to your mother and tell her to buy you some pretty dresses and make 'em nice for you to wear in this mill." I was mighty proud of that.

Her story was by no means unique. An old folk song (or perhaps quasi-folk song) has as its chorus:

It's hard times, Cotton Mill Girls.
Hard times, Cotton Mill Girls.
It's hard times, Cotton Mill Girls, hard times everywhere.

A couple of stanzas reinforce the message:

Us kids worked 14 hours a day
For 13 cents of measly pay.
It's hard times, Cotton Mill Girls. It's hard times everywhere.

When I die don't bury me at all.
Just hang me up on the spinning wheel wall.
Pickle my bones in alcohol. It's hard times everywhere.

This, then, was the industrial revolution historians have come to admire, the one that brought prosperity to the South and its emancipation from the torturous drudgery of farm life. Of course, children worked on subsistence farms. But that was seasonal, and they were still able to attend school for much of the year. In fact—as advocates of a longer school year now point out—a lengthy summer vacation is a relic of the nation's agrarian past, originally built into the school calendar so children could work in the fields.

Eventually, child-labor laws came South, after much finger-wagging and lecturing from New England, which—by the early 20th century—had forgotten its own history, just as, in an earlier time, it had forgotten who first brought slaves to America. Strikes came South as well. In 1929, violence erupted in Gastonia, North Carolina, in one of the bloodiest labor-management confrontations of that era.

INDEED, THE WORLD THE TEXTILE INDUSTRY MADE was quite different from the agrarian world the South was leaving behind. Among other things, industry produced a substantial blue-collar class that had not existed before. The millworkers—also known as "mill operatives"—became a political bloc and were mobilized by such historically significant South Carolina Democrats as Cole Blease and Olin D. Johnston, each of whom served as governor and as U.S. senator, largely because of their appeal to textile workers.

Yet after more than 50 years of the redemptive textile industry and other industrial ventures, the region was still poor. In fact, in 1938, in the midst of the Great Depression, President Franklin D. Roosevelt called the South "the nation's number-one economic problem."

World War II took care of the Depression and the economic backwardness of the region. Today, the South is thriving—not only because of increased manufacturing but because of its expanding service economy, its financial institutions, and its tourism. Northern companies have migrated to Florida, North Carolina, and Texas to escape Northern cities, which have become dangerous and unlivable. Caught up in the euphoria of greed, Southern city councilmen, mayors, governors, and congressmen are knocking one another down, pulling hair and gouging eyes in their attempt to attract new companies to their respective jurisdictions. Members of Southern chambers of commerce have become, like ancient Jews, the watchers at the gate, scanning the northern horizon, looking for the Messiah to come roaring down I-95, driving a Lamborghini.

IN THE MIDST OF ALL THIS PROSPERITY, the textile industry has all but disappeared from South Carolina and neighboring states. In 2005, Spartanburg textile magnate Roger Milliken warned:

> Since January 2001, nearly 300,000 textile and apparel jobs have been lost—and that number does not even include the job losses from the tragic Pillowtex bankruptcy. Moreover, the United States ran a $61 billion trade deficit in textile and apparel goods in 2002. If the federal government refuses to change the flawed trade policies that generated those numbers, the U.S. textile and apparel industry is in grave danger. The government needs to act now to save South Carolina and Georgia textile jobs.

Indeed, in 2001 alone, 62 Carolina mills closed. Many now blight the South Carolina landscape, windows broken, skirted by head-high weeds—red-brick eyesores waiting to become rubble heaps. As if to mock its own fate, a textile mill in Anderson has been transformed into a dinosaur museum.

No one knows for sure why dinosaurs disappeared from the face of the earth. But everyone agrees that the textile industry has died out because of international competition, principally from China. Spokesmen demand the return of quotas, arguing that China has been able to undersell American manufacturers by using slave labor and by subsidizing their industry.

Free-market economists reject this argument. Thus, Robert Barfield of the American Enterprise Institute has said: "The textile people have seen this coming for 10 years. The government should do something about trade adjustment assistance for workers whose jobs are put in jeopardy, but I don't think we ought to re-institute quotas."

The history of textile mills in South Carolina—and in several other

Southern states—gives new meaning to Robert Frost's line "Nothing gold can stay." A once-lucrative industry is moribund. Mill villages—monuments to the idea that human beings are as alike as Ford carburetors—have become ghost towns, covered by green blankets of kudzu, or else salvaged by wrecking crews.

A century ago, the New South crowd would have bet their sacred fortunes that the textile industry would last until men and women stopped wearing clothes. Today, the same bunch is hailing the advent of high-tech companies and the automobile industry. After all, for New South adherents, paradise is always just around the corner, just over the next hill.

When presidential candidate John McCain was confronted by a textile worker who complained that his children would not be able to follow in his footsteps, Senator McCain replied:

> Sir, I did not know that your ambitions were for your children to work in a textile mill, to be honest with you. I would rather have them work in a high-tech industry. I would rather have them work in the computer industry. I would rather give them the kind of education and training that's necessary in order for them to really [*sic*] have prosperous and full lives.

Putting aside the effrontery of publicly lecturing a father on what's best for his children, Senator McCain was up to his chin in shallow water. Like earlier boosters of textile mills, he clearly believed in the immortality of present economic conditions, the inviolability of the fragile industrial dream. He drew the wrong lesson from the father's complaint. The global marketplace is just as dicey as Las Vegas, whether the industry be textiles or high-tech or computers.

Economist Paul Craig Roberts recently [in 2006] wrote:

> The declines in some manufacturing sectors have more in common with a country undergoing saturation bombing during war than with a super-economy that is "the envy of the world." Communications equipment lost 43% of its workforce. Semiconductors and electronic components lost 37% of its workforce. The workforce in computers and electronic products declined 30%. Electrical equipment and appliances lost 25% of its employees. The workforce in motor vehicles and parts declined 12%.

The father who addressed Senator McCain saw a world disappear before his eyes, one he had taken for granted his entire life. He may have lived in a mill village; been a textile machine setter and operator since graduation from high school; fed yarn, thread, and fabric through guides, needles, or rollers; and eaten a peanut-butter sandwich for lunch. But for him, those things constituted a precious reality, his own piece of God's created order—even more so, perhaps, than the check at the end of the week. He could not believe that such fine particularities could be gone forever, stolen by people chattering in a strange language on the bottom side of the earth. He just asked Senator McCain to explain why this had happened and what could be done to bring back that lost world. He is still waiting for an answer.

The irony of this history—shorn of ideology and boosterism—should be apparent: Whatever light the textile industry brought to South Carolina and its neighbors, most of the same conditions existed that led William Blake to wonder if Jerusalem could be built "among these dark Satanic mills." From nine-year-old Fannie Miles to that bereft father, the victims are scattered across a hard century like so many stars. None of us has the wisdom to measure accurately the worth of the light against the darkness. If you took a survey, most people would vote for the light. But then, they probably never heard the children singing in high, frail voices: "It's hard times, Cotton Mill Girls, hard times everywhere."

# The Old South, the New South, and the Real South

I N APRIL OF 1968, the University of Dallas Literature Department hosted the Southern Literary Festival, a gathering of college students who submitted poetry, fiction, and essays for evaluation; listened to addresses and readings by published writers; and met editors of literary journals. Mel Bradford, Louise Cowan, and I were teaching at UD. We had all done graduate work at Vanderbilt, studied under Donald Davidson, and knew some of the Fugitive-Agrarians well. So we were able to put together a program featuring John Crowe Ransom, Robert Penn Warren, Allen Tate, Andrew Lytle, and Donald Davidson. In addition to the festival, where they read their works, we invited all five to remain on campus for two extra days to talk about the history and meaning of the Agrarian movement. Ransom, Warren, Tate, and Lytle accepted. Davidson was too ill to attend. Less than two weeks after the events, he was dead.

Lytle and Davidson had changed their views little if at all since 1930. Ransom in his published essays and in his comments as editor of the *Kenyon Review* had seemingly left Tennessee and Agrarian preoccupations far behind. Robert Penn Warren was a self-styled liberal who had published two books on the race question: *Segregation: The Inner Conflict of the South* and *Who Speaks for the Negro?* And Allen Tate was like a Civil War-era sutler (a peddler who traded with both sides). When he was in the North, he wrote haughty, scolding letters to Southern apologists like Donald Davidson. When he was visiting in our part of the country, he made racist wisecracks.

Face to face, no one wanted to fight. They were like long-lost cousins at a family reunion—vaguely affectionate and reluctant to tell on each other. The tape wasn't worth transcribing.

What a shame. Warren came to Dallas having thought about *I'll Take My Stand* in terms that were far more original and broad-ranging than anything written before or since. While the others were attending a cocktail party, I met his plane at Love Field. As we drove to the motel, he said something that I thought put the Agrarian's view of the South in an entirely new perspective.

"The overarching question of our time," he said, "is whether the modern tendency to think abstractly is a good or a bad thing. That's a question I'd like for us to discuss." Unfortunately, the dialogue never turned in that direction.

The harsh criticism of *I'll Take My Stand* was, from the very beginning, grounded in an abstraction—an already existent paradigm that had infatuated Southerners and Northerners alike since the War and Reconstruction—that of the "New South." In creating this concept, True Believers attempted to transcend an ignominious past and a demeaning present by inventing a utopian future. The most famous 19th-century use of the phrase was by Henry Grady in an 1886 speech before the New England Society of New York. Full of jokes and anecdotes, the speech nonetheless has at its heart a juxtaposition of two abstractions—the Old South and the New South. Thus Grady says:

> The Old South rested everything on slavery and agriculture, unconscious that these could neither give nor maintain healthy growth. The New South presents a perfect democracy, the oligarchs leading in the popular movements, social system compact and closely knitted, less splendid on the surface but stronger at the core—a hundred farms for every plantation, fifty homes for every palace, and a diversified industry that meets the complex needs of this complex age.

As Grady presents them, both the Old South and the New South are constructs of an impatient mind rushing to a preordained conclusion. The Old South—the one that "rested everything on slavery and agriculture"—was familiar to the New Englanders whom Grady was addressing. If they didn't create it, they certainly believed in it as surely as they believed that the Pilgrims had invented Thanksgiving. They also hated it. The South they conquered was a real society, infinitely more complicated (and therefore more troublesome) than Grady's speech suggests. That they never understood this reality is verified by the actions of New England schoolmarms who came down South during Reconstruction and established segregated schools and churches.

As for Grady's "New South," the New Englanders who heard his highly decorative oratory may have believed in that as well. Did Grady know New England's Ramistic passion for dichotomizing and pull a fast one on his audience?

> Now, what answer has New England to this message? Will she permit the prejudices of war to remain in the hearts of the conquerors, when it has died in the hearts of the conquered? [Cries of "No! No!"] Will she transmit this prejudice to the next generation, that in their hearts, which never felt the generous ardor of

conflict, it may perpetuate itself? ["No! No!"] Will she withhold, save in strained courtesy, the hand which straight from his soldier's heart Grant offered to Lee at Appomattox? Will she make the vision of a restored and happy people, which gathered above the couch of your dying captain, filling his heart with grace, touching his lips with praise and glorifying his path to the grave; will she make this vision on which the last sight of his expiring soul breathed a benediction, a cheat and a delusion? [Tumultuous cheering and shouts of "No! No!"]

This was the first New South, the "perfect democracy, the oligarchs leading in the popular movements, social system compact and closely knitted." Ask Harvard University if that New South ever existed or ever will. Yet it was very real to those New Englanders who cheered Grady's speech in 1886 and dreamed of a more perfect Union—real because it only existed *in potentia*.

The second manifestation of this utopian concept—Son of New South— was abroad in the first half of the 20th century, and is still with us. It was the New South the Agrarians faced when they published *I'll Take My Stand*. Again, it was utopian. The South, after decades of poverty, induced as much by Reconstruction as by the War, was captured by the vision of a society in which Atlanta, Nashville, and Birmingham would become industrial giants like Pittsburgh, Cleveland, and Detroit, their stacks belching fire and smoke like concrete-and-steel dragons. This was before the environmentalists had recognized what the Agrarians had told them a generation earlier—that the overbuilding of plants and factories tends to ruin the landscape.

BOTH THE OLD SOUTH AND THE NEW SOUTH are constructions that appeal to the New England mind, which is obsessed with intellectual polarities. In part, this tendency has its origins in the writings of Petrus Ramus, a 16th-century neoplatonist, who attempted to create a Protestant logic to replace Aristotle's, which had been incorporated into Scholasticism and was part of the medieval university's curriculum. Ramus's system contained, among other things, a schema or pattern—based on the principle of dichotomy—that could be superimposed on existence like a transparency. This schema looked like a family tree with members who had odd Latin names. To oversimplify its uses, Ramus's system divided ideas into two parts, then divided those parts into two more, and so on—*e.g.*, us and them. Ramus was killed in the St. Bartholomew's Day Massacre (1572), but unfortunately not in time. His system, promoted by no less a Puritan figure than John Milton, found its way to the Massachusetts Bay Colony and, like a spirochete, bored deep into the New England mind. Thus, parsing the South into abstractions like the Old South and the New South made perfect sense to them, even if neither one existed.

Ransom makes the Agrarians' animosity toward abstraction abundantly clear in his discussion of Humanism:

> The "Humanists" are too abstract. Humanism, properly speaking, is not an abstract system, but a culture, the whole way in which we live, act, think, and feel. It is a kind of imaginatively balanced life lived out in a definite social tradition. And, in the concrete, we believe that this, the genuine humanism, was rooted in the agrarian life of the older South and of other parts of the country that shared in such a tradition. It was not an abstract moral "check" derived from the classics—it was not soft material poured in from the top. It was deeply founded in the way of life itself—in its tables, chairs, portraits, festivals, laws, marriage customs. We cannot recover our native humanism by adopting some standard of taste that is critical enough to question the contemporary arts but not critical enough to question the social and economic life which is their ground.

Here he is not talking about the Unitarian clergy and social scientists who, in 1933, issued the highly utopian Humanist Manifesto, with its anti-religious declamations and its exaltation of human intelligence. He is talking instead of the "New Humanism," inspired in great part by the writings of Irving Babbitt, who suggested that the soul of America could be saved by great art and literature. Ransom makes it clear in this passage that the South the Agrarians are defending is a region of concrete particulars. He names them: tables, chairs, portraits, festivals, laws, marriage customs.

The 12 Southerners who wrote *I'll Take My Stand* knew that region from firsthand experience. Some critics have dismissed them by saying that none had ever farmed. In the first place, that wasn't true. Both Tate and Lytle were at one time farmers. However, most if not all had lived in small towns where agriculture was the chief economic enterprise. They knew the sparse pleasures and considerable virtues of such communities. It was these things they wanted to preserve, not the actual act of hoeing and weeding, though such labor lay at the heart of the South they knew.

In 1930, 30 million Americans lived on farms—about 25 percent of the population. In the South, the percentage was considerably higher.

The "Old South" is defined in terms of plantations and platoons of slaves.

New Englanders, and their latter-day intellectual followers, would add cruelty, economic exploitation, and miscegenation. They are hard at work keeping the abstraction alive today. For one thing, the War—which, like all great historical events, was infinitely complex—has itself become the great dichotomy of our past: a nation half slave, half free, with freedom finally winning out. Such was not the case.

When the War began with the firing on Fort Sumter, a majority of the slaves and a majority of slave states were in the Union, not the Confederacy. Throughout the War, five slave states remained in the Union—Missouri, Kentucky, Maryland, West Virginia, and Delaware. In fact, the slaves in these states were not freed by the Emancipation Proclamation, but were forced to wait until the passage of the 13th Amendment, which had a mighty hard time making its way through the Congress of the United States. It took almost a year for three fourths of the states to ratify it, and it took the Union state of Delaware 36 years.

The New England mind won't permit such complexities in defining the Old South. Life must not intrude to spoil the purity of its vision. Thus, in its fairy-tale account of the Irrepressible Conflict, the word "tariff" never appears. That debate remains beyond the purview of the storyteller, like Red Riding Hood's parents. And the phrase "states' rights" becomes no more than an excuse for economic repression and the exercise of brutality. The early 19th-century debates on a wide variety of issues suggest otherwise.

CURRENT ATTACKS ON THE OLD SOUTH have reached an intensity no one could have predicted 20 years ago. The symbols of the Confederacy have evolved from quaint evocations of the Lost Cause into reminders of slavery and racism. Old South antagonists are particularly hard on the battle flag, in part because it was used by the racist rabble in the fight against segregation in the 50's and 60's. Ironically, when the rabble hung the flag on automobile aerials or flew it at Klan rallies, they were affirming the New England interpretation of their region's history, a point of view that Robert E. Lee, Jefferson Davis, and Stonewall Jackson would have regarded as alien to everything they believed.

Speaking of Lee, he too has been dehumanized by the abstractionists. He opposed slavery as unequivocally as Harriet Beecher Stowe, and wrote in 1856: "There are few, I believe, in this enlightened age, who will not acknowledge that slavery as an institution is a moral and political evil." Yet he is now depicted as chief defender of that institution, wearing a black cape, twirling a black mustache, and tying golden-haired freedom to the railroad track. Lee said he was defending his country, by which he probably meant

Virginia, which he could look out of his window and see. The New England mind tells us otherwise. He was defending the Old South, and no one belonging to that two-dimensional world could possibly be kind or modest or brave, qualities attributed to the three-dimensional Lee. His portrait, displayed along the Canal Walk in Richmond, was recently [in 1999-2000] removed by the city fathers, restored, and then burned up by some anonymous Yankee of the spirit.

The playing of "Dixie" is now equated with the singing of the "Horst Wessel Song." In Germany, the latter is against the law. In First Amendment America, the former might as well be. Yet the song—written by a Northerner for performance in a Northern creation called a minstrel show—does nothing more than express nostalgia for a region known for its buckwheat cakes and Injun batter.

Schools and streets named for Confederate generals have been renamed. Marble-eyed statues of Confederate soldiers have been removed from public squares. Angry Puritans have even demanded that Gen. Nathan Bedford Forrest and his wife be exhumed from graves in a Memphis public park and reburied on private property far from the hypersensitive eyes of out-of-state tourists.

To be sure, this hatred of the "Old South" has been fed in part by 50-60 years of legalized segregation in the region. Again, Northern states had such laws as well. "Board of Education"—as in *Brown* v. *Board of Education*—governed schools in Kansas, which entered the Union as a free state. However, the Southern states were by far the chief offenders, and the Supreme Court ruling affected the Southern states disproportionately. According to the region's critics, the Old South had reared its abstract head again.

However, it was not "Old South" defenders who produced Jim Crow. It was the small farmers and industrial workers of Henry Grady's "New South," those who inhabited "a hundred farms for every plantation, fifty homes for every palace." As C. Vann Woodward pointed out in *The Strange Career of Jim Crow*, genteel Southerners—and most particularly large plantation owners—opposed segregation laws because they ended the "Era of Good Feeling" and offended "our colored friends." The Apostles of the New South segregation—men like Tom Watson of Georgia, James Vardaman of Mississippi, and Pitchfork Ben Tillman of South Carolina—plotted to overthrow the Old South landed gentry and restrict blacks to a parallel and inferior world. Under their leadership, virtually all Jim Crow laws were passed between 1895-1905, not—as many have erroneously assumed—immediately after Reconstruction.

By the way, the Agrarians were not preoccupied with race, as are most present-day historians of the region. Robert Penn Warren was chosen to write the single essay on the race question to be included in *I'll Take My Stand*. Years later, in a famous *Partisan Review* dialogue, he said his contribution, "The Briar Patch," was a defense of segregation. He also admitted he hadn't read it in decades. Had he done so, he might have found that it was a remarkably "moderate" essay for the time, not defending segregation, but accepting its existence as a disturbing but unchangeable part of the political and social landscape. I remember an elderly racist acquaintance commenting years ago on Warren's liberal polemic, *Segregation: The Inner Conflict of the South*, saying: "Doesn't surprise me a bit. When I read 'The Briar Patch' back in 1930, I knew he was a nigger lover."

THE OLD SOUTH LIVES ON IN HOLLYWOOD FILMS, made-for-TV movies, and in news clips of civil-rights marches screened incessantly on public TV. (It sometimes seems as if PBS runs the deviously edited Selma confrontation seven nights a week.) Apparently they are determined to keep the animosity alive.

Meanwhile, the real South—the one the Agrarians cherished and wrote about—is doing quite well these days, despite the efforts of the media, the NAACP, and the Southern Poverty Law Center to prop up and refurbish the stereotype of the Old South. A few years ago the Gallup organization ran a poll on race relations nationwide. The South was the only region where a majority of blacks said they were treated equally.

The press is constantly reporting that a large proportion of white Southerners (some say a majority) attend segregation academies. In fact, Southern attendance at private schools is slightly below the national average, and a recent Harvard study reported that the South was the only region where a majority of white children attended integrated schools. An even more recent report by the U.S. Census Bureau pointed out that the South was the only region where more blacks were moving in than moving out. The ratio was about two to one.

When I called the Gallup organization to ask for the results of its poll on race relations, the man who took my call said, "You'll be surprised." I told him I didn't think so. Gallup doesn't deal in abstractions either. The polls are remarkably accurate, and the numbers they generate come from real people who live in real places and lead real lives. The same with the U.S. Census. I don't know about Harvard studies. The information on schoolchildren mentioned above was contained in a subordinate clause.

The South of 1930 has undergone catastrophic changes, as has the rest of the country. It is still the most religious region in the country and the most politically conservative—all red in the last election [2004]. However, it has embraced the meretricious image of the New South without seeing the skull beneath the skin—and renounced the image of the Old South as if it had really existed.

Several years ago, students at Brattleboro High School in Vermont began flying the Confederate battle flag. After all, Brattleboro is in *southern* Vermont. Several white students (almost everybody in Vermont is white) objected, but the local school board said it was an issue of free speech and refused to ban the flag. Every Southern school board in recent memory has branded that same flag "divisive" and "racist" and ordered its deportation. Behind this attitude lies the fear that any reminder of the Old South will frighten away Northern and foreign corporations, who are relocating in our region daily, hourly. Mayors, city councils, and chambers of commerce are forever fighting the ghost of the Old South, which haunts their dreams of prosperity.

Seventy-five years ago, John Crowe Ransom noted the same attitude: "How may the little agrarian community resist the Chamber of Commerce of its county seat, which is always trying to import some foreign industry that cannot be assimilated to the life-pattern of the community? Just what must the Southern leaders do to defend the traditional Southern life?"

So some issues and responses haven't changed, and the intellectual descendants of the Agrarians are still fighting many of the same battles, though they no longer attempt to save the South from a fate that has already overtaken the region and transformed it into something that even Andrew Lytle could not recognize, despite the fact that he lived through 65 years of change after the publication of *I'll Take My Stand*. "We were better prophets than we realized," he said, near the end of his life.

On the other hand, Southern scholars and polemicists have begun to reclaim territory lost to the opposition in earlier years. One example should suffice.

M.E. Bradford, who died at the age of 58, two years before Lytle, was one of the most brilliant political theorists the region has produced. His career was a vast reclamation project, consisting of books and articles that reexamined the lives and writings of the Framers and exposed the brazen distortions of the ideologues who dominated the academy during the last three decades of the 20th century. His four articles on Abraham Lincoln—there were only four—caused scholars of several intellectual persuasions to pour out of their ant beds, stingers quivering, ready to swarm over Bradford's feet.

Where Lincoln was concerned, Bradford—who studied under Donald Davidson, and knew Tate and Lytle well—let the cat out of the bag. Others began to find in the Great Emancipator's deeds and rhetoric a flawed character and a devious mind. Anti-Lincoln studies have become a thriving business in the academy and even in the realm of practical politics, where black activists are echoing neo-Agrarian charges.

I could name a dozen or more Southern historians, political philosophers, and literary critics who have made major contributions to the current debate over the South, America, and the future of republican democracy.

At Vanderbilt University the politically correct faculty and administration are ashamed of the Agrarians. A recent issue of the alumni magazine catalogued 25 contributions the university has made to the nation and the world. The Agrarians didn't show up on the list, though Robert Penn Warren was cited for his three Pulitzer Prizes in literature. The magazine did include on the list a homosexual psychiatrist who appeared masked at the 1971 meeting of the American Psychiatric Association and told his assembled colleagues how painful it was to live in the closet.

Apparently, the current Vanderbilt crowd has yet to learn that the Agrarians are heroes of hippiedom. Indeed they have been sympathetically featured in an issue of *Mother Jones*. Their criticisms of industrial capitalism were eerily similar to those found in the Communist Manifesto, and the Cato Institute would probably find *I'll Take My Stand* equally dangerous, equally naive.

At the Agrarian reunion at the University of Dallas, Warren called me aside during a break and said, "Why don't you ask us whether or not we knew anything about economics in 1930?" I asked the question, and Tate, Lytle, and Ransom were bewildered. Tate said, "Certainly not!" as if I had asked him if he knew anything about building an internal combustion engine. They weren't interested in economics any more than Wordsworth was. Like that great poet, they believed that, getting and spending, we lay waste our powers.

In that respect, they were like the radical environmentalists of today: They were interested in morals and aesthetics rather than dollars and cents. For this reason alone, politically correct Vanderbilt should scatter bronze statues of them throughout the campus and do something with the all-too-prominent statue of Cornelius Vanderbilt, who expressed his contempt for the very mission of the University he endowed when he said, "If I had learned education, I would not have had time to learn anything else." When asked if he didn't think the railroads he owned should be run for the good of the public, he said, "The public be damned."

THE CONSERVATIVE MOVEMENT, if such a thing still exists, has no use for such archaic ideas. The Agrarians are never discussed at strategy sessions of the Club for Growth or by speakers at the Heritage Foundation. It's as if the movement were buried long, long ago in some Middle Tennessee cemetery, the words on its headstone almost worn away by the wind and rain. No women in mourning bring flowers to the grave. Not too long ago, *National Review* printed an article bashing Mel Bradford, but that's as close as the Agrarians come to having a life—or so it would seem to those who run the salons of the fashionable right.

In fact, the Agrarians are very much alive and inhabiting the most unlikely places, teaching in Northern as well as Southern universities, publishing articles and books, editing journals of opinion. It would take only one bright latter-day Agrarian to wipe out the abstractions and redeem the past.

# The Fugitive-Agrarians: Personal Recollections

WHEN RICHARD WEAVER CAME TO VANDERBILT to get his M.A. in English, he was a committed socialist. Someone had indoctrinated him in undergraduate school. In those days it happened all the time. It still does. Socialism is too easy to explain, too easy to understand, and, at first glance, too easy to love. You can be certain that Little Goody Two-Shoes, Snow White, and the other heroes and heroines of fairy tales were all socialists. Shorn of romantic illusions, a grown-up Weaver remembered his socialist mentors as "dry, insistent people of shallow objectives."

In the mid-30's he came to Vanderbilt University, where he met and fell under the spell of the Fugitive-Agrarians. John Crowe Ransom, Donald Davidson, and Allen Tate (I believe) were still on the faculty, and Weaver would later transfer to LSU, where he met and studied under Robert Penn Warren. They were anything but dry and insistent. In "Up From Liberalism," he wrote, "I liked them all as persons. They were humane, more generous, and considerably less dogmatic than those with whom I had been associated under the opposing banner."

It took him a while to move from left to right, but his perception of those men worked inside him like an antibiotic, engaging the virus he had picked up as an undergraduate. Eventually he came to understand that he was cured: "I recall very sharply how, in the autumn of 1939, as I was driving one afternoon across the monotonous prairies of Texas . . . it came to me like a revelation . . . that I did not have to go on professing the clichés of liberalism."

I understand how he felt. I came to Vanderbilt in 1949, a liberal of sorts, with half-formed ideas of just about everything. I had read *Time*, the *New Yorker*, and books like *Black Boy* by Richard Wright. I thought that Southerners were bigoted racists, despite the fact that neither my parents nor their friends ever exhibited such unattractive qualities. I had not yet learned to put ideas and people together, like Weaver.

I came to Vanderbilt in part because of the Fugitives, whose poetry I had read in anthologies; and I wanted to take a creative-writing course the day I arrived. Donald Davidson taught the course, and he didn't admit underclassmen, so I had to wait two years. Meanwhile I heard stories about him— that he wanted to put everyone back on farms, that he was a right-wing ideologue, that he was a fire-eater in class.

Then one day a friend pointed him out to me as he trudged slowly across the campus, slight of figure, hunched over, plodding carefully along the sidewalk like an old man walking on ice. He had no-color hair; wore a mudbrown suit; and carried his books in a green bag.

"Are you sure that's him?" I asked my friend.

"I'm afraid so," he said.

The following year I registered in two of his classes, The Ballad and Creative Writing. At first I thought his Ballad class was dull. His delivery was low-key and matter-of-fact, with none of the ranting and raving I'd been led to expect. I sat in the back row and drew caricatures of him and other students in the class, hardly paying attention. Then something he said caught my attention, and I began to listen more carefully. He never talked about anything except ballads and ballad scholarship. No mention of politics or the South. In those days professors were expected to keep their political and social opinions to themselves. Davidson subscribed to that professional ethic and followed it to the letter.

However, several of us came to understand that, while lecturing on English and Scottish border ballads, he was also creating a parallel world for our consideration. It was a world we recognized as the one we lived in, yet he was making us see it for the first time. Most of the students missed it entirely. I remember a girl telling me as we walked out of class, "Mr. Davidson just rattles on about those ballads. I almost went to sleep this morning." I tried to explain what he was doing, but she dismissed my explanation with a wave of her hand and breezed off to her next class.

Like scores of Davidson's disciples, I was enthralled. He changed my life in a matter of three months. Having grown up in a sophisticated little resort town in Florida filled with what the Chamber of Commerce called "winter visitors," I never thought of myself as a Southerner. Yet halfway through the ballad class, I went to the library and checked out Douglas Southall Freeman's *Lee's Lieutenants*.

Some of his disciples went even further. A graduate student in English was dating a Nashville girl, one who—as the old saying went—was no better than she should be. His intentions were thoroughly, unambiguously dishonorable. Over dinner one evening she told him that her parents were out of town and that she would be home alone all night. He was certain his time had come. Later that evening, as they were seated on a sofa in her parlor and he was whispering entreaties, he looked up at a painting on the wall and saw a familiar face scowling at him.

"My God," he said. "That's John Singleton Mosby, the greatest guerrilla fighter in the Confederacy."

"Oh," she said, "you mean great-granddaddy?"

Without a moment's hesitation, he went down on one knee and proposed to her. (I might add that I married a farmer's daughter.)

Davidson never mentioned Lee, the Confederacy, or the South the entire time I was in his classroom. Never. All he talked about were ballads, lyrics, the modern novel, modern poetry, and the poems and short stories his creative-writing students submitted.

Across Hillsboro Avenue, the education professors at Peabody College were also wondering how he did it. They knew he inspired students, turned their thinking upside down, sent zealots charging into the world armed with quivers of knowledge and arrows of rhetoric. Since to Peabody, teaching was no more than the application of a set of diagrammable techniques, the teachers of teachers wanted to analyze and reduce Davidson's method to a formula that could be bottled and sold. So they registered students in his class and sent them scuttling across the street every morning with notebooks and pencils. Invariably they came back with blank pages.

"But what does he *do*?" the teachers asked.

"He just talks."

"About *what*?"

"About ballads."

I BELIEVE I UNDERSTAND PART, THOUGH NOT ALL, of how he drew students to him. In the first place, he was astonishingly learned. He had read everything—not just in literary studies but in all other disciplines as well. One year—looking for the modern equivalent of a hair shirt—he devoured dozens and dozens of sociology books so that he could reduce the worst of them to their absurd essence, as he did in an essay called "Why the Modern South Has a Great Literature." He knew as much about music as did Cyrus P. Daniel, the chairman of that department at Vanderbilt. And he could recite the history of the world if need be. It goes without saying that he knew Greek and Latin. A man who could display that kind of erudition, with all the sprezzatura of a Renaissance courtier, was bound to command the respect of brighter students.

But he did something else. He left subtle clues in his discussions of ballads, poetry, and literary scholarship. One day he was summarizing—not criticizing but summarizing—the work of scholars who attempted to promote a social and political agenda by doing violence to the text of ballads. A feeble light went on in my half-formed mind. After class, I rushed up to him and said, "Mr. Davidson, they're doing the same thing in the religion department with biblical scholarship."

He nodded. "I know. I know. Maybe that's why I brought it up."

"Oh," I said.

Those clues weren't for everybody. They were just for those whose heart was already open to their secret message. At one time, scores of us, maybe hundreds, were teaching in English departments around the region, and even in the world of outer darkness, like the University of Chicago. And the marvelous thing about Davidson's clues—the thing that fed the undernourished egos of the dispossessed—was the illusion that we had discovered these truths all by ourselves.

**I KNEW ANDREW LYTLE BETTER THAN THE REST.** I visited him a number of times at his home in Monteagle, and he visited us both in South Carolina and in Dallas. He was my son's godfather. Andrew never deserted, never surrendered. It has been said by critics of the Agrarians that they never farmed, so they had no right to praise agriculture. (That's like saying you can't admire flowers unless you're a gardener.) Andrew was a farmer. As a young man, he ran the family farm and could talk for hours about the problems he encountered. One of his hens fell in love with him and followed him wherever he went, refusing to roost with the others. Finally, Andrew climbed up on the bar himself and squatted there. The hen followed his example but never laid eggs because he couldn't show her how.

When asked why he quit farming, he said that it required the same kind of creative energies that writing fiction required. He couldn't do both, so he chose fiction.

Andrew was probably the best conversationalist alive. He was a treasury of anecdotes about his family, about his friends, about his region. He could talk every evening for a lifetime and never repeat himself. When he taught at Sewanee and edited *The Sewanee Review*, he lived in a cabin in nearby Monteagle and would hold an informal open house on Friday and Saturday evenings. The Sewanee boys would flock there in brigades to sit around on the floor, drink Heaven Hill bourbon out of antique julep cups, and mostly listen or ask questions. In earlier times they may have come in part to see his three beautiful daughters, who would occasionally float through the living room, retrieve something from the kitchen, and float back to the bedroom.

Even more than Donald Davidson, Andrew was unreconstructed. Mr. Davidson admired rural New England and wrote a famous essay called "Still Rebels, Still Yankees," in which he praised the similar virtues of the rural South and small-town New England. Andrew never said a kind word about New England.

He didn't hate the contemporary North. He just didn't think about it.

To him it was as remote and irrelevant as Finland. He felt quite differently about the Yankees who invaded the South in 1861, one of whom gratuitously shot his five-year-old grandmother. To him more than to any of the others, the War was still raging. On quiet summer nights, between the occasional grinding down of gears as trucks made their way slowly up the steep grade, you could sit on Andrew's front porch and almost hear the parrot guns and napoleons echoing from Lookout Mountain, where the Battle in the Clouds was still taking place. As he told the Sewanee boys, Nathan Bedford Forrest could have won the War had it not been for the stupidity and arrogance of Braxton Bragg and the incredibly poor judgment of Jefferson Davis. All this highly partisan history enfolded as he sat beneath a Confederate flag almost as big as a football field.

You must understand that his fierce devotion to the Confederacy had nothing to do with slavery, nor did it lead to animosity toward the contemporary North. He understood and wrote brilliantly about the political conflict that lay behind the Civil War, which some folks down our way refer to as the War Between the States, or—when their blood begins to simmer—the War for Southern Independence, or—when it boils over—the War of Northern Aggression. But, like many of us, Andrew's eyes fired up when he remembered the battles and heroes—Lee, Jackson, the Gallant Pelham, and most of all—because he was a Tennessean—Nathan Bedford Forrest. *Bedford Forrest and His Critter Company*—Andrew's biography of that great general—is one of the best narratives ever published about the War. Like Shelby Foote's three-volume account, it is history meticulously researched and beautifully written by a world-class novelist.

But most of Andrew's anecdotes—the things he talked about those evenings—were about his family, and often what he told was unflattering and even scandalous. He lived in a typical Southern family of that era, where the only entertainment on long winter evenings was conversation, and most of the conversation was gossip. You didn't spend too much time talking about the saints in the family. They were much too bland and dull. Imagine *Gone With the Wind* as a novel devoted exclusively to the married life of Ashley and Melanie. You'd throw it across the room after the first 25 pages.

On those interminable evenings, families talked instead of their disgraceful, perverse, eccentric members—the drunks, liars, card cheats, adulterers, thieves, and certifiable idiots. All families had them, and they made the most entertaining conversation, provided the children were already in bed.

Allen Tate, in a famous essay, explained the explosion of Southern literature in the 1920's, 30's, and 40's. He said that the South had reached a moment of self-consciousness, when it was forced to look backward to what it had been and to look forward to what people were urging the region to become. Out of the tension between those two visions, he said, the novelist and poet had created literature.

It was a brilliant theory, typical of Tate's critical genius; and it became canon law among devotees of the so-called Southern Renaissance. It was a valid theory to explain *I'll Take My Stand*. As an explanation for the out-pouring of Southern fiction and poetry, it was, I've always thought, a lot of high-blown nonsense. When literature turned away from New York City and began to focus on small-town America—a trend for which Sherwood Anderson was in part responsible—Southern poets and fiction writers suddenly found their voice. That's where they were born, what they knew.

The Southern Renaissance came into being because of the kind of conversation carried on in Andrew's living room and, in the summer, on his front porch—simply a continuation of the family or town gossip so prevalent in the region before radio and television. Faulkner sat on a bench on the square in Oxford, Mississippi and listened to old men talk. And make no mistake, when they get the chance, men are just as prone to gossiping as women. That's where Faulkner got the ideas for many of his best stories—from the communal memory of old codgers who knew anecdotes about great-great-grandparents who had been dead a hundred years. People who live in big cities are less likely to know their family history. As Mr. Davidson once said in discussing this same phenomenon, "Can you imagine a Heming-way character *having* a grandfather?"

When you grew up in a small town like Murfreesboro, Tennessee—as Andrew Lytle did—you knew not only the secrets of your own family but also the secrets of everybody else's. In such a world, you couldn't be too proud. While it was natural to think your folks were better than anyone else's, you could never say so except to your own kin, because everybody in town knew that your great-uncle Joe had been an embezzler (as mine was) or that your Aunt Effie had gotten pregnant and had visited cousins in Charleston for the better part of a year. Knowing this, Andrew told all the ugly family stories himself. In so doing, he recreated the world the Agrarians had attempted to preserve—not in any abstract or idealized way, but in the concrete particulars of his own experience. In his published family history, *A Wake for the Living*, he recaptures that world and entertains the reader as few writers could do.

He often told these anecdotes in lectures, and usually got a standing ova-tion at the end. He had the timing of a stand-up comedian and the presence of a seasoned actor, probably because, in his youth, he had appeared on the Broadway stage. His impact on women was extraordinary.

Once, after such an appearance at the University of Dallas, Mel Bradford and I were talking to him in his motel room when the phone rang. It was one of our English majors, a pretty blonde of 20 who had written her senior paper on some aspect of Andrew's work. She was engaged to be married, but she begged Andrew to let her come to his motel room—alone. "You've got to give me something to remember," she said. From snatches of conversation we could tell what she was proposing. He tried to explain that he had no intention of allowing such a meeting to take place, and she began to cry. He finally handed the phone to Bradford and said, "Here, Mel. You handle this."

At the time Andrew was 67.

The last time I saw him, he was 90. I had flown down to Tennessee from Washington to gather notes for a biography of him that I still hope to write. His voice was no more than a whisper. His skin was drained of moisture, like old leather. He could barely walk. It was the first time I'd seen him when he looked his age.

But the anecdotes still tumbled out—his boyhood, an early romance with a girl in Virginia, his first year at Vanderbilt. He had lost his daughter Kate to cancer, and he told me about a recent visit her husband, their children, and the husband's new wife had made to Kate's grave. The new wife had stepped into a sudden and inexplicable hole and had broken her leg right there on Kate's grave. "I know who was responsible for that," he said.

A few months later, Tam Carlson—his all-time favorite student and a member of the Sewanee faculty—brought his wife over for their daily visit. In the middle of the conversation, Andrew smiled and closed his eyes. He never reopened them.

WHEN I WAS TEACHING AT CONVERSE COLLEGE in Spartanburg, South Carolina, several of us persuaded the administration to fund a creative-writing workshop during both summer semesters. Students would take an eight-week course taught by poet-novelist-critic Marion Montgomery. Then the group would move to a mountain lodge owned by the college, where they would be joined by a fiction writer and a poet, who would discuss student manuscripts and otherwise discourse on the supreme theme of art and song. It was a good way for both faculty and students to use up a summer.

By then I knew Andrew quite well and asked him to be our fiction writer. And since he knew Allen Tate quite well, we decided that Tate would be our poet.

Allen had been a Phi Delta Theta at Vanderbilt—my father's fraternity—and I had a picture of the brotherhood that included both Allen and my father. In order to play on his heart strings, I sent the picture along with an invitation to join our summer faculty. He wrote back a gracious letter, telling me how touched he was to receive the photo, and agreeing to come that summer. (I later learned that he already had a copy of the fraternity photo.)

At Converse we put together a brochure, mailed to English departments throughout the country, and waited for applications. We got some—enough to justify the program. A week before the scheduled arrival of our novelist and poet, I got a call from Andrew.

"I ought to tell you. I don't think Allen is coming."

"Of course he's coming," I said. "I have his letter."

"I think he plans to go to Italy instead. He told me so."

I was shocked. (Had I known Allen a little better, I wouldn't have been shocked at all.)

Andrew managed to get an old friend, Brewster Ghiselin, to take his place. He was a charming man who did a fine job with the students. However, when next year rolled around, I was determined to get Tate. Again, he agreed to come. Again I got the call from Andrew.

"He's hiding out from his wife. He isn't coming. But I enlisted a back-up a couple of months ago."

My heart sank. There were—and are—more poets out there than the sands of the desert. Most of them mediocre at best.

"Whom did you get?" I asked.

"John Ransom."

Had I known that Ransom would come, I would never have bothered with Allen. At the time, Ransom's work was in every anthology of contemporary poetry, whereas Tate's was not. In form, diction, and tone Ransom's spare, carefully chiseled lyrics were as readily identifiable as those of A.E. Housman or John Donne. I believe they will be read 100 years from now, assuming anyone can read. At that time, Ransom was one of the first poets journeymen imitated on their way to discovering their own voice. Some of the early poetry of Sylvia Plath sounds like it was written by Ransom on a bad day.

He all but stopped writing verse before the end of the 1920's and published only criticism from then on. When someone attending his public lecture asked him why he had forsaken poetry, he said in his quiet still-Southern voice: "It's a free country."

When he arrived in Spartanburg, he charmed everyone with his quiet courtesy and apparent sweetness. He was short and plump, with white wispy hair and the smoothest skin I ever saw on a man his age. He had a cheerful disposition, seemed to enjoy the students, and was quite convivial over a drink in the late afternoon.

He was gentle-natured, spoke softly and never carried a stick, big or small. Or so we concluded. At the time, he was editor of *The Kenyon Review*, one of the two or three most prestigious literary quarterlies in America, and we wondered how anyone so kind and considerate could have had the heart to reject a manuscript.

Our plan was to allow students to eat breakfast, lunch, and dinner with these men, discuss literature and other important matters, and then—in private sessions—have their manuscripts critiqued: the fiction by Lytle, the poetry by Ransom.

I remember one student, a boy named Spear, who was barely an apprentice in the art of poetry. He came to the campus sporting a beard—not as common a practice in the early 60's as it was a few years later. I remember that in one of his poems he compared himself to Christ, arguing that Jesus was probably crucified because he wore a beard. He asked one of the Converse girls for a date, and she said she wouldn't go out with him unless he got rid of that beard, whereupon he immediately went to the dormitory and came back clean-shaven. The next day, Marion Montgomery—who taught the eight-week course—asked the boy if he didn't think Jesus might have shaved His beard to avoid crucifixion. It was a valid literary question, challenging the integrity of the poem and poet.

So when Spear took his portfolio into the room to discuss it with Mr. Ransom, we shook our heads. Spear didn't return to poolside after the two-hour conference, but Mr. Ransom joined us with a benign smile on his face.

"Well," he said, "Young Spear tells me he intends to devote his life to poetry."

We were stunned. How could he possibly think that Young Spear had talent, or even rudimentary skill? More to the point, how could he encourage an inarticulate, self-centered boy to waste his life writing bad verse? At that point, we concluded that Mr. Ransom was in his dotage, that the Jesus-beard poem would be appearing in the next issue of *The Kenyon Review*.

At dinnertime Young Spear was nowhere to be seen. One of the other students told us he was sulking in his tent.

"Why?" we asked.

"He came back pumped up with enthusiasm, but the more he thought about what Mr. Ransom had told him, the more depressed he became. He says he'll never write another poem."

Mr. Ransom furrowed his brow. "Oh, dear," he said, and asked for another ear of corn.

As for his tenderhearted inability to exercise critical judgment as editor of *The Kenyon Review*, I remembered that I had already tested that proposition several years earlier. I had written three poems I thought would surely be anthologized. I decided to give first crack at them to *The Kenyon Review*. Having missed the mail at home, I took them down to Union Station in Nashville so they would go out that night, which was Tuesday. Thursday morning I looked in the mailbox and found the envelope containing the poems. Obviously the postman had sent them to the return address rather than to *The Kenyon Review*. Then I noticed the postmark: Gambier, Ohio. And opening the envelope, I found the poems inside with a standard rejection slip from *The Kenyon Review*. My opinion of the U.S. Post Office rose a couple of notches. Years later I told Mr. Ransom how quickly and efficiently he had handled my manuscript; he shook his head and said, "Oh, dear."

IN 1970, the University of Dallas hosted the Southern Literary Festival; and with Louise Cowan, Mel Bradford, and I well connected with the group, we decided to ask the surviving Fugitive-Agrarians to read their works at the festival and then stay over for a private recorded session on Agrarianism. Andrew Lytle, Donald Davidson, John Ransom, and Allen Tate accepted immediately, but Warren refused. By then he had won a Pulitzer Prize in fiction and one in poetry, and his price was more than we could muster. However, Henry Salvatori, a noted conservative philanthropist, sent us a large check, and we were able to bring Warren as well. Davidson was too sick to attend.

Warren read from his poetry to an audience of well over 1,000. When he came to the podium, he looked down to see Ransom, Lytle, and Tate sitting on the first row. He stepped back and shook his head.

"I'm not sure I can read these poems with those cold eyes staring up at me. Those are the hardest critics in the world."

Then he pointed a trembling finger. "There's John Ransom. You all think he's a sweet old man. But he's not. He's as mean as a snake."

After the Agrarian session was over—and for the most part it went badly—I took Mr. Ransom back to his motel. He was to celebrate his 80th birthday in a few months, and I thought he might want to rest, but he insisted that I come in. He wanted to talk—to gossip, mostly. We talked about Vanderbilt in the old days, about Dr. Mims, the dictatorial English department chairman who had made life so hard for the Fugitives. Dr. Mims was a notorious lecher, even in his late 80's. When I was at Vanderbilt, some 30 years after the Fugitives, Dr. Mims was still stumping around the campus, eyeing the coeds. The young women at the library learned to issue him books by sliding them across the counter, because, even at his advanced years, his hand was as quick as a young boy's catching flies. I told Mr. Ransom about an incident in which my mother was forced to burn the old man's hand with a cigarette.

Mr. Ransom smiled and said, "You mustn't be too hard on him, because, you know, Mrs. Mims denied him the privileges."

That sounded too charitable. Knowing the history of the department—and the fact that when Kenyon made Ransom an offer, Mims saw to it that Vanderbilt didn't match it—I asked him how the Fugitives really felt about the old guy.

He replied very gently, "Dr. Mims kept coming around, saying 'Why don't you boys love me?' And we would always say, 'Oh, Dr. Mims we do love you.' But of course we didn't. We hated him."

I brought up Warren's remarks, and he said, "I admire his poetry greatly. I believe he's one of our finest poets." Then he began to reminisce about Warren the young man and about his first marriage.

"His wife, Cinina, was an Italian girl," he said, "and very high-strung. I remember that when we would play croquet, if someone struck her ball and knocked it away, she would throw herself on the ground and begin kicking and screaming."

He told me that eventually she had what they called a nervous breakdown and became suicidal. Her psychiatrist told her that her animosity toward Warren was the root of her problems. So they separated and eventually divorced.

"He was so concerned about her," Ransom said, "that he rented the apartment across the street and watched over her until she went to sleep each night. That's the kind of man he is."

Later, I told Mr. Warren how much Mr. Ransom said he admired his poetry. Warren laughed and shook his head. "Don't believe a word he says."

I took Mr. Ransom to the plane the next day; and as we were sitting, waiting for his flight to be called, somehow our conversation turned to dying.

"I think we're meant to die so others can take our place," he said. "When my time comes, I'll be happy to make room for somebody else."

His flight was called, and I watched him walk through the gate, waving to me, nodding and smiling to the strangers also boarding. That's the last time I saw him. He died a few years later, apparently of Alzheimer's disease. But as I remember that last conversation—the one about dying—I can't help thinking that if I were the Lord, I would be willing to trade several million Baby Boomers just to keep a place for a mind and wit that subtle, a manner that courtly, and a heart as deep and dangerous as quicksand.

If there's a place for good poets in heaven, Ransom will surely be there, sitting at a round table, smiling, listening more than talking, as Dante, Shakespeare, and Keats hold forth. But every Friday, God will lend him to the devil so that he can torment the bad poets in hell, by proving to them, in the kindest way possible, just how unacceptable, how absolutely dreadful their work really is.

ROBERT PENN WARREN was the youngest member of the Fugitive-Agrarians. His essay in *I'll Take My Stand* was on the race question. Years later, when interviewed by the fiercely left-wing *Partisan Review*, he said the essay was an apology for segregation, that he had not read it since it was published, and that he had been uncomfortable with the subject matter from the outset. By then he was a self-styled liberal who had written a famous book-length denunciation of Jim Crow called *Segregation: The Inner Conflict of the South*.

Had he really failed to reread his early essay as he claimed, or was this just a ploy to avoid having to discuss its content with a member of what he called "the Bully Boys of Virtue?" I believe he was telling the truth—and for two reasons. In the first place, from personal experience I know that writers don't like to confront things published many years earlier, knowing that, in all likelihood, they will, from a current perspective, be written in barbaric prose. (My Vanderbilt M.A. thesis, four short stories, seemed so bad in later years that I persuaded a former student to steal it from the library and burn it.) In the second place, Warren's essay is not an apology for segregation. It is, instead, a sympathetic portrayal of black life in the region, given the immitigable fact of segregation and the likelihood then that the arrangement would continue until the archangel Gabriel blew his horn. In fact, 30 years later, some segregationists were outraged by what Warren had written.

When we hosted the Agrarian reunion at the University of Dallas, Warren posed the greatest threat to an harmonious discussion. Ransom and Tate were no longer militantly Southern, but neither were they militantly anti-Southern, as Warren seemed to be. We imagined him savaging Davidson and Lytle, heaping scorn on *I'll Take My Stand*, and attacking the reunion and the university in the *New York Times*. But if the reunion was to be credible, we had to have him.

We finally scraped up enough money to lure him down from Yale, and I was assigned the task of picking him up at Love Field, while the others, already in town, were enjoying a dinner at the house of one of the university's rich patrons. I was honored to pick him up, but wary. Among other things, he was the only one I had never met. I needn't have worried. He was one of the warmest, most charming men I'd ever met. From the beginning I understood why Weaver, who studied under Warren at LSU, was so impressed by him and so tempted to give up socialism for such a man. I wondered if, with renewed exposure to the liberal Warren, Weaver would now reconvert to socialism.

As we rode to the motel, Warren talked about the problems the Agrarians might discuss at these sessions. "The overarching question," he said, "is whether or not man's capacity for abstraction is a good thing or a bad thing." He spoke with a Kentucky twang in his voice that sounded earthier and less cultivated than the accents of the others, all of which were still identifiably Southern, despite the fact that Ransom and Tate had spent most of the intervening years in the North, as had Warren.

When we reached his hotel room, he took off his shirt and unselfconsciously washed under his arms with water from the lavatory. On the way to Dallas, he told me, he had stopped to see his brother, a tobacco farmer, and he talked about the problems the brother was facing. He could have been a farmer, so detailed was his knowledge about crops, the soil, and the marketplace.

He greeted the others as warmly as if they had met in the Vanderbilt dining hall only yesterday. All of them had a sense of loyalty to one another that transcended mere politics and social theory. Recently I read somewhere that Warren's son had said contemptuously: "Donald Davidson was never mentioned in our house." He might have been surprised to learn that Warren had stopped in Nashville to see Davidson on the way over, and that he had told the others with tears in his eyes, "He's dying. He's dying."

When the Agrarian conversations began—behind closed doors, tape recorder running—the participants were unresponsive. It soon became clear that they didn't want to talk about *I'll Take My Stand*. Ransom was diffident. Lytle was willing but could elicit little response with what he said. Tate was almost belligerent in his curt answers. Warren seemed unwilling to attack the past. Our plan had been to devote the first session to factual questions about how the project got started, and the manner in which they did or didn't work together. They'd forgotten all those details.

At the first break, Warren called me aside.

"Why don't you ask us if we knew anything about economics?"

It was a loaded question. Except for one of the contributors—the late H.C. Nixon—you could be certain not one of them had read Adam Smith or Keynes or Samuelson or the emerging free-market theorists who would soon begin capturing Nobel prizes.

I asked the question, and it fell on the table like a dying fish, eyes bulging, gasping for air.

At the next break, Warren said, "Ask us about the minority psychology, that overdefends itself."

I asked. Another dying fish.

Then John Crowe Ransom started talking, not about *I'll Take My Stand*

73

or the Agrarians, but about one of his colleagues at Kenyon who was a foot fetishist. The story went on and on about this man's obsessive attraction to women's shoes, which got him into all sorts of difficult situations and a marriage he had not intended. We realized then that the discussions could never be transcribed and published as the Vanderbilt Fugitive Reunion had been—not without a lawsuit from this foot man in Gambier. But the ice was broken.

At that point, Warren asked his own question and answered it in what I can only describe as the most brilliant off-the-cuff conversation I have ever heard. He spoke not only in perfect sentences but in perfect paragraphs. It was formal discourse but filled with concrete images and anecdotes, vivid, earthy, original. We sat there and listened in awe. I can't remember what he was talking about. I tried to get the transcript in preparation for this talk, but the University of Dallas couldn't locate it.

At some later time, Warren also discussed the founding of *The Southern Review*, a world-famous literary quarterly that he and Cleanth Brooks initially edited. The idea for an LSU-based literary journal came not from Brooks and Warren but from a highly unlikely source.

As Warren told us during that session, one day the two English professors got a call from the office of Huey P. Long, then governor of Louisiana. Long's secretary said the governor would like to meet with them, today if possible. They agreed on a time, and the secretary told Brooks and Warren to go down to the Baton Rouge town square and wait for a long black Packard to pick them up. They were there at the appointed time, and sure enough the car came slowly around the corner and stopped. They got in, and there sat the Kingfish himself.

The car began to move slowly and made a right turn, as Governor Long asked them, "Do you fellows think a literary magazine would bring prestige to the university?" They both assured him that it would. The Packard made another right turn. "Do you two think you could put one together?" They assured him they could. The Packard made yet another right turn. "How long do you think it would take to get it up and running?" They told him pretty quick. The Packard made a final right turn and stopped. "O.K.," Long said. "You figure out how much you'll need and I'll get you the money real quick." They thanked him and got out of the car—on precisely the spot where they'd been picked up, maybe two minutes earlier.

Warren and I talked at some length, between sessions and at meals. He told me of an early 19th-century manuscript he had found in a Midwestern university—a nonfiction autobiography. "I'm desperate to publish it under my own name," he said, "but it's so perfect that I'm afraid if I touch it, I'll ruin it." Among other things, it was the story of a young man who had not as yet been saved. An enemy was angry with him, and he was afraid his adversary would kill him before he received the Lord, so in order to save his immortal soul, he bushwhacked and killed the other guy first. The autobiographer said this murderer was the holiest man he'd ever known.

"If I publish it as a novel under my own name, will you tell on me?" he asked.

"As soon as it hits the bookstore," I said.

We talked about his use of historical figures and narratives, and I mentioned *All the King's Men.*

"I read somewhere that you denied Willie Stark was based entirely on Huey Long. You said you also had in mind the rise of fascism in Italy."

With the trace of a smile, he nodded. He knew I didn't believe him.

"If you wanted to make that connection," I asked, "then why didn't you name him Willie Linguini?"

"I should have," he said. "I should have."

AFTER THE SESSIONS HAD ENDED, we agreed that our private discussions weren't worth publishing. Because we couldn't afford to bring in others— and also because we had wanted them all to ourselves, all the intimacy, all the glory—we had excluded people who could have driven the conversation more authoritatively in the right direction: Cleanth Brooks and Walter Sullivan, for example. Later Vanderbilt held its own Agrarian reunion, and it went much better.

They're all fading names now—12 men who shared for a while the illusion that they could stop the inevitable unraveling of a great society. Like Cassandra, they predicted the future, and no one listened. Lytle told me in his last years, "We were better prophets than we knew. Things are worse now than we ever imagined. The problem was, no one believed that the society they knew could ever be taken from them. Now it's gone forever." Perhaps the greater tragedy—more modern than Aeschylean—is that people today don't even know it ever existed.

# An American Dilemma:
# The Episcopal Church (1976-2006)

IN 1976, THE EPISCOPAL CHURCH, U.S.A., met in General Convention to consider, among other things, two questions: the adoption of a new Book of Common Prayer and the ordination of women. Whether they knew it or not, the delegates were actually resolving a deeper, more disturbing dilemma: whether to remain orthodox or to remain respectable.

From its beginnings and well into the 20th century, the Episcopal Church had enjoyed the luxury of being both. While theological debates raged in other branches of Christendom, Episcopalians agreed on the tenets of the historical creeds and quarreled instead over high church and low church. Though, in some locales, other denominations brought social status to their membership, nationwide the Episcopal Church was the place to be if you wanted to join the country club or meet the president of the bank. At Saint Albans, orthodoxy and respectability were old friends and sat in the same pew on Sunday mornings.

Then, in the second half of the 20th century, a rift occurred; and, soon enough, the two were no longer speaking. The nation suddenly found itself in the grip of social revolution. The civil-rights movement, peace movement, women's movement, and sexual revolution quickly changed America from a stable, traditional society into a political and cultural war zone. The media and the academy quickly sided with the revolutionaries and began to exert an ever-increasing influence on Christian churches. Soon, it became unfashionable to adhere to creeds and traditional ways. The chic, educated crowd was ready for new ideas, new social arrangements, a new church.

Episcopalians were told that the Book of Common Prayer—dating back to the 16th century—was too penitential, too focused on sin. When praying, people knelt like cowering serfs instead of standing straight and tall. They repeated phrases like "have mercy upon us, miserable offenders" and "there is no health in us." Even worse, the Episcopal Church had an all-male clergy in an emerging era of militant feminism. If a woman could be the CEO of a Fortune 500 company, she should be able to be a priest or a bishop in the Episcopal Church.

Indeed, elite Episcopalians concluded that, if they did not slough off their gauche orthodoxies and enter the Age of Aquarius, the Church would no longer be a fashionable place to promenade on Sunday mornings. At the beginning of the cultural revolution, the leading spokesman for such hetero-doxy was the Rt. Rev. James Pike, who became a celebrity clergyman while serving as dean of New York's Cathedral of St. John the Divine—the most con-spicuous pulpit the Episcopal Church had to offer. And, as far as the main-stream media were concerned, he was saying all the right things: He rejected the Virgin Birth; he dismissed the doctrine of the Trinity as false and irrele-vant; and he endorsed the ordination of women. An accomplished phrase-maker, he called for "more belief and fewer beliefs." He was "refreshing," "outspoken," "brilliant." His thoughtful face appeared on the cover of *Time*.

This notoriety won him the see of California and the growing disapprov-al of his orthodox fellow bishops, already a shrinking number in the Epis-copal Church. In 1966, a group led by Henry I. Louttit, bishop of the Cen-tral Archdeanery of South Florida, demanded that Pike be tried for heresy.

John Hines, presiding bishop of the Episcopal Church, met with Lout-tit and a small delegation in New York and told them he had polled key fig-ures in the mass media, who had declared unanimously that a heresy trial would severely, disastrously damage the Church's image. Most of the bish-ops agreed. The bishop of New York expressed the feelings of the majori-ty: "Of all the methods of dealing with Bishop Pike's views, the very worst is surely a heresy trial! Whatever the result, the good name of the church will be greatly injured."

Hines asked Louttit and his cohorts to allow an *ad hoc* committee to address the problem more informally, less visibly. Louttit reluctantly agreed. Members of the committee met, engaged in a great deal of handwringing, and came back with a report that said (in part):

> It is the opinion that this proposed trial would not solve the prob-lem presented to the church by this minister, but in fact would be detrimental to the church's mission and witness. This heresy trial would be widely viewed as a "throw back" to centuries when the law in church and state sought to repress and penalize unaccept-able opinions. It would spread abroad a "repressive image" of the church and suggest to many that we were more concerned with traditional propositions about God than with the faith as the re-sponse of the whole man to God.

At Wheeling, West Virginia, the House of Bishops adopted this state-ment by an overwhelming vote, though they also agreed to "censure" Bish-op Pike—a small, dry bone tossed to Christian orthodoxy. In the above passage, two phrases—"unacceptable opinions" and "repressive image"—revealed what was really going on.

In the first of these phrases, the bishops suggested that Pike's dismissal of the Trinity was mere "opinion" rather than a denial of eternal truth. For decades, high and low churchmen had been arguing heatedly over the practice of garnishing the liturgy with sanctus bells and incense. Following this decree, they could also argue over the doctrine of the Trinity in the same earnest but harmless way.

In the second phrase, "image" is elevated to the level of First Principle. Once he had made short work of the Trinity, Bishop Pike refused to say "in the name of the Father, Son, and Holy Ghost" during services he conducted. Given the unique centrality of this doctrine to Christianity, what Pike professed was a modern version of the Arian heresy. Yet to say so officially, the bishops agreed, would be to expose the Episcopal Church to the charge of "dogmatism"—an unacceptable alternative to looking the other way.

The bishops came together in Wheeling as one kind of church and parted ways as quite another. Henceforth, the Episcopal Church would have no theology to anchor its speculations and enthusiasms, no commitment to immutable truths, no real mind—only a deepening concern for public opinion, which its defenders euphemistically called "tolerance."

AT THE TIME OF THE PIKE CONTROVERSY, the Episcopal Church had no formal catechism. Its theology could be found in the text of the Book of Common Prayer (1928 version)—embedded in the Apostles' and Nicene Creeds, in the Prayer of Consecration, and in services such as Baptism and Ordination. This theology was orthodox in every respect, which is why the modernist bishops and priests saw the Prayer Book as a dinosaur, at best, and a dire threat to "progressive thinking," at worst. It had to go.

Even as the liturgical debate raged, a parallel controversy was developing—one that would again threaten the Church's respectability. The feminist movement had captured the imagination of the media; and, suddenly, an all-male clergy was giving the Church a "repressive image." A debate emerged; but even before the 1976 General Convention could resolve the issue officially, three retired bishops, acting in defiance of then-current canon law, ordained female priests. And why not? No compelling authority existed to restrain them. And hadn't Bishop Pike received a mere slap on the wrist?

The orthodox forces had been too preoccupied with the Prayer Book to think seriously about the feminist movement. The General Convention—stacked with anti-Prayer Book activists—stunned the Church by canonizing the ordination of women.

Nor could this new Church defend Christian moral teachings. A year after the ordination of women, Bishop Paul Moore of New York—a high-profile Pike-alike—ordained an open and practicing lesbian. A brief and fruitless furor ensued. Moore issued an "apology" of sorts, and the ordination of open homosexuals was put on the shelf for several decades.

This transformation from orthodoxy to theological anarchy by no means occurred without damaging consequences. Hordes have left the Episcopal Church. No one knows for sure how many or where they went, but, clearly, a substantial portion—wounded and disillusioned—sit at home on Sundays, watching *Meet the Press*. Others have "gone to Rome" or the Greek Orthodox Church. A few have even ended up in evangelical congregations—a far cry from the solemn liturgy they loved in the old Episcopal Church.

However, a significant number formed what are now called "continuing churches," most of them using the 1928 Book of Common Prayer, with bishops and clergy who can trace their apostolic lineage back to one of the 12 apostles. The growth of these churches has been slow and strife-ridden. When Moses led the saving remnant out of Egypt, he probably took with him a ragtag band of pagans, pickpockets, and murderers—anyone who wanted out of Egypt. Later, he took a branch, dipped it in the blood of a lamb, and sprinkled everybody, making them all Jews. When the 1976 General Convention ended, the best and the worst left the Episcopal Church together: the true believers who could no longer tolerate fashionable heresy and, with them, the ideologues, misfits, and power-seekers.

A volatile mix of the orthodox and half-sane, these defectors have wandered in the wilderness for decades, bickering among themselves, splitting into even smaller fragments held together by certitude and memory. Indeed, to cynical observers, they have become what the Episcopal hierarchy predicted: excessively dogmatic and finally irrelevant.

However, at least one man believes that these disparate factions can find enough common ground to form a single unified church—Bishop Paul Hewett of the Diocese of the Holy Cross. A trim, dark-haired man in his late 50's—convivial, articulate, and often eloquent—he takes the orthodox position that the Christian Church exists in unity with Christ, no matter how often we carve up its temporal jurisdictions or deliver it for a time to heresy.

"The Church's unity," he says, "is the sign to shattered, splintered humanity of wholeness and new life in Christ. Our unity is a given. We cannot make the Church one. It already is one. What we do is reveal this unity, or obscure it."

Bishop Hewett sees his first order of business as the melding of eight separate continuing churches into one organic whole—a freestanding and orthodox "province." The chief obstacle to the unity of these communions is not really doctrinal, canonical, or liturgical. With some serious and self-effacing debate, a consensus might be reached on the ways and teachings of the Church. So what is the biggest stumbling block to unity?

Bishops.

Each branch of the continuing church has its geographical jurisdictions, and they tend to overlap. In one state, for example, two rival bishops reign in cathedrals a mere 30 miles apart. So which one, in the interest of reunion, would be willing to put his purple tunic in mothballs and surrender his crook and miter? The probable answer to that question is "neither"—as Bishop Hewett well knows. Thus, in his drawing-board province, all current bishops would retain their episcopal status, able to confirm laymen, ordain priests, and even participate in the consecration of new bishops.

However, it might be necessary to ask that some bishops allow other bishops to become head dog in these new geographical jurisdictions. As Bishop Hewett has said, "We recall the example of the Antiochian Orthodox Church, which at one time had two separate jurisdictions in the United States. They became a single jurisdiction when one of the bishops said to Metropolitan Philip, 'You are a better man than I. So you look after the whole thing.' That kind of courage and humility is a miracle of God's grace."

*Miracle* is the right word. Yet he counts on precisely that kind of grace to reconstitute at least a portion of the fragmented Anglican Communion in America. "The Holy Spirit," he says, "is not very interested in our territorial squabbles."

"If we can't do this," he told a reporter for the *Philadelphia Inquirer*, "then I think Anglicanism in this country is lost. Everyone who has left [the Episcopal Church] will either become Roman Catholic or Eastern Orthodox or go nowhere. We have one more five-year window if we're going to put the thing together right."

To this end, he is constantly on the road, talking to bishops in other communions, meeting with like-minded clergy and laity in Great Britain, even traveling to Norway and Sweden, where a chilly remnant is struggling to keep the flickering flame of orthodoxy alive. Fishing for true believers in Scandinavia may seem like trolling for marlin in a wading pond, yet the Swedes and Norwegians periodically come to London to join Hewett and others in strategy talks. So maybe the grace Bishop Hewett seeks is beginning to work its quiet magic in the most unlikely places.

As for the Episcopal Church, it is still on a collision course with historical Christianity. Its positions on women's ordination and homosexual rights are irrevocable. If its bishops were to back down now and reaffirm traditionalist views on these subjects, they would lose the respectability they have so tenaciously retained over the last 30 years.

**Bishop Pike's spiritual heirs are everywhere**; but, over the past decade, the most prominent has been the Rt. Rev. John Spong, bishop of Newark, now retired. Bishop Spong has discussed his militant unbelief in several books, including *Why Christianity Must Change or Die*, in which he argues, point by point, that all of the historical doctrines specified in the creeds are nonsense and that the Christian Church must reject them or shrivel to irrelevancy and be swept away by the winds of change. Bishop Spong is by no means as bright or as learned as Bishop Pike; but, in an age when pagan ignorance is in fashion, he does not have to be.

Bishop Spong's highly publicized sanctification of homosexuality helped to pave the way for the 2003 consecration of Bishop Gene Robinson, who, years earlier, had left his wife and children to live openly with a male lover. When the General Convention put its imprimatur on this rejection of biblical morality, the Episcopal Church found itself seriously at odds with worldwide Anglicanism. Indeed, Episcopalians may soon find themselves out of communion with Anglicans in other countries. Bishop Robinson did not help matters when, in a recent [2000] interview with Planned Parenthood, he trumpeted his own moral relativism. When asked if he was "pro-choice," he answered: "Absolutely. The reason I love the Episcopal Church is that it actually trusts us to be adults. In a world where everyone tries to paint things as black or white, Episcopalians feel pretty comfortable in the gray areas."

Indeed, they do. These days, that is the place to be, the most respectable part of town. The entire popular culture has moved into the gray house next door and throws block parties every weekend. The stern folks who live way over on Black-and-White Street—such as Bishop Paul Hewett and his followers—do not know what they are missing.

# Sex, Propaganda, and Higher Education

**O**VER THE PAST FEW YEARS, college administrators and faculty committees have been tackling a relatively new ethical question raised on campuses across the nation: What about sex between faculty members and students? Older professors can remember when the answer to that question would have been obvious. Some can even recall a time when the question would never have been asked.

Today, however, with mixed dorms and mixed roommates, how can the old-fashioned barrier that separates teacher and student be permitted to stand? After all, if engaging in sex has become a right enjoyed by all consenting adults, then what possible objection can anyone offer to a consenting student and a faculty member exercising that right together? While the academy has not yet reached a consensus on this question, the fact that it has been raised at all is symptomatic of a sea change in higher education, a substantive redefinition of the idea of a university.

For generations, the university was regarded as a free market of ideas, a place where diverse opinions were encouraged and where students learned to think by weighing one point of view against another. Hence the concept of academic freedom, the doctrine that a professor had a right to express whatever ideas he championed, both in the classroom and in the community at large. This doctrine was grounded in the assumption that the academy as an institution didn't take sides. Even Cardinal Newman, when describing the ideal Catholic university, insisted that no indoctrination take place, that the student be taught *how* to think rather than *what* to think. This view prevailed in American universities up until the 1960's—or, at least, the academy paid lip service to it.

While faculty members came to believe that the twin doctrines of academic freedom and the free market of ideas were invented solely to protect them, these ideals protected students as well, given their intellectual naiveté and, hence, their vulnerability to manipulation. After all, the university did not exist so that teachers could prance about campuses, expressing eccentric opinions, quarreling with one another and the world. It existed to train the minds of the young. Thus, it was originally student-centered rather than faculty-centered. Somewhere along the way, professors forgot for whom the university existed.

In his 1965 book *Repressive Tolerance*, Herbert Marcuse became the philosopher of late 20th-century academia. In essence, he advocated the repeal of academic freedom and the suppression of all ideas hostile to social and economic revolution. As he put it, "Certain things cannot be said; certain ideas cannot be expressed; certain policies cannot be proposed, certain behavior cannot be permitted without making tolerance an instrument for the continuation of servitude." It was a typically Marxist pronouncement—blunt, arrogant, and without so much as a rhetorical bow to conventional wisdom.

This statement still seems outrageous to professors over 70 and to their graying former students. However, few current academics share this sense of outrage. Indeed, in this single sentence, Marcuse produced a new creed for higher education in America and helped to inaugurate a vision of a new institution—no longer a university in the traditional sense but an opinion mill, an arm of the revolution.

THE MOTIVE BEHIND THIS CRUSHING OF ALL DISSENT was the drive to recruit students in a Second American Revolution, which, in the 1960's and 70's, seemed all but inevitable. For generations, American students had behaved themselves—except for periodically swallowing goldfish, conducting panty raids, or jamming themselves into telephone booths. Then the war in Vietnam followed on the heels of the civil-rights movement, and leftist professors became professional agitators, seizing on the opportunity to use students in the same way their counterparts had for decades used them in Europe and South America—to destabilize an orderly society. The students were predictably pliant; when manipulated by their professors, they always are.

Why? Because when they go off to college, young people leave a relatively complex world and enter a relatively simple one—a kingdom where abstractions rule. In that world, those who do what is most valued are the professors, with their advanced degrees, their intellectual fiefdoms, their air of certitude. A few examples of *argumentum ad misericordiam*, a few tales of oppression, a line or two from John Lennon's "Imagine," and young people charge into the streets, teeth grinding, nostrils flaring, waving whatever insolent banner their teachers hand them. So, by the late 60's, middle-class students were rioting on campuses all over the country, heaving rocks at police, vandalizing buildings, issuing nonnegotiable demands—full of carefree, self-righteous zeal.

Few people noticed that the rapid transformation of the university into the opinion mill dramatically altered the attitude of teacher to student. In the university, students were treated as ends rather than as means to ends. The integrity of their malleable minds was regarded as inviolable. Ideally, the chief aim of instruction was to nurture their critical ability to the point at which they could make judgments independent of others, including their instructors. By contrast, the opinion mill treats students as means to an end, bodies to hurl against the ramparts of authority. They are taught to embrace a prescribed view of society without considering the possibility that alternative views might have merit. In such an institution, students are rewarded for intellectual laziness, for failing to challenge received opinions, for their reluctance to ask pointed questions.

As for the subject matter, in the university, knowledge was regarded as an end in itself—a unique and discrete reality. As such, neither professor nor student could mess with its essential nature. It was not to be manipulated any more than a student was to be manipulated. It had a right to life, liberty, and the pursuit of happiness.

In the current academy, the professor regards the materials of his discipline as means to an end. They possess only instrumental value. Thus, he has the right to torture and eviscerate them to make them work in behalf of whatever revolution he hopes to start that particular day.

In history, facts may be omitted or invented if omissions and inventions serve the cause. Subject to such malicious tampering, the past becomes simpler and simpler—its complexities eliminated through ruthless refinement until all that remains is pure propaganda.

Likewise, in literary studies, novelists and poets who do not lend themselves to misinterpretation are dropped from the syllabus. The rest are compelled to serve in the revolutionary army. Some do so willingly; others are cruelly conscripted. Jane Austen, with her 18th-century love of symmetry and order—a woman in perfect harmony with the world into which she was born—is thus transformed into a modern feminist, at war with the patriarchy, longing to tear out Mr. Darcy's throat.

In today's opinion mills, classes are no longer conducted as they were in universities. Professors make political speeches in class, and often do so while ignoring the discipline they are paid to teach. Some teachers ridicule or savage anyone who refuses to submit to the prevailing orthodoxy. A few even use the grade book to punish dissent. But most rely on the aura of infallibility that follows professors into the classroom and hovers above them as they lecture. They can accomplish more by quietly asserting their authority than by threats and intimidation. In the classroom, they speak *ex cathedra*.

In *A Portrait of the Artist as a Young Man*, Stephen Dedalus, attending a Catholic boys' school, is told by the teacher, a priest, that his essay is heretical.

Humiliated, Stephen is forced to restate his position to conform to Catholic theology. As presented by the anti-Catholic Joyce, the orthodoxy of the school is a harsh, intractable discipline against which the protagonist eventually rebels. This is precisely the kind of intellectual bullying that goes on in thousands of classrooms throughout higher education in this country. The orthodoxy of the left is as rigid and merciless as any theology ever devised. It has its own finely tuned dogmas, its Torquemadas, its instruments of torture.

*Portrait* is a work of art rather than a book of wisdom, and its hero is often arrogant and wrongheaded. However, in one passage, he makes an important distinction between proper art and improper art. What he says could also be used to differentiate between proper and improper education.

> The feelings excited by improper art are kinetic, desire or loathing. Desire urges us to possess, to go to something; loathing urges us to abandon, to go from something. The arts that excite them, pornographical or didactic, are therefore improper arts. The esthetic emotion (I used the general term) is therefore static. The mind is arrested and raised above desire and loathing.

Stephen argues that a work of art whose sole purpose is to make an impact outside its own aesthetic dimensions has no intrinsic worth; it is a servant to sexual desire or to some commitment or cause. In higher education today, knowledge is likewise the servant of ideology, and its worth can be measured only by its impact on the body politic. Therefore, it, too, is intrinsically worthless.

Such knowledge—like improper art—also has a limited shelf life. Today, few if any literate people read novels of social protest written in the first half of the 20th century. Upton Sinclair's *The Jungle* may have led to government inspection of meat, as its author clearly intended, but you would be hard-pressed to find a denser, duller book on the shelves of the Library of Congress—dense and dull precisely because of its didactic purpose. Besides, who has time to worry about the meat-packing industry when we are fighting a war in Iraq and the North Pole is melting away?

You have to feel sorry for the young men and women who will graduate from such institutions with majors in women's studies, black studies, or even English, history, psychology, and sociology. Many will reenter a world of complexity knowing nothing that is valuable or relevant or true. They will find that no one is hiring leftist demonstrators, not even *MoveOn.org*. Mere opinions bring nothing in the marketplace. People are giving them away all over town.

ONE MORE POINT. Stephen Dedalus's linkage of didacticism and pornography suggests a link between the way today's professors promote ideology and the question of whether professors should have sex with students. As the academy addresses this question, the debate is confused and nonsensical, a higher-decibel version of the average faculty meeting.

Few of these academics dare to make statements that might be termed "judgmental," either about the morality of such conduct or its propriety. In the opinion mill, where sex is concerned, there are no absolutes. Some schools ban these liaisons for prudential reasons: "to avoid exploitation and lawsuits." Others lay down guidelines: not if the student is currently in the professor's class. The relationship must be consensual. Discretion.

Feminists tend to oppose faculty-student liaisons because they see male professors as wielding the same old patriarchal power over female students. They cite a history of exploitation, back-alley abortions, and high-strung girls leaping off bridges.

Barry Dank, professor of sociology at California State University, Long Beach, is outraged by the feminist arguments: "This is simply another attack against men, who [sic] they see as being powerful. It's also an attack on young women . . . [denying them the] freedom to decide what they want and what they don't want." Professor Dank has organized a group called Consenting Academics for Sexual Equity (CASE) to fight for the right to have sex with students.

The feminists come closest to understanding what is going on here, though they miss the mark because they can only think in terms of their own self-serving slogans. This debate could take place only on a contemporary campus, where ideology has replaced common sense and—most importantly—where students are now regarded as means to ends. The same arrogance that allows feminists to indoctrinate young women also allows male professors to bed them.

The professor comes to such relationships with the identical advantages he enjoys in the classroom. He is a member of the ruling class, one of the heroes of this closed intellectual society. Young people are attracted to heroes. In the outside world, he would be another face in the crowd. Behind ivy walls, he is Achilles, and the blue-eyed girl on the front row is Briseis, the prize given to Achilles for heroism and then arbitrarily taken away by Agamemnon. In Homer's epic, she has only instrumental value. In the contemporary classroom, she is likewise a prize, a perquisite that comes with an academic appointment, a thing to be used.

# Punishment for Your Sins

A S AMERICA DRIFTS AWAY from orthodox religious belief, God becomes less and less personal and more and more political. The secular world surrounds and absorbs the spiritual. In the 21st century, the Lord joins political parties, circulates petitions, stumps for candidates. The Rev. Jesse Jackson, in a *Chicago Sun-Times* column, tells us that "[a] conservative Christian is a contradiction in terms . . . Jesus was a liberal . . . "

Small wonder that evangelical Christians—accustomed to seeing God's hand in the workings of the world—attributed the devastating consequences of Katrina and Rita to God's anger over a variety of misbehaviors. You would expect Pat Robertson to blame the winds and flooding on abortion, and he did (though he did not say—as reported by *Dateline Hollywood*—that Katrina was God's punishment for allowing New Orleans-reared Ellen DeGeneres to host the Emmy Awards). Michael Marcavage, director of Repent America, went even further: "[W]e must not forget that the citizens of New Orleans tolerated and welcomed the wickedness in their city for so long . . . May this act of God cause us all to think about what we tolerate in our city limits, and bring us trembling before the throne of Almighty God."

Surprisingly, however, many commentators attributed these disasters to a left-leaning deity, one who punishes both our domestic wrongs and our sins abroad. Environmentalists claimed that God was chastising America for SUVs and aerosol cans. Others saw the hurricanes as retribution for social injustice. Thus, Rabbi Michael Lerner wrote that "this is a classic case of the law of karma, or what the Torah warns of environmental disaster unless we create a just society, or what others call watching the chickens come home to roost, or what goes around comes around."

Some saw Katrina and Rita as punishment for America's intervention in the Middle East. Muslim websites were filled with triumphalist rhetoric: "Allahu akbar. Soldiers of God, Hurricane Katrina demolishes America. Don't think that God doesn't care about the injustices of tyrants."

Conversely, supporters of Israel claimed that God sent the devastation to chastise America for her role in forcing Jewish settlers to withdraw from the Gaza Strip. Rabbi Ovadia Yoself (cited on Al Jazeera's website) put it this way: "Bush was behind the (expulsion of) Gush Katif. He encouraged Sharon to expel Gush Katif . . . [W]e had 15,000 people expelled here, and there

150,000 [were expelled]. It was God's retribution."

Black political leaders mixed divine retribution with the usual attacks on white racism. Lewis E. Logan, a Los Angeles AME pastor, shouted:

> [I]t is not a coincidence that it is exactly 50 years from the time of [inaudible] lynching and murder. That it is not a coincidence that the storm's name is a sister. Katrina. For she represents the collective cries of mothers who have lost their sons [applause] to the brutality [louder applause] and the murderous grip of this racist white supremacist American culture [frenzied applause].

In far-off California, it was easy to ignore the obvious: that blacks suffered disproportionately from Katrina and Rita. At ground zero, Mayor Ray Nagin of New Orleans avoided that mistake. In a diatribe laced with obscenities and snarling accusations, he warned of future wrath, saying, "I have no idea what [federal officials] are doing. But I will tell you this: You know, God is looking down on all this, and if they are not doing everything in their power to save people, they are going to pay the price."

APPARENTLY, NOT ONE OF THESE COMMENTATORS entertained the idea that his people could be responsible for God's wrath—or for the chaos that followed. Only political enemies were to blame. Thus, while denouncing the President, Nagin excused looters by saying they were merely looking for food and water. (The TV cameras caught black policewomen in an abandoned Wal-Mart, leisurely filling their shopping carts with clothes.) Snipers shot at rescue teams with the same moral certitude that the mayor displayed, and the corpses of hundreds of drowned school buses yellowed the water, while the mayor called on Washington to send every available Greyhound to New Orleans.

At this point, God—hearing each faction claim His favor—must have regretted stirring up those hurricanes in the first place.

# Envy and the Consumerism of the Have-Nots: Against the Chicken Snakes

YOU CAN MAKE A GOOD ARGUMENT that, by the late 20th century, the Seven Deadly Sins had become the Seven Lively Virtues. In the 1960's, the media lauded the anger of students who bombed police stations and set dormitories on fire. Hollywood glorified lust the way it had once glorified chastity. Government at every level subsidized sloth. As for gluttony, for years the *Guinness Book of World Records* celebrated eating and drinking excesses, including such categories as "heaviest cat." An ex-president of the United States said on national television that "greed is good." Black pride came to be regarded as the quintessential virtue of that community (though white pride is still the deadliest of all sins). But envy is the little engine that drives left-wing politics in America, the cash cow of the Democratic Party, Pavlov's bell.

In the rush to denounce the consumerism of the middle class, we often forget the degree to which the folks who live in untidy neighborhoods and buy groceries off the discount table likewise share in our national obsession with getting and spending. As a country, we've always forgiven the poor for wanting things that bankers and doctors take for granted—indeed, congratulated them for their raw envy. At the same time we've condemned the rich for enjoying those very same things. One of the unspoken assumptions underlying our democracy is that until you're "well off," you're miserable. Our popular songs repeat the phrase "as happy as a king," and nobody seems to question the simile. Charles I? Louis XVI? Nicholas II?

I remember sitting in an Army infirmary, waiting for a pill (that's all they ever gave you) while doctors performed an autopsy on a major. The nurse told us that he'd committed suicide, and that the procedure wouldn't take much longer. I was sitting next to a private who looked to be in his late 40's, the Man With the Hoe in fatigues.

When he heard what was going on, he turned to me, shook his head, and said, "Jeez, why would a major want to kill himself?" He couldn't imagine a problem that being a major wouldn't solve. I suspect a reservoir of unacknowledged envy lay behind that question—a desire to be a dues-paying member of the officer's club, to be chauffeured about in a jeep, and (above all) to buy the things a major's pay would buy.

Poet Edwin Arlington Robinson deals with the same phenomenon in "Richard Cory," a poem that increasingly tricks ideological critics into regarding it as an attack on wealth and privilege. It is anything but that.

In the first stanza, the anonymous speaker tells us he represents the poor folks, who view the rich, polished Richard Cory with unapologetic awe:

> Whenever Richard Cory went down town,
> We people on the pavement looked at him:
> He was a gentleman from sole to crown,
> Clean favored, and imperially slim.

Through the use of the words *crown* and *imperially*, the poet hints at a submerged metaphor that almost surfaces in the third stanza: Richard Cory as king and the people as subjects.

> And he was rich—yes, richer than a king—
> And admirably schooled in every grace:
> In fine, we thought that he was everything
> To make us wish that we were in his place.

Rich and debonair, Cory becomes for the "people on the pavement" the ideal to which they can only aspire. Is their attitude simply wistful fantasizing, or is it envy—bitter, pure, and unappeased? The next stanza answers that question and also by implication rebukes the people for their mulish belief in the superficialities of life.

> So on we worked, and waited for the light,
> And went without the meat, and cursed the bread;
> And Richard Cory, one calm summer night,
> Went home and put a bullet through his head.

Why did Richard Cory kill himself? Unrequited love? It happens even to the rich and debonair; but not, insofar as we can tell, to Richard Cory. Mental illness? No evidence of that. Latent homosexuality? A popular choice today, I'm sure, though nothing in the text even hints at a motive for suicide. That's because the poem isn't about Richard Cory. It's about "the people," about the proletariat that Karl Marx and Walt Whitman and Carl Sandburg so shamelessly sentimentalize—and about a pervasive envy, rooted in simplistic materialism.

We recognize and condemn this materialism in, say, Ebenezer Scrooge, and all the more easily because it is totally absent in Bob Cratchit, who, living in poverty, offers a toast at Christmas dinner to his money-grubbing employer: "I'll give you Mr. Scrooge, the Founder of the Feast." No envy there. But when we see Scrooge's vice alive and well in the poor, we immediately begin to manufacture excuses, to transform vice into virtue, even to baptize a deadly sin and welcome it into the Body of Christ.

SECULAR SOCIETY DEALS WITH THAT BROILING ENVY in at least two ways. The free market—trafficking in illusion—offers imitations of the luxuries the upper-middle class and rich enjoy. Suburban developments feature three-bedroom, two-bath houses, with gables, turrets, and jacuzzis. Garages built on the side extend the width of the house and appear from the street to be extra rooms, particularly when the garages have curtained faux windows.

Rich folks have hideaways in exotic places. Therefore, blue-collar workers and retirees, living on fixed incomes, can buy one fiftieth of a condominium through a time-sharing plan. They can use their tiny square of heaven for a specified week once a year—just so Madge can tell the girls at the beauty parlor, "Clyde and I are flying down to Florida to spend a week at our condo."

You can buy knockoffs of Rodeo Drive clothes on the streets of major cities and in flea markets everywhere. On Pennsylvania Avenue in Washington, Hermès scarves go for a ten-dollar bill; and a flea-market dealer in South Carolina sells Ferrari fold-up sunglasses for three bucks, while the same pair is selling for $100 to $200 in New York City. Fake designer purses (Kate Spade, Chanel, Prada) are everywhere, supercilious smiles on their faces, pretending to be the real thing.

The Franklin Mint can turn a trash collector into a collector of fine art for only three payments of $19.95—plus shipping and handling.

At discount furniture stores you can get sleigh beds, Chippendale chairs, Charles X recamiers, and handwoven Indian rugs. And you won't have to pay a penny for the next 18 months—nothing down, no interest.

This is what the free market offers: to bridge the perennial gap between haves and have-nots in America. It seems like a pretty good solution to the problem of rampant envy—that seemingly irrepressible urge to have what you can't afford. It's like the Wizard of Oz giving the Tin Man a mechanical heart that ticks away but pumps no blood. The Tin Man is happy as a king. "God's in His Heaven— / All's right with the world!"

Yet viewed from another perspective, this hawking of the American Dream is outright fraud—the sale of delusions and debased dreams, the mainstream equivalent of those greasy little men who step out of alleys and offer you a genuine Rolex for only $50. Thus the left cries: "American business shouldn't prey on lower-income Americans by encouraging them to believe they live in a classless society. Where is government, our old leveler, when we need it?"

And government replies: "Over here. Leveling as hard as we can": subsidizing housing for middle-income renters so they can rub elbows with a better class of neighbors; subsidizing certain farms, eight percent of which are owned by honest-to-god farmers, so they can compete with the other eighty percent (down-home folks like Archer Daniels Midland and Prudential Life); providing scholarships and loans for the semiliterate, so they can learn in college what they failed to learn in elementary school and become doctors, lawyers, and billionaire computer geeks like Bill Gates; and electing our 44th president, who tells us he intends to "spread the wealth around."

It took the old socialist George Bernard Shaw to epitomize this too-familiar philosophy of government: "When you rob Peter to pay Paul, you will always have the support of Paul." Indeed, these days Paul is legion; and tens of millions of Pauls are receiving stolen goods. The levelers call it social justice.

They claim the free market is too cruel to be legal. It's like standing by, watching a chicken snake swallow a mouse. What chance does the poor mouse have in a merciless, God-abandoned world? Let's outlaw chicken snakes! Or better yet, impose a 40-percent food tax on mice so that chicken snakes can barely afford to eat them. Then use the tax revenues to fund an ad campaign warning mice to steer clear of chicken snakes.

This analogy assumes that social and economic manipulators intervene in nature purely out of sympathy for the mouse. This is not necessarily the case. Indeed, all such interventions may be motivated to some degree by a deep-seated, visceral envy of the chicken snake.

DESPITE PROTESTS TO THE CONTRARY, deep in their soiled hearts, American leftists hate a winner and desperately want to see him toppled. Their attitude is something more than a natural sympathy for the underdog. You sometimes get a glimpse of green-skinned malice in their political rhetoric and actions.

For example, in 1962, collector Leonard Sherman of New Jersey bought three sheets of U.S. four-cent stamps honoring Dag Hammarskjold. On one sheet, the yellow background was printed upside down. The estimated value of that one misprinted sheet: $500,000. Sherman made the mistake of telling the press about his purchase; and before sundown, J. Edward Day, Kennedy's postmaster general, heard about Sherman's good fortune and immediately ordered the postal service to print an additional 400,000 of the upside-down sheets for sale to the public. In so doing, Day reduced the worth of Sherman's misprinted stamps to just a little more than four cents each.

Note that collectors—who in four hours gobbled up 320,000 sheets of Day's supplementary printing—got nothing of real value. With the snap of one bureaucrat's finger, a rarity became a commonplace. Day couldn't have believed he was enriching anybody. He must have known he was arbitrarily confiscating the newly acquired wealth of a single collector, who, as it turned out, was a man of modest means. Here was that rare situation in which he could actually allow one person to prosper without depriving someone else as a consequence. He wasn't robbing Peter to pay Paul.

So what motivated Postmaster Day to rob Peter? It wasn't empathy for low-income stamp collectors. Day did not come from the wrong side of the tracks to go from rags to riches, like Horatio Alger's Jed, the Poorhouse Boy. He graduated from the University of Chicago and Harvard Law School, and then practiced law and made a lot of money. Regardless of how rich they are, these leftists always seem to empathize with envy, which has become the chief political virtue of their Democratic base, the one quality that turns out their voters in hailstorms and blizzards. Their slogan: Don't let the filthy rich get in!

With Day it had to have been a kind of vicarious envy, a pinched vision of the world as consisting of wicked exploiter and powerless victim. If he couldn't give all impoverished stamp collectors a half-million dollars, at least he could sell them the same sheet of stamps and deny that son of a bitch Leonard Sherman something he, by God, didn't deserve. Be assured that Postmaster Day—who'd never met Leonard Sherman—knew precisely what evil lurked in the heart of a stamp collector worth $500,000. Wouldn't it be nice if every stamp collector had exactly the same stamps? Wouldn't those philatelist conventions be love-fests?

Underlying the apotheosis of envy are the unspoken assumptions that the ills of society are the result of economic exploitation, that everyone is playing an inevitable role in a gray historical drama, that no player is responsible for what he does. In the end, all of us will have everything or nothing. Either way, we will live in a just society. In the meantime, however inevitable all this may be, the envious will remain virtuous, and the rich wicked. Obviously, Americans in huge numbers believed in some part of that odd account of the world this past November [2008]. It will be interesting to see what they believe four years from now.

# To Each According to His Need

To you who live with no autumn—
Except for the sudden wind that meets
You headlong around a corner—
I am airmailing a dead leaf.
This morning it swung like a frantic bell
On a low branch of my tulip poplar,
And from the dining room it was burning
Star-yellow against the sky.
Immediately I thought of you,
Sitting in your firm brownstone,
Drinking frozen orange juice
And reading the prose of the *New York Times*.
He needs that yellow, I told myself,
As I stepped outside to pull it down.

But alas the yellow was more in the sunlight
Than in the leaf, which had already turned.
For a moment I started to throw it away,
Since God knows there is brown enough
For serious thought in your architecture.
But then I remembered your brown was stone,
So durable it seemed to grow
With the cold years instead of diminish;
I recalled your pious grandfather,
Who lived to the age of ninety-seven
Before the day he failed to awake;
And I thought of your prosperity,
How your father converted capital gains
To blue chips and government bonds.

So I am sending it anyhow,
This brown leaf, with all the affection
Of an ill-used friend and in hopes you'll vote
Against utopian programs this fall,
Remembering the world is run by power
So terrible it can blight a thing
As green and righteous as a leaf.

# Marvin "Popcorn" Sutton, R.I.P.

WHEN POPCORN SUTTON DIED in mid-March [2009] at the age of 62, the national press ran obituaries. Though he was just an old moonshiner who'd plied his trade for half a century and done nothing else of consequence, a whole bunch of folks in Tennessee and North Carolina grieved more than they would have over the death of a military hero, movie star, or ex-president. A few lamented the disappearance of the best 180-proof whiskey available on planet Earth. More mourned the loss of a dogged warrior who'd fought the enemy's merciless legions, held them at bay for nearly a lifetime, and finally yielded to overwhelming numbers and resources.

You can see photographs of Popcorn on the world-wide web, a scrawny old man wearing overalls, a faded flannel shirt, and the wreck of a brown hat—the splay of his red-gray beard covering his chest, sad eyes seared by the gaze of the Beast. One snapshot shows him standing by his Model A Ford, with MOM CORN and POP CORN painted on the front bumper. Another with Willie Nelson's arm around him. A third with him holding a copy of *Me and My Likker*, his autobiography.

You can even go to YouTube and see a snippet of *The Last One*, a film about Sutton, made by Neal Hutcheson, whose North Carolina company, Sucker Punch Pictures, features Appalachian stories and themes. *The Last One* is a step-by-step workshop on how to make a still and run off your very own moonshine, with Popcorn and assistant J.B. Rader as instructors.

It's like watching a segment of Paula Deen on the Food Network. Popcorn talks you through the exacting process, starting with the selection of a site and ending with the sampling of the finished product. You can sense the true artisan's quest for perfection in his careful explanation of each step. This is no hustler, out to make a quick buck. Scuttling around the copper kettle and tubing, sealing the contraption with his skeletal thumb, he is the master of a great craft, cooking one more batch for posterity, "the last run of likker I'll ever make."

By the time Hutcheson shot this film, Popcorn was already a mythic figure.

Everybody in that part of the country knew who he was and what he did. Of course, he had no intention of stopping, any more than Michelangelo considered stopping after finishing the ceiling of the Sistine Chapel. Sutton went right back to the old copper cookery, and no one seemed to mind—except for the Bureau of Alcohol, Tobacco, Firearms and Explosives (ATF). Perhaps for them he had become the embodiment of surd evil. Perhaps his local fame reflected poorly on their competence and relevance. Whatever the case might be, last year they swarmed all over his three-still operation and heaped numerous charges on his back, already bent double from hauling 25-pound sacks of sugar to mix with the sour mash.

FOLLOWING POPCORN'S ARREST, ATF Special Agent James Cavanaugh proclaimed, "Moonshine is romanticized in folklore and in the movies. The truth though is that moonshine is a dangerous health issue and breeds other crime."

Not as dangerous to health as the ATF. You will recall that this same agency was complicit in killing 78 people at Waco, including 21 children and 2 pregnant women. When it came time to investigate this federal massacre, the chief of ATF operations at Waco said there were no guns on the government helicopters. Under questioning, he changed his story, admitting there were indeed guns, just no mounted guns. A bullet from a handheld gun is just as lethal as one from a mounted gun.

Who was the leader of the ATF at the Waco massacre, whom critics have charged with lying to investigators? The same James Cavanaugh. Question: Over the years, who has posed the greater threat to human life—poor old Popcorn Sutton or the federal government, led by trigger-happy hotshots like Cavanaugh? The evidence seems clear. The score is at least 78-0, not counting Ruby Ridge.

Here's what Popcorn said about moonshining, in general, and his own operation, in particular: "If you ain't got the proper equipment to start with, then you don't need to get in the business, because you don't need to kill a bunch of people and make 'em sick . . . I wanted to make a product that they'd come back and see me when they got that drunk up."

Apparently, he knew more about the equipment he was using to make whiskey than Cavanaugh knew about the equipment the government used to kill civilians at Waco.

Following Popcorn's arrest and subsequent death, plain folks expressed their anger on the world-wide web. On a site called Smokey Mountain Breakdown the following appeared:

[R]evenuers suck. Like our federal government doesn't have better things to do. But we keep making them bigger and fatter, and creating new departments for them to run and staff. Defend the country, deliver the mail, I'm thinking that's about enough for them to handle.

I HOPE YOU BASTERDS ARE HAPPY NOW YOU HAVE DONE TOOK A DAMN GOOD MAN FROM US WHY BOTHER OLD TIMERS LIKE THIS I DONT CARE WHAT ANYONE HAD OR HAS TO SAY POPCORN YOU ARE THE MAN BE CAREFULL WITH THE SWEETNESS IN HEAVEN DONT GET ST.PETER TO DAMN DRUNK LIKE THAT DAMN BIG FROG LOL A TRUE REBEL CALLED HOME TO BE WITH GOD REST IN PEACE POPCORN YOUR MEMORY WILL LIVE ON IN US ALL

East Tennessee has been robbed of a man who was a part of history. I met Popcorn a few years back, and I thought he was precious[.] I never heard tale of any time he ever hurt a soul[.] They should have just let him be to continue his craft. Well, I'm sure ole Popcorn knew he had many freinds and aquaintences that will be missing him. I bet he is in Heaven tending a Golden Still.

While many attitudes and values have changed over the past 200-plus years, some have remained constant. Government still wants to tax sin, in general, and whiskey, in particular. Ordinary people believe fiercely, unequivocally that such taxes are wrong, indeed downright wicked. What we see in the case of Popcorn Sutton is the continuation of the Whiskey Rebellion, which began in George Washington's administration and threatened the very existence of the new nation.

IN THE LATE 18TH CENTURY whiskey was more than merely a solace against bone-chilling winter and—with an average of seven children per house—a way to sweeten the lengthy confinement between harvest and spring planting. ("Maude, tell them children to shut up, and bring me my jug.") It was also a money crop and, along the frontier, a medium of exchange.

"How much is that cotton dress in the window?"

"Three gallons, Ma'am. But it's been there for a while. I'll give it to you for two."

It was Alexander Hamilton's idea to impose an excise tax on whiskey—to raise revenue to pay off the war debt of the colonies and to establish the right of the federal government to jerk the chain of the newly freed citizenry. As Hamilton put it, the whiskey tax was "more as a measure of social discipline than as a source of revenue." Hamilton was the quintessential apostle of Big Government. Aaron Burr did the right thing for the wrong reason.

The law specified that small producers of whiskey would be taxed at a rate of nine cents per gallon, while large producers would pay only six cents per gallon. President Washington—who was a large producer—thought Hamilton had a good idea. So did Congress. Again, some things haven't changed.

On the other hand, small farmers, who remembered fighting a revolution in part over the Stamp Act of 1765, felt betrayed. This was the first time the new government had flexed its muscles, and folks in the boondocks didn't like it a bit. In the hills and hollows they concluded that this was just the kind of situation for which the Second Amendment was created. Their struggle for independence began in South Park Township, Pennsylvania, and spread southward and westward. Soon a loosely organized but well-armed resistance movement was flourishing nationwide, directing their attacks against the likes of tax collectors, mail carriers, and courts—*i.e.*, government agents.

George Washington—who had fought and defeated the armies of a tax-mad king—wasn't about to let the same thing happen to his own duly constituted government. He declared martial law, recruited some 13,000 men, and appointed Lighthorse Harry Lee as their commander, with written instructions to fight those "who may be found in arms in opposition to the National will and authority." It was the first time a president assumed that the will of his government and the will of the people were identical—but by no means the last. To underscore that proposition, he even rode out at the head of the army, which was just about the size of the force he'd led against the British.

Instead of Braddock, Washington's army pursued a folk hero—nameless and faceless—called Tom the Tinker. To this day, no one knows for sure who he was or if, indeed, he ever existed. In a sense, it doesn't matter. In many states, groups organized, calling themselves Tom the Tinker's Men. They narrowed their focus to target whiskey-tax collectors and those who collaborated with them, if only by complying with the law. Of the latter group, historian William Hogeland wrote:

> You might find a note posted on a tree outside your house, requiring you to publish in the Gazette your hatred of the whiskey tax and your commitment to the cause; otherwise, the note promised, your still would be mended. Tom had a wicked sense of humor and a literary bent: "mended" meant shot full of holes or burned. Tom published on his own, too, rousing his followers to action, telling the Gazette's editor in cover notes to run the messages or suffer the consequences.

Though the army was effective in Western Pennsylvania, Washington didn't even attempt to enforce the tax in the hills and valleys of the outlands. Today history books concentrate on success in Pennsylvania and ignore failure in the rest of the country. As Murray Rothbard explained,

> Washington, Hamilton, and the Cabinet covered up the extent of the revolution because they didn't want to advertise the extent of their failure. They knew very well if they tried to enforce, or send an army into, the rest of the back country, they would have failed. Kentucky and perhaps the other areas would have seceded from the Union then and there.

In 1802, Congress repealed the law that precipitated the Whiskey Rebellion. However, today it is still illegal to make whiskey, even for your own consumption—a law that defies common sense. As a consequence, the spirit of Tom the Tinker lives on, particularly in the mountains of Appalachia, where white lightning remains a respectable beverage.

TO HIS ADMIRERS, Popcorn Sutton was the reincarnation of Tom the Tinker. Had he been a purveyor of pornography or methamphetamine he would have been a pariah, loathed by the very people who found him quaint and heroic. Whiskey is different from smut and dope. It just is.

Popcorn was arrested because somebody couldn't keep his mouth shut. One of his "still sheds" caught on fire; and both the county and local fire departments came to put out the flames. Before they had completed the job, Popcorn showed up and asked the firefighters to please not mention the presence of three stills, coils of copper wire, bags of sugar, sour mash, and more than 800 gallons of moonshine stored in the remains of an old school bus. Somebody ratted him out, and the feds swooped down on his property and hauled him away, along with his paraphernalia.

He hadn't been arrested since 1998; and in the past he'd been given probated sentences, since no one took what he'd been doing too seriously. This time Popcorn promised never to do it again; he pled ill health, saying, "I'd like to die at home rather than in a penitentiary." The court was unforgiving. The prim judge said he'd heard no expression of remorse and sentenced Popcorn to 18 months in prison.

Popcorn waited until the word came to surrender. Then he did what he believed he had to do. He climbed into his old Ford Fairmont—the one he'd traded three jugs of moonshine for—shut the windows, and cranked up the car. That afternoon, his wife, Pam, found him, dead of carbon-monoxide poisoning.

"He got his letter to report Friday, and he just couldn't handle it," she said. "We tried everything we could to leave him on house arrest, and they wouldn't do it. So I thank the federal court for this."

Some of his admirers have said that the making of moonshine is a dying craft, that Popcorn was the last great practitioner. They complain that there's no money in moonshine anymore, that soon enough no one will even know how to make the stuff.

Don't you believe it. The spirit of Tom the Tinker and Popcorn Sutton will rule the mountains until the final trumpet echoes in smoking valleys. Raw-boned mountain boys already know it isn't just the money. It's the incomparable thrill of thumbing your nose at Alexander Hamilton. Popcorn has left them the how-to DVD. A dozen young towheaded adventurers are back in the mountains right now, soldering coils together, cooking sour mash, listening to the drip, drip, drip of their own fierce defiance. And they don't give a damn for George Washington's army.

# Notes on a Dedication, Edgefield

**F**ALL CAME LATE THIS YEAR, and in the final days of October the leaves, still a pale shade of green, clung to the branches of the huge oak trees that we passed before we eased around the square in Edgefield and looked for a place to park. We were early, but already 40 or 50 people were standing around at the foot of the courthouse steps or else seated in two's and three's before a large wooden platform draped in red, white, and blue.

And on a pedestal behind them, reared against the sky like an unorthodox ghost, stood a figure draped in a scarlet sheet, one arm outstretched, the wind whipping the cloth like a battle flag. Any Yankee who had taken the wrong turn off I-20 and blundered into this little town might have been terrified. For an instant we too were startled. Then we remembered. Underneath the blood-red sheet was Maria Kirby-Smith's undedicated bronze of J. Strom Thurmond, the reason for our trip to Edgefield.

Of course several of us were curious to see the senator as well as the statue. We'd heard from friends that he was finally coming apart, that he could no longer walk or talk, that he was being programmed by his staff, which was why his voting record had been so erratic in recent years. Well, we got to see him sooner than we expected.

Following a stream of people dressed in their Sunday best, we mounted the steep stone steps of the courthouse to attend a meeting of the Edgefield County Historical Society— not part of the official unveiling but carefully calculated to coincide with it. The courthouse, which dates back to the 1830's, looked like an old Baptist church with its long wooden pews, its pulpit-like judge's bench, and its choir-loft jury box. The walls, painted the same green you find in filling-station restrooms, were hung with portraits of Edgefield County's most distinguished fathers, their sad and severe faces darkened with age, their frames askew as if the building had just been rattled by the 1896 earthquake. At the rear, to the right of the front door, was a more recent portrait of Strom Thurmond, a young man with smooth skin and a balding head. He too had a sober look on his face, as if to reflect the mood of the proceedings that habitually went on inside these four walls.

Then Thurmond himself entered, with his young wife and young children, and for the first time we began to have the sense that we'd been misled. Trimmer than we'd seen him some 12 years ago, he walked with a straight back and a quick step, his head miraculously covered with hair, his face full of color and relatively free of wrinkles. He and his family sat on the second row, patient and submissive as the meeting was called to order.

After the reading of the minutes and the treasurer's report, Rick Booraem, a local high school teacher, spoke briefly about each of the portraits on the wall; and as he talked you suddenly realized that from this tiny rural county, still hiding out from the modern world, had come ten governors of South Carolina, five U.S. congressmen, and five U.S. senators. Benjamin Tillman, Preston Brooks, Strom Thurmond. Indeed the more Booraem went on the more you had the odd sensation that the insubstantial spirit which had produced such an extraordinary succession of men had lived a good deal of its life in this room, and even now was stretching itself and yawning somewhere in the audience on this bland October day.

**AFTER THE MEETING HAD ENDED,** we moved outside and joined the crush of people waiting for the dedication to begin. Clustered there on the square we must have looked like a camp meeting or else guests at a huge country wedding. Then the speeches began.

When Thurmond finally rose we expected to see the hand of time lying heavy on his shoulder. And while he strode to the microphone with a good deal more vigor than most of the other speakers, we knew you could fake it for eight or ten steps but you couldn't fake it for 30 minutes, not on a public platform.

Well, Thurmond took care of any doubts we had in the first 60 seconds. He was incredible. He was magnificent. He stood there in the slant of late autumn sunlight and put together the jigsaw puzzle of time as if he had invented it. He talked about the people who had spoken before him on the platform, remembering their families, their connections, their acts of kindness. He talked about the Historical Society meeting, the woman who was its president, some of the figures on the wall, the people in the crowd whose faces he recognized. He even joked about his age. And he ended with a glance to the future, a charge to the young people of Edgefield County to make something of their lives.

All of this seemed just fine to the home folks standing there under the crape myrtles—and also to the rest of us, who had somehow forgotten about the votes in the U.S. Senate and were wondering how a man as old as Strom Thurmond could sound so vital and strong and certain of who and where he was.

But the senator soon supplied the answer in what he said: His strength came from something back in that courthouse, from the faces glaring out of those old frames, their eyes fixed with a certitude that is somehow missing from the world outside the narrow boundaries of this county. If the men in the portraits could give their approval to him, as well as the crowds of old friends in the square, then who were we to raise impertinent questions?

# LITERATURE

# Punk Rock, Prufrock, and the Words We Live By

**I**F YOU'RE A BUSINESSMAN you don't have time for poetry, unless, of course, you happen to enjoy it the way other businessmen enjoy Monday Night Football. Certainly you don't feel you have to read it. There's no poetry in the *Wall Street Journal* or *Barron's*, unless you are one whose heart is stirred by the language of the New York Stock Exchange, where on occasion "To be or not to be . . . " is the drabbest kind of prose compared with "up two points." No, poetry has nothing to do with business and the more important aspects of modern life.

Well, what about "popular poetry?" What about song lyrics? What about punk rock? If in addition to being a businessman you are also a middle-aged parent—particularly one who gave up listening to disc jockeys in the 1950's—you've been reluctant to think about punk rock, much less to listen to it with any degree of seriousness.

You've heard it screeching and pulsating under the doors of your teenagers' rooms; maybe it suddenly shattered your eardrums one morning when you turned on the automobile ignition; or you became aware of it more gradually as you drove along with your daughter and realized that you were about to scream because the four-speaker stereo had been playing just below the level of conversation for the last ten minutes.

Yet the time comes when the one-eyed monster dragging itself up and down the hallways of your house has grown so hulking and raucous that you can't ignore it any longer. It seems to have possessed the souls of your once-angelic children. They walk and talk differently. They give you surly looks at the dinner table. Your son gets a Mohawk.

So one night—despite the fact that poetry is irrelevant to business—you charge downstairs, pound on the door, and say, "O.K. I want you to tell me what you see in this noise anyway!" After their inarticulate explanation— punctuated by long silences and heavy breathing—you snatch up a stack of albums, haul them off to your study, and begin to listen to them with your best critical ear.

The result is—to say the least—disturbing. It occurs to you that the TV evangelists who shout and wave their arms may be right about one thing. As the gospel song says, "We need a whole lot more about Jesus, and a lot less rock and roll."

In addition to the music itself, most of which is childlike in its simplicity, you are struck by the monotony of the lyrics, the heavily ironic denunciations of the social order or else the shrill affirmation of the glory and centrality of self. It's nothing like the good, wholesome music you used to listen to.

As best you can recall, in the songs of Irving Berlin the chief pronoun was the second-person plural. In rock and roll it is more often the first-person singular; there are all sorts of songs about the necessity to be your own kind of person, to do your own thing, celebrations of the self and its intensely felt experience of sexual joy and political pain. Or else there is no *I* or *you* at all but a sinister *they*, a third-person plural which seems to be responsible for all discomfort and inconvenience on the face of the earth, to say nothing of mere injustice and oppression.

Realizing all this you go back downstairs and tell your children to listen to Mozart or Scarlatti; but they answer that punk rock is where the spirit of the age lives—curled up on a littered floor, its head resting on a stack of empty beer cans, whining about the oppressiveness of society. Punk rock, you are told, is America. If Mozart and Scarlatti were just starting out these days they'd be punk rockers. So would Byron and Shelley. So would the Prophet Isaiah.

## From Irving Berlin to Sid Vicious

YOU HAVE TO AGREE that there's a little of each of these in the songs you've listened to (Mozart and Scarlatti used some of the same notes), but there's something else as well, besides the incorrigible ignorance of the young. You see evidence of a pride that sets itself against the most basic prescriptions of Western civilization without so much as the slightest blush or apology. You see it in the eyes of the performers as they glare out at you from angry album covers, filled with graphic oddities, pretentious satanic symbols, and casual obscenity. Mostly the rock groups are pictured in performance, dressed in outright costume or else ersatz shabby. Their names suggest their contempt for the things that others hold in highest esteem: Crass, the Clash, Social Distortion, the Circle Jerks, the Dead Kennedys. And more to the point: Bad Religion, Crucifix, the Lords of the New Church.

Is it all a bad joke or are these people serious? In one sense, of course, they couldn't possibly be serious any more than a ten-year-old could be seriously in love. In another sense—the more obvious sense—it's hard to tell. You can see the black humor in someone calling himself "Sid Vicious," as did one of the Sex Pistols. But when he murders his girlfriend and then dies of an overdose, perhaps we should begin to assume that the symbolism of these names is serious indeed.

But the only way to tell for sure is to examine the lyrics of punk rock and try to see what it claims for itself. Here are a couple of examples, the first from the Lords of the New Church, the second from the Clash.

> The City eats its children of dust from the cradle to grave.
> Drag their captives through the deep-sleeps of life.
> Ghosts of dream-dwelling slaves.
> The stranger scares the creatures of night.
> Corpse of sluggards fall.
> First you called it experiment, and then the terror called.
> The subterranean escapes the light to an empty space.
> I'll do my time prowling in the streets behind a human face.

and

> Thank God for the rain to wash the trash off the sidewalk.
> Listen, here is a man who would not take it anymore,
> A man who stood up against the scum.
> The filth now I see clearly.
> Personally I know the alley
> Where Jack feeds on the birds of night.
> Not even bobbies on bicycles, two by two,
> Can stop the blood and feathers flying.

The more you examine these lyrics the more you realize that you've heard this kind of talk before. Thirty, maybe forty years ago—in an English class on modern poetry. The memory eludes you like—like voices dying from a dying fall. Who was it who wrote this way, with that marvelous discontinuity of images, the fine illogic, the ironic tonal qualities that excited you when you were 19 or 20 years old? There is nothing, you suddenly remember, quite so exciting as being young and world-weary. And 30 years ago no one spoke so persuasively to your imagination as did T.S. Eliot in "The Love Song of J. Alfred Prufrock" and *The Waste Land*.

It was T.S. Eliot who invented this kind of verse! The revelation takes you by surprise. You're shocked; then skeptical. You take out your *Norton Anthology*, and sure enough—there it is, on page 1786: *The Waste Land*.

> What are you thinking of? What thinking? What? I
> never know what you are thinking. Think.

113

I think we are in rats' alley
Where the dead men lost their bones.

"What is that noise?" The
Wind under the door.

Eliot, of course, is a classic American poet, one whose mature commitment to traditional Christian institutions and attitudes was central to an understanding of his overall achievement as a man of letters. Yet it is surely from his early work and from the work of his followers and imitators that punk rock derives much of its poetics, if *poetics* is not too foolish a word to use here.

## Waste Land of Language

NOTE, FOR EXAMPLE, THE LINE, "The city eats its children of dust from the cradle to grave." First, there is the balancing of the genuinely innovative phrase with the cliché. Such ironic juxtapositions were characteristic of Eliot (see the seduction and pub scenes in *The Waste Land*), and were derived, at least in part, from his early contempt for everyday life and for the community at large, which he suggested was either effete (as exemplified by Prufrock) or brutal (as exemplified by Sweeney). He seemed to believe that modern society was made up of human beings toward whom he could feel morally as well as intellectually superior, and he mocked such people by throwing their banal language back in their teeth. So did Sinclair Lewis. So did Hemingway. So in more recent times has Walker Percy. Today it's old hat. Yet Eliot's use of debased slang and middle-class cant was new to poetry in the years immediately following World War I, and the ironic tone produced by the introduction of such language was to affect virtually every major American poet for the next 25 or 30 years. It was fresh and exciting 65 years ago, and it fed the tendency of many educated people to think themselves a higher breed than the Prufrocks and Babbitts. They adopted Eliot's irony, and with it they put on the mantle of skepticism as well; because you can't use rhetoric for long without assuming the virtues and vices that lie behind it. Soon several generations of college graduates were speaking and thinking according to the example of Eliot's voices.

The second characteristic of Eliot's poetry which one finds in the punk-rock passages quoted above is a kind of deliberate vagueness of diction that is maddening to a literalist and exciting to a certain kind of poetic sensibility.

114

The sentence "The subterranean escapes the light to an empty space," for example, can't be paraphrased or even completely explained. Indeed Eliot himself, in responding to bemused questioners at public lectures, was perfectly willing to accept any reading that was suggested to him.

The origins of this view of language are multiple and mysterious. But one point stands out for purposes of our discussion: Eliot believed that language was by definition vague and imprecise, and that the poet's task was not to imitate and explain the world but to stir up associations and feelings, to deal with the subjective rather than the objective. For him and for a whole generation to follow, the word was one thing, the thought a second, and the object a third—and there was no necessary connection between any two of them.

Such a theory of language might well lead one to question whether or not experience has any concrete meaning that can be stated in words. If the tree you think you see is not necessarily there, and if other people don't necessarily think they see the same tree that you do, then how can we possibly say that the word *tree* has any meaning? (If all this seems a little difficult to understand, it's not merely because I'm not explaining it very well, since at least some of the difficulty lies with the maddening subjectivity of modern philosophy.)

The third characteristic of Eliot's poetry that is also a trait of punk rock is the abrupt shifting of focus from one image to another without benefit of conventional transitions. Note in the examples above how fragmentary everything seems, as if the poem or song had been cut up with scissors, then a few of the phrases and sentences pasted back together in no particular order. Again Eliot's discovery and use of such a device tells us something about the way he wants his readers to perceive the world of the poem. The mind of Prufrock and the observer of *The Waste Land* are, by strong implication, fragmented and incoherent. Prufrock is what we would now call a "wimp," a man who is so intimidated by the world around him that he can neither love nor act in the way he wishes but is finally paralyzed by his fear of social convention, despite the fact that he regards society as empty and hypocritical. Likewise Teiresias (or the speaker) in *The Waste Land* sees the present as a broken mosaic of the past, a meaningless collage of unpleasant sensations which might take on renewed significance only when rejuvenated by a vital past or the infusion of values from another culture, one in which religion and sexuality play an important role.

Thus the world as viewed in these poems is incoherent and sordid—sordid, in part, because it is incoherent. Eliot is suggesting that the loss of any sort of metaphysical orthodoxy makes it impossible to find vitality and purpose in life; yet modern man, while recognizing his predicament, can do very little about it, except perhaps to flirt with Eastern religions or to re-read the classics.

These three technical aspects of Eliot's work—the ironic use of language, the vagueness of imagery and diction, the disjointed movement of the poem—all combine to emphasize his thematic concerns at this stage of his career; and if you don't draw too neat a picture you can show that the technique and the meaning of the poem are perfectly wedded to one another, not only in Eliot's work but in the songs of the Clash and the Lords of the New Church as well.

## Undressing the Old Order

FOR AN UNDERSTANDING of what Eliot was saying about the world in 1917 you have only to examine the following passage in "The Love Song of J. Alfred Prufrock," the one which tells us all we need to know about the hero's physical appearance:

> And indeed there will be time
> To wonder, "Do I dare?" and, "Do I dare?"
> Time to turn back and descend the stair,
> With a bald spot in the middle of my hair—
> (They will say: "How his hair is growing thin!")
> My morning coat, my collar mounting firmly to the chin,
> My necktie rich and modest, but asserted by a simple pin—
> (They will say: "But how his arms and legs are thin!")
> Do I dare
> Disturb the universe?
> In a minute there is time
> For decisions and revisions which a minute will reverse.

One of the most important things that Eliot tells us in this segment of the poem is the way that Prufrock dresses and the manner in which the reader is supposed to respond to this mode of dress. The description means less and less to us as the memory of even the recent past fades, but Eliot's first readers would have understood that Prufrock was following a very rigid and explicit code for dressing before the hour of six: black morning coat, gray vest, ascot tie, striped pants, black shoes, spats. And on the head nothing else but a bowler.

All the men wore the same thing. It was like a uniform at a military academy, and the implications of wearing it were essentially the same: the individual was less important than the community. Oh, you could wear a highly personal stick pin if you wanted to, though nothing too flashy, nothing that would set you apart radically from the other men at the occasion, whether tea dance or music recital. It all sounds bizarre to those of us who live in an age when shirts and slacks are as colorful as the plumage of Australian birds.

And in contrast to the conventionally dressed Prufrock, whose inhibitions and frustration are expressed in his conformity, you have only to look and listen to understand how different is the world of punk rock. Everyone is dressed according to his own private code. Everyone is therefore in costume—bizarrely, uniquely himself in the fatigues of Che Guevara, or tight jeans with only a vest for a top, or at times near nakedness, and public nakedness at that.

And the same might be said of "characters" in punk-rock songs, most of whom, when they are rendered visually, are depicted in the act of sexual intercourse. In effect they are "dressed" or "undressed" in stark contrast to Prufrock. It might even be argued that they are the men that Prufrock is longing to become—rebellious, self-assertive, sexually aggressive. All ego.

The more you think about it, the more you realize that, like the punk rockers he spawned, Eliot in his ironic juxtapositions, his vague language, and his disjointed imagery was attacking civilization itself, or at least society as he understood it in his own time. He was suggesting in his portrait of Prufrock that the manners and conventions of the social order—as symbolized by its clothes—were empty and inhibiting, mere form without the vitality that human institutions must exhibit in order to nurture the heart and the soul. The attack is a linguistic one and has as its ultimate intent the destruction of an older decorative language, the sort of rhetoric used by most 19th-century public men and in the 20th century only by such splendid anachronisms as Douglas MacArthur and Winston Churchill.

That the attack was successful is evidenced by the obscene irreverence for all things traditional that is so widespread and so much a part of our world that it blares over our children's radios 16 hours per day and leers at us from every TV and movie screen. "Get rid of those clothes," Eliot told a small readership in the years immediately following World War I. "Get rid of those clothes," say the punk rockers in four-letter words and obscene gestures. And today all over America and Europe people are doing just that—and by the millions.

Prufrock was stilted and diffident in his relations with women because of the outmoded restraints of social convention; today, while punk rockers scream the same message that Eliot spoke so quietly and archly, we're no longer worried about the strictures of society so much as the spread of AIDS and herpes and a rate of illegitimate births that soars in direct proportion to the amount of contraceptives, birth-control pamphlets, and abortions sponsored by government at every level.

And clothes today are so clearly a mockery of traditional modes of dress that our schools and colleges are all too often a battleground on which armies of polo players and alligators march into a kind of sartorial Armageddon, fighting it out with rock T-shirts and black chrome-ringed bondage pants ordered from the ads in the back of *Rolling Stone*. Of course the dress is just as stylized as it ever was: One army defends an ignorant, *nouveau-riche* consumerism, while the other fights for the enthronement of garbage-man chic. Neither would wear a morning coat because, on the one hand, they wouldn't be able to tell its quality without an outside label, and, on the other hand, they couldn't wear it thin enough to affect proletarian poverty.

## Selfishness, Earth Deity of Oz

To SUMMARIZE, THEN, the language of the first half of the 20th century has brought us to a crisis in the second half, when the world of punk rock and the world of Middle America are more and more indistinguishable from each other, as evidenced by the increasingly formless way in which most Americans live their lives, their almost immeasurable self-indulgence as revealed in statistics on alcoholism, drug addiction, shoplifting, divorce, suicide, murder, rape.

The truth is, the society that Eliot satirized and the punk rockers are attacking doesn't really exist anymore. It's been done in. In recent years the apparent triggermen have been the opinion-makers of the media: the earnest-eyed, deadpanned news correspondents who, for the sake of a Higher Good, have hidden or distorted opposing opinions, jerry-rigged film clips, faked news events, made up entire histories, staged demonstrations, and above all turned the English language into a graduate assistant in sociology in order to bring about a political change with which everybody will be immediately dissatisfied; the filmmakers and TV producers who have recognized the potential for prurience in all human communities and for money have made us believe that lust, which was once regarded among the seven deadly sins, is in fact a great virtue among free people or at best an amusing and harmless overflow of natural appetite; the holding companies which now own most of the major publishing houses and as a matter of course demand that editors seek books which will yield a high short-term profit by appealing to the public's growing addiction to sensationalism; the recording studios which are doing the same thing, even in areas like country music, which was once more closely attuned to the sensibilities of small-town America than the other segments of popular music.

But as much as the explanation may satisfy us, it's wrong to blame the media for this phenomenon of disintegration. In the first place, "media" is a plural noun (though most people don't seem to know it), and there is every opportunity for a diversity of opinion, style, and taste to assert itself. The *New York Times*, MGM, the television newscasters, and Norman Lear have not entered into a conspiracy to corrupt a good and simple people.

With almost no exception that comes immediately to mind, the men and women whose work appears on the editorial pages of the great Eastern opinion mills or on the screens of your television set are badly educated and ill trained. Their attitudes are conditioned by four years at what are still called (and once were) "the best schools," followed by life in one of the great coastal metropolises, which is a little like living in the Emerald City— it's the biggest, flashiest thing around, but its way of life and its philosophical attitudes are controlled by a wizened little charlatan who hides behind a screen and pretends he is the Great and Powerful Oz. His name, as some of us know, is really Selfishness.

These people are mostly too ordinary and unimportant to be responsible for the tremendous changes that have taken place in our time. None of them is Genghis Khan. They're not even privates in the barbarian army. They're merely camp followers, tagging along behind, hoping to turn a trick and make a buck, all the while absolutely certain they're serving some marvelous earth deity who will liberate the human spirit from its old enemy, the Lord God Jehovah.

No, the real destroyers of our society, as I have already suggested, are words, which are the clothes we wear to tell the world and God who we are. And if we want to find out what kind of dress the next generation will choose we had better consult the poets, in whose hands the language is always resting, like a still-beating heart waiting to be transplanted into the body politic.

## Civic Duty of Poets

AND HOW IS THIS SO? Ezra Pound gave as good an explanation as any when he wrote:

> Good writers are those who keep the language efficient. That is to say, keep it accurate, keep it clear. It doesn't matter whether the

good writer wants to be useful, or whether the bad writer wants to do harm. Language is the main means of human communication. If an animal's nervous system does not transmit sensations and stimuli, the animal atrophies. If a nation's literature declines, the nation atrophies and decays.

Let me hasten to explain that Pound is not saying the poet should write about the ills of society, that he should prescribe solutions to problems. To the contrary, he says that those things don't matter as much as the poet's responsibility to purify and reinvent the diction and syntax of literature in accordance with the true world in which he lives, as opposed to the false world created by false language. The poet, he tells us, restyles our rhetorical clothing constantly so that practical men and women can go into the community as competent human beings and carry on its business. If the poet does his job well then presidents, businessmen, and plumbers can do their jobs well.

So how long does it take the poet to reclothe the community? Well, the day after "Prufrock" was published the American flag still flew over the Boston post office. It flies there today, but it doesn't quite stand for the same thing it stood for in 1917. Yet such change takes place slowly. At first it affects only a few literate and highly influential people. Later it reaches a wider and less esoteric audience. Eventually it seeps down to the lowest level of society, which is where popular music lives. At that point it is still alive culturally but intellectually dead. Thus the lyrics of Irving Berlin were late 19th-century Romanticism, served up as hash for the most mawkish of sensibilities; while, as we have seen, the Sex Pistols follow Eliot by a mere 60 years.

But the punk-rock composer is not like the genuine poet. He is merely a reflection of popular political attitudes turned sour, the revolution of the 1960's nostalgically revisited. The revolution itself was the major catastrophe caused by the poetry of the 20's and 30's. Read the slogans in the signs of anti-war demonstrators and gay-liberation paraders. They are the greeting cards of the past, messages from poets dead and buried in the grave of memory.

But what can we do about it? Just knowing that Eliot and his generation are responsible for the punk-rock element in America doesn't really help us, does it, any more than it would help a man dying of rabies to be introduced to the rat that bit him?

It's a desperate situation. If the problem is language then no ordinary political solution is possible—no program, no decision by the Supreme Court, no amendment to the U.S. Constitution. Can't you imagine the President's Blue Ribbon Commission on the Restoration of Good Language reporting to the nation on what the government ought to do to spur the poets into performing their civic duty? No, it wouldn't even work if we held guns to their heads and said to them, "Write us poems that will clothe us in the language of hope and love and peace." A good poet would rather be shot than to work under such circumstances.

It must all happen quietly and secretly in the souls of a few men, but it can and does happen, always it happens, if the situation is desperate enough. As an illustration of this final point let me remind you that the first great poet of Western civilization wrote an epic narrative which was in part about the need for the right language in order to create the proper clothing for society. The poet is Homer, and the poem is *The Odyssey*.

You may remember that as the narrative opens Odysseus, the hero, is living on an island with Calypso, a woman who looks surprisingly like Bo Derek and will never look any worse since she is an immortal goddess. She is in love with Odysseus, a mere man, and she has a great deal to offer him. She owns a liquor store, all the fast-food franchises, a 25-inch Curtis Mathes with a Betamax. It goes without saying that she offers herself as well. But there is one more gift, the most precious of all—that of eternal life. She has connections in high places. She will make him a god. Who here today could refuse that offer?

## Clothed by the Living Word

BUT ODYSSEUS DOES REFUSE. He's had propositions like this before. Circe, who turns men into pigs, wanted him to stay with her as well; but Odysseus was as adamantly opposed to being a pig as to being a god. He chooses instead to be a man and return to his wife and son. That is, he chooses to die. (And remember that he has heard Achilles down in Hades tell him that he would rather be a living slave than a dead shadow floating in that perpetually doomed twilight. Odysseus knows as well as we do what it means to die.)

Yet he puts to sea, only to suffer one last indignity. He is caught up in a terrible storm. His clothes are stripped from his body. Finally he is tossed on the shores of Phaiakia, where he is discovered by the princess of the realm and her retinue. What is he to do? Though a king, he appears to be no more than a worm—naked, completely naked, dirty, covered with the salt slime of the sea, divested of the fine trappings of civilization. For all the princess knows, a barbarian. A lesser man might have turned and fled.

But Odysseus is no coward. He begins to speak, and she is enchanted by the clear beauty and high formality of what he says. Though the handmaidens flee with the first words, the princess remains—to listen, then to offer him the hospitality of the palace itself; for she is convinced that he is a man of great nobility and stature.

What he has done on this primitive island, literally thousands of years ago, is something we must do through our poets in our own time. He has reclothed himself with nothing more than language so that he stands before her in the ancient and uniquely human robes of rhetoric, a creature of dignity, something more than the pig that Circe (the punk rockers) would make of him, something less than the arrogant gods of Calypso's (Eliot's) promise. That is what Odysseus's language says of his nature, that he holds firm to that middle ground in the hierarchy of Being where man has always stood, where he is something more than animal, something less than angel.

Make no mistake—it is a place of splendor, and it belongs to us no less than to Odysseus, and perhaps we will reaffirm it soon, not because we have earned it, not because we ever could, but because it was given to us graciously, out of an Infinite Mystery that finally demands of us more than we ourselves would presume to be.

For before time began we were clothed by the Living Word, by God Incarnate, accepting the humanity of words, condescending to define Himself by noun, verb, adjective—by all the finite parts of speech that through Him bind us forever and inextricably into the Wonder of Being. It is a mystery that He would want us to speak at all. It is glory enough, after all, to make us keep absolute silence, this knowledge that whenever we speak we speak His Name.

# Homage to a Friend:
## Russell Kirk's Book on T.S. Eliot

YEARS AGO, when a Vanderbilt graduate-school party was careening toward promiscuity, a quiet young woman, an English major, suddenly shocked everyone by saying: "Tell you what let's do: Let's all name the books we've never read." Suddenly it was time to go home. In five minutes the room was empty, except for the host and hostess, hauling half-filled glasses to the kitchen and dumping cigarette butts out of ashtrays.

I for one could have mentioned a number of "essential books" I hadn't read, among them Russell Kirk's *Eliot and His Age*, a study I'd frequently recommended to students as "the best single work on the subject." I made that pronouncement without reservation. I knew Russell Kirk.

When the Intercollegiate Studies Institute reissued the title, I was asked to review it. After having actually read it, I can confirm my original assessment: It's the best book on Eliot ever written. And, more than that, it is a brilliant performance, the finest literary biography I've ever read.

First of all, it is gracefully written, yet full of linguistic surprises—witty and imaginative. Kirk was one of the premier stylists of his generation—and that means more to me than all the footnotes in the Library of Congress. In addition, his commentary on the poetry and the age is clear and precise, nothing like the academic prose that ruins most literary histories, even for other academics. Herbert Read once observed that "style is the ultimate morality of mind." No style illustrates that truth better than Russell Kirk's. The clarity of his mind is mirrored in the clarity of his prose.

And the book is full of Kirk's own memories of T.S. Eliot. It's as if the reader had come across a photograph album filled with snapshots of a long-dead friend. Kirk knew Eliot well. When in London—and he spent a lot of time there—he called on the great poet, had lunch or dinner with him, and discussed the important matters that later critics and biographers would have to address only through the reading of verse, essays and reviews, letters, and the testimony of others. As Kirk wrote: "He was thirty years older than I, but we had read the same books, knew the same places, were almost as one in literary preferences and social convictions, and had several old friends in common." Both were committed Christians who had come to orthodoxy after a period of doubt, and both had discovered England about the same time, though Kirk remained a disgruntled American while Eliot became a British subject. So no one born in the second half of the 20th century could possibly know Eliot the man and poet as well as did Russell Kirk.

In fact, many early critics who tackled poems like "The Love Song of J. Alfred Prufrock" and *The Waste Land* concluded that they were pure literary constructs, that Eliot was writing poetry unrelated to his private life. Had they known him better, they would have seen the neurotic face of Vivienne Haigh-Wood Eliot, his first wife, peering out from behind key allusive images and ironic dialogue. As Kirk shows, Eliot's problem with the world was both philosophical and personal—a bad ontology and epistemology on the world's part, a bad marriage on his part.

You can understand the poetry without knowing about the marriage, but the philosophy is crucial, and Kirk, like Eliot, was steeped in it. As this book suggests, both men had sifted through and parsed the work of the important philosophers—classical to modern. T.S. Eliot's dissertation—begun at Harvard, completed at Oxford—was an abstruse display of learning: *Knowledge and Experience in the Philosophy of F.H. Bradley*. When it was published in 1964, shortly before his death, Eliot wrote: "Forty-six years after my academic philosophizing came to an end, I find myself unable to think in the terminology of this essay. Indeed, I do not pretend to understand it." Kirk understood it and showed the reader just how much of Bradley was essential to a full understanding of Eliot's poetry—and how much was irrelevant.

**BOTH KIRK AND ELIOT** were deeply interested in social history, and particularly those works that shed light on what Eliot-oriented critics would come to call "the modern predicament." A whole generation of intellectuals would begin to see the present as Eliot saw it—as a falling away from certitude, a loss of tradition and hence of faith, an aimless wandering in self-doubt. In such a world, the individual could no longer identify with a rich and vital past—or shrug off a sparse and decadent present.

"Prufrock," *The Waste Land*, and *The Hollow Men* render 20th-century society in imagery and dialogue that reflect the fragmentation of modern consciousness. Eliot's first readers didn't think of themselves as solipsistic until they read "Prufrock." Then many recognized their own shriveled souls as reflected in Eliot's protagonist. At the same time, they experienced a sharp sense of loss, enhanced by the ironic tone of the poem, which pricked the conscience of an entire generation. That tone—or something akin to it—was replicated by a generation of poets writing in a "period style" that dominated the literary scene for decades. Everybody wanted to sound like—indeed to *be*—T.S. Eliot.

Following *The Waste Land*, which ends in hope, he wrote poetry that was less ironic and more overtly Christian. Eliot had thought his way out of a despair that to him was both highly personal and endemic to the society around him. In 1927, he was baptized in the Church of England and a year later published a collection of essays, *For Lancelot Andrewes*, saying in the introduction: "The general point of view [of the essays] may be described as classicist in literature, royalist in politics, and anglo-catholic in religion." On that platform he stood unyielding for the next 38 years.

As for Eliot's contact with the literati of London, as Kirk shows, most instantly recognized his genius and began calling him Great Tom long before the world had heard of him. A few of them—Roy Campbell, Wyndham Lewis—became lifelong friends and encouraged his principled break with the self-satisfied but effete literary establishment of that day. In several key references Kirk captures the essence of this literary malaise—for example, a dinner presided over by Sir Edmund Gosse, the rich, self-appointed Lord High Chancellor of English letters. Evelyn Waugh said of him: "To me he epitomized all that I found ignoble in the profession of letters . . . I saw Gosse as a Mr. Tulkinghorn [a character in *Bleak House*], the soft-footed, inconspicuous, ill-natured habitué of the great world, and I longed for a demented lady's-maid to make an end of him."

In addition to making several good friends, Eliot got a close look at the enemies of the permanent things. Surprisingly, as a newly married banker, he hung out with the Bloomsbury crowd, a squawking nest of atheists, socialists, and sexual adventurers, epitomized by Bertrand Russell, who wrote of Eliot: "It is quite funny how I have come to love him, as if he were my son."

Funny indeed. Soon Eliot would become one of the chief defenders of Christianity (*The Idea of a Christian Society*). Russell, a social revolutionary and chronic adulterer, was already a chief adversary of the Church, albeit an astonishingly inept and simplistic one. Of Russell's feel-good, substitute religion, Eliot wrote, with heavy irony: "I cannot regret that such views as Mr. Russell's, or what we may call the enervate *gospel of happiness*, are openly expounded and defended. They help to make clear, what the nineteenth century had been largely occupied in obscuring, that there is no such thing as just Morality; but that for any man who thinks clearly, as his Faith is, so will his Morals be."

Eliot's writings on religion and politics are by no means confined to quarrels with his contemporaries. In *Notes Toward the Definition of Culture*, among other things, Eliot defends a concept popular in 2008 [when this essay was published]—that of "diversity." Both Eliot and the politically correct of the 21st century believe that diversity is best served by an overarching unity.

As Kirk observes: "It is to Christianity that Eliot looks for a unifying power; to Christian culture, within which much diversity is possible." Contemporary advocates of a unifying structure tend to look to the United Nations. Perennially dissatisfied with America, these believe that a benign, chirpy, all-powerful global government would somehow create a world culture more vital than any existing regional or national culture. Of that attitude, Eliot wrote: "[Any world culture] which was simply a *uniform* culture would be no culture at all. We should have a humanity de-humanized. It would be a nightmare." His words, written in 1948, still speak to us as we argue over the same irresolvable issues with the same prophets of the coming millennium. (Which millennium? Any millennium, except, of course, the true one.)

As for a summary of T.S. Eliot's achievement, Kirk admits that the poet-critic failed to accomplish the great goal of his life:

> He had endeavored consciously to redeem the time; at the end, he was under no illusion that he had succeeded. Self-censorious always—in this very like his ancestral connections John Adams and John Quincy Adams—Eliot entertained no inflated opinion of his abilities or his achievements. His best poems had seemed only preludes to some splendor of concept that he never wholly contrived to voice; his best plays had been experiments, unperfected; his best essays had been challenging, rather than magisterial; his social criticism had been an exercise in definition, not a grand design. "These fragments I have shored against my ruins." Had he been meant, like Coleridge, for something greater? Like Coleridge, had he procrastinated and lingered in reverie, while time ran out? Were his the sins of omission?

If T.S. Eliot failed in accomplishing the impossible, Kirk, in a splendid assessment of his subject's career as poet, playwright, and essayist, rescues Eliot from latter-day critics, biographers, and other bottom-feeders who say he was homosexual, antisemitic, elitist, fascist, cranky, religiose, strait-laced, and—the most absurd charge of all—irrelevant. It takes Kirk just ten paragraphs to set the record straight: Eliot wrote a substantial body of poetry that perfectly captured the spirit of the 20th century and "renewed that age's moral imagination." His plays revived English verse drama and made it work again on the 20th-century stage. And his essays and reviews—some 600 of them—"rescued the critic's art from personal impressionism" and "stripped the follies of the time" without sparing "the morals of his age, or its politics, or its economics, or its notions of education, or its strange gods."

Kirk states these conclusions without offering argument, facts, or illustration. They need no support. The entire book stands behind his chiseled generalizations, rendering them self-evident. In writing this monumental study, Kirk built a bridge from the future to the past, from tomorrow's readers to yesterday's greatest poet, from ignorance to understanding.

In the 1940's, Eliot was regarded as "too hard" for students. Today he is regarded as "too reactionary." In both cases, blame the teachers, and be assured that as long as Russell Kirk's matchless book is in print, neither excuse will suffice.

# James Joyce and Aesthetic Gnosticism

**T**HE PLIGHT OF THE ARTIST in the modern world has been the topic of too much fiction, poetry, and commentary to require extensive definition. I would only point out what is already obvious to members of the academy: that the haunting sense of alienation attributed to urban residents of the 1960's and 70's was precisely analyzed and rendered by a number of poets and novelists even before the turn of the century; and between 1900 and 1950 virtually every major literary figure addressed himself to this question. Among the most important of these was James Joyce, one of the few genuinely influential figures in the development of 20th-century fictional technique. His three novels—*A Portrait of the Artist as a Young Man, Ulysses*, and *Finnegan's Wake*—mirror, as well as render, the significant plunge into the pool of self that has been a predominant subject of the novel since the late Victorian period.

*Ulysses* and *Finnegan's Wake* are undoubtedly the most ambitious of Joyce's works, for in their radical departure from conventional modes of narration they suggest the triumph of individual consciousness over the traditional ordering of action—the subjugation of time and space by the active imagination in league with the will. To a lesser degree *A Portrait of the Artist* suggests the same modernist tendencies, though its meaning is rendered more often in discourse than in the implications of formal complexity; and for this reason *Portrait*, Joyce's first novel, provides us with one of the purest examples in modern literature of the gnostic impulse as it manifests itself in the artistic imagination.

On its most obvious level the central action of the novel is concerned with the intellectual and spiritual growth of Stephen Dedalus, a pattern of development that seems to some critics to include no more than an abnormally painful childhood followed by adolescent rebellion, maturity, and a satisfying sense of true vocation. To such commentators, Stephen is simply Everyboy, his sensibilities heightened by an acute and instinctive awareness of the created order that surrounds him. But he is something more than a Wordsworthian poet, however Romantic his own conception of himself. For Wordsworth conceived of the imagination as responding to some great force from without (call it nature or call it God); and while Joyce's artist has a keen eye for the natural image, he is more interested in the universe of words, for him a realm of existence that transcends the merely given of the created order. In one sense, then, the meaning of *A Portrait of the Artist* can be found in the progression of Stephen Dedalus's soul from the mundane to the supramundane, a journey of the spirit that finally culminates in a tenuous flight from the constitution of being itself, a "gnostic" escape in which the author imperfectly believes and which the reader can finally accept only if he is highly credulous or very young. I say "finally accept" because this novel is one of the most carefully wrought in all of English literature, and in the tightly woven texture of the narrative Joyce is able to ensnare even the wariest and most meticulous of readers.

PROFESSOR ERIC VOEGELIN has told us that the central element in all gnostic experience is that of "the world as an alien place into which man has strayed and from which he must find his way back home to the other world of his origin"[1]; and such an attitude is implicit in the first sentence of *A Portrait of the Artist*, for, as several critics have noted, through the suggestive use of sounds Joyce has implied an external frame of reference with important meaning:

> Once upon a time and a very good time it was there was a moocow coming down along the road and this moocow that was coming down along the road met a nice little boy named baby tuckoo.
> His father told him that story: his father looked at him through a glass: he had a hairy face.
> He was a baby tuckoo.[2]

Although this bit of childish nonsense seems to have been taken from Joyce's own experience, it has additional significance in terms of Stephen Dedalus's evolution; for in the jumble of words one can discern an allusion to the cuckoo which lays its eggs in the nests of other birds.[3] This reference suggests that Stephen's story may be read as a variant of "The Ugly Duckling" in which the young boy, awkward and strange, is raised among an alien brood and suffers painful abuse until he finally matures and then flies away to join his own kind in the community of a finer species. This ancient folk tale in its various versions clearly embodies the potential for a gnostic sense of alienation as defined by Voegelin and others. The implied image of the earthbound cuckoo or duckling, struggling among inferiors who taunt him for his failure to conform to their communal norm, is a precise analogue to Stephen Dedalus's incipient sense of his own superiority over family, nation, and Church. The potential for rebellion against the prison of his world is realized both in the resolution of the ancient tale and in Joyce's development of his central action. The bird flies away, transcending the earth to which he has been confined, and seeks his place in the sky where he sings or soars with a grace and beauty beyond the capabilities of those whom he has left behind.

In *A Portrait of the Artist as a Young Man* Stephen eventually rejects the communal world into which he has been born, a world filled with creatures who are human and hence fallibly annoying to his sensibility. His rejection manifests itself in two ways analogous to the movement of the folk tale. First, he makes a figurative flight into aesthetic gnosis, devising a "theology" of his own which occupies his attention in the latter portions of the novel. Second, he literally abandons Ireland for the freedom of Paris, which was just beginning to serve at this time as the international gathering place for expatriate artists.

It is important to note that the nature of Stephen Dedalus's early alienation is further reinforced by the abundant implications of his name. As "Stephen" he is the counterpart of the first martyr of the Christian Faith, stoned to death by Pharisees, the intractable adherents of the old religious order. "Stephen" is the sufferer of corporate abuse, the visionary who preaches a special truth to a world which responds with vindictive hostility. Joyce does little more with this first name than assign it to his character, but Stephen himself recognizes his identification with Daedalus, whom he calls "the old artificer," creator of the labyrinth and escapee from the island prison of Crete. This myth, which, like the cuckoo story, has many potential meanings, may also embody the essentials of gnostic experience. For in Joyce's version the maze which his hero begins to build is his own aesthetic, a private system whose meaning he partially shares with fellow students, lesser intellects incapable of grasping its full significance. The flight of Daedalus, however, is obviously an analogue *in potentia* of the gnostic impulse, particularly when one considers the fact that the mythical artist is accompanied in his ingenious escape by Icarus, whose proud flight too near the sun results in the melting of artificially constructed wings and a consequent fall to his death.

In the initial stages of Joyce's narrative, the folk tale and the Greek myth coalesce into a single action which prefigures the "epiphany" of the hero, that moment when he comes to the realization that he has at last put behind him all of the communal concerns which have bound him to the world:

> Now at the name of the fabulous artificer he seemed to hear the noise of dim waves and to see a winged form flying above the waves and slowly climbing the air. What did it mean? Was it a

quaint device opening a page of some medieval book of prophecies and symbols, a hawklike man flying sunward above the sea, a
prophecy of the end he had been born to serve and had been following through mists of childhood and boyhood, a symbol of the
artist forging anew in his workshop out of the sluggish matter of
the earth a new soaring impalpable imperishable being?

His heart trembled; his breath came faster and a wild spirit
passed over his limbs as though he were soaring sunward. His
heart trembled in an ecstasy of fear and his soul was in flight.
His soul was soaring in an air beyond the world and the body he
knew was purified in a breath and delivered of incertitude and
made radiant and commingled with the element of the spirit.[4]

This passage, which forms a portion of the novel's peripety, renders in
unmistakable terms the "religious" nature of this important moment in Stephen Dedalus's life. In the first place, the figure of the flying man is not a
creature of this world but is generated in the imagination of the hero/artist as
a result of the spoken word, the name "Daedalus." The relationship between
the word and the image (word) is immediate, like the leap of an electric spark
from pole to pole. The world of concrete things does not seem to intervene,
and in the higher order into which his soul has ascended he is transfigured.

The vision of the winged man, whose identification with Horus as well
as Daedalus has been noted, is an absurdity that the reader may accept only
with a "willing suspension of disbelief," despite the equivocal word "seemed."
Do Stephen's eyes actually participate in a delusion or does the flying form
exist only within his imagination? In either case, the moment exemplifies
Stephen's rejection of the constitution of being which, as Voegelin has written, "is what it is, and cannot be affected by human fancies." "Hence," he continues, "the metastatic denial of the order of mundane existence is neither a
true proposition in philosophy, nor a program of action that could be executed. The will to transform reality into something which by essence it is not
is the rebellion against the nature of things as ordained by God."[5]

And indeed both Stephen and Joyce seem to understand this point precisely, when the hero speculates about the origins of his vision as "a quaint
device opening a page of some medieval book of prophecies and symbols."
He has, after all, been reared by scholastics who recognize magic for what it
is—a tool of the devil. The allusion to such sorcery as the alchemical, cab-
alistic, and hermetic traditions is unmistakable and suggests the degree to
which the reader is to understand this scene as the rendition of a desire to
transform the given world into something more pleasing to the will, and to

do so on a higher level of being.

On the next page the same idea is reintroduced, in even more specific terms: "Yes! Yes! Yes: he would create proudly out of the freedom and power of his soul, as the great artificer whose name he bore, a living thing, new and soaring and beautiful, impalpable, imperishable."[6] Here there can be no mistake about what moves Stephen, if not Joyce. He now believes he has transcended the given world and has become God the Father, able to create *out of himself* a living thing which is to be the beautiful, impalpable, imperishable *logos*. Having been affronted by the alien world into which he has been born, he has successfully escaped into a reality of his own creation where mythological figures can fly above the Irish Sea in response to the implacable urge within him that requires them to do so. And along with the image of Daedalus, his soul also takes leave of its prison, as he sees it, "soaring in an air beyond the world."[7]

But what can he do with the magical powers he has gained? Can he actually control being, reconstitute it? He believes he can, has always coveted such powers. In the first few sentences of the novel, for example, he sings a childish song about a rose, altering its natural color to green in order to suit his fancy. Later, while still a small boy, he acknowledges the impossibility of the green rose in the world as it is constituted; yet he holds out the promise to himself that "perhaps somewhere" such a thing might exist. The union of the rose with the color green is a state of being which the poet, the free soul, has the power to create, just as he is able to make the image of Daedalus fly in order to symbolize his own aspirations.

Having rejected the constitution of being, then, he is ready to exercise the new potential that he has acquired in the course of discovering his true vocation; and in one of the most celebrated passages of modern literature we see him in the process of performing such magical transformations. He is walking along the beach, in the throes of his newly discovered gnosis, feeling that he is about to be introduced to "strange fields and hills and faces," when he sees a girl, "in midstream, alone and still, gazing out to sea." During the course of the novel Stephen has been defined in terms of his changing relationships with women, and thus far his attitudes toward his mother and toward the girls he has known are recognizable as normal developments in the life of a young man. But at this point he looks at the beautiful stranger with a new precocity born of his rejection of the world, and in his eyes she undergoes a miraculous transformation:

> She seemed like one whom magic had changed into the likeness
> of a strange and beautiful seabird. Her long slender bare legs

were delicate as a crane's and pure save where an emerald trail of seaweed had fashioned itself as a sign upon the flesh. Her thighs, fuller and softhued as ivory, were bared almost to the hips where the white fringes of her drawers were like featherings of soft white down. Her slate blue skirts were kilted boldly about her waist and dovetailed behind her. Her bosom was as a bird's soft and slight, slight and soft as the breast of some dark plumaged dove. But her long fair hair was girlish; and girlish and touched with the wonder of mortal beauty her face.[8]

Again, as with the image of the flying man, what *seems* to be is confused with what is; and an alteration of the order of mundane existence takes place. It is possible, of course, to argue that Joyce is merely making use of conventional metaphor here in an effort to render the excitement of Stephen's active imagination. But what follows this extraordinary moment of perception is too charged with abnormal meaning to support such a view, for Joyce makes it explicit that the transformation that Stephen effects is magic and that the girl indeed has been changed (or half-changed) into a winged creature, something like an Egyptian bird god, an analogue to the winged man of the young artist's earlier fancy.

It is important to note that she is no longer herself at all but has become a creature made in the image of her creator. Whatever integrity she has as an object in the real world gives way to the machinations of the artist's will. Therefore the accidental properties she displays are altered in Stephen's perception of her and become a significant contribution to the transformation of her substantial being.

Thus has the gnostic imagination, freed from its prison, captured and subjugated the phenomenal other-than-self and then recreated it on a "higher level" in the image of the ego—Eve reverted to the status of rib, with Stephen, the newest Adam, performing the role of God. The girls whom he has known, desired, failed to win, or else paid for in the marketplace: these have coalesced into one image and become the passive instrument of the artist's stricken pride. As he contemplates her standing "in quiet sufferance of his gaze," the passive feminine spirit accepting the form imposed by the active masculine impulse, Stephen is overcome with a fervor which can only be described as that of the religious pagan:

Heavenly God! cried Stephen's soul in an outburst of profane joy. Her image has passed into his soul forever and no word had broken the holy silence of his ecstasy. Her eyes had called him and his soul had leaped to the call. To live, to err, to fall, to triumph, to recreate life out of life. A wild angel had appeared to him, the angel of mortal youth and beauty, an envoy from the fair courts of life, to throw open before him in an instant of ecstasy the gates of all the ways of error and glory.[9]

The diction in this passage clearly and intentionally suggests the degree to which Stephen's experience is to be understood as the founding of an ersatz religion in which he is both creator and a portion of the "recreated" order of existence as well. In speaking of the urge to "recreate life out of life" and in designating Stephen's joy as "profane," Joyce gives his reader (and himself) some hint of the mischief that his character is up to. However, the young convert has yet to understand the full implications of his religious zeal, though he is, at this point, thoroughly committed to its authenticity.

Notice that even in the passages quoted above, when Stephen is immersed in the transformations wrought by his own imagination, the reader never quite loses the sense of an old order still surviving and coexistent with the new; for at this stage Stephen still submits partially to the images of color, shape, and motion that in some respects root his experience in the events of a world of particularity.

The awareness of things as they are, however, is increasingly compromised as the novel unfolds; and the latter pages are not dominated by scenes in which Stephen's experience of the concrete is the avenue by which the meaning of the action is explored. Instead, Joyce gives the reader a series of "Platonic dialogues" punctuated by occasional interior monologues, a few fully rendered moments of dramatic confrontation, and (at the very end) entries in the hero's diary that somewhat ambiguously present his thoughts and feelings as he is about to fly from Ireland. And it is in these passages of argumentation between Stephen and his philosophical adversaries that the author attempts to suggest the final stage of his young rebel's development as an artist—a stage in which the youth uses his scholastic training to forge an aesthetics that will serve him as a credo in lieu of the traditional pieties he has chosen to reject.

AT FIRST GLANCE Joyce's motives in creating a discursive resolution to his action may seem obvious. Stephen wants to be a writer above all else; he must reject other considerations as secondary; and of greatest importance, he needs a well-formulated aesthetic theory in order to undergird his attempts to "recreate life out of life." But, as Walter Sullivan has observed, there are more basic reasons for Joyce's decision to end his narrative in a flurry of discourse. Mr. Sullivan has suggested the use of the Faustian legend as an analogue to *A Portrait of the Artist*[10]; and though in his discussion he is substantially right, I would merely like to approach the same structural problems with a somewhat different comparison in mind.

In the first place, the desire to be a literary artist is distinctly different from a poet's urge to write poetry; and Stephen's preoccupation with literary theory as a mode of pure speculation is an important indication of what impulse really lies behind his aspirations. In order to write, poets do not need to understand a well-developed literary theory any more than they need to master the discipline of formal grammar, though I suspect the latter would prove more useful than the former, since literary theory of a purely *a priori* nature might tend to lead the would-be artist away from the genuine problems he needs to confront in the act of composition. I would suggest, then, that Stephen the artist does not necessarily benefit from the aesthetics he insists on devising. Certainly the poetry he offers in evidence would tend to refute such a claim.

But Stephen the religious convert absolutely requires this system, because it becomes for him a new theology to replace the old. In lecturing the dean and his friend Lynch on the nature of art and tragedy, Stephen is really satisfying a religious rather than an aesthetic need, and therefore the full implications of this segment of the novel might be better understood after an examination of the faith he has rejected and the manner in which his new religion is defined.

The "old religion," of course, is not merely Roman Catholicism but a more all-encompassing *pietas* that includes a devotion to family, Ireland, and the Church. Stephen's alternative faith is one in which the artist is God the Father, God the Son, and God the Holy Spirit, his own family and community as well as transcendent being. This new vision is born out of the failure of the former orthodoxy, which, as Joyce presents it, has become effete and corrupt, a religion of empty forms and endless hypocrisies. Its priesthood is composed of liars, bullies, drunkards, dullwits, and false rhetoricians. Some of the spokesmen for this moribund establishment speak for the Church, some for Ireland, and some for the family; but all are the Pharisees of the *status quo*. Smug or shortsighted, they propagate the cant of a faith which, through Joyce's meticulous rendition, the reader must reject as decadent while applauding the prophet who can proclaim a gospel of regeneration. The moment of that prophet is at hand when Stephen sees (or seems to see) the image of the winged Daedalus and undergoes his ecstatic conversion.

The analogue between the development of Stephen's New Testament and that of first-century Christianity is striking and significant. Forgetting for a moment the idea that Stephen is both creator and incarnate word, let us consider him as a convert become exegete, the Saint Paul of his own divine revelation; for in the spiritual journey of Saul of Tarsus is embodied the fullest range of the religious founding that Joyce imitates in this novel, the movement from absolute commitment to the old order to a creative formulation of the theology of the new.

As Stephen becomes in early maturity the chief pride of his Jesuit instructors, so was Paul a brilliant and dedicated Pharisee who held the coats of those who stoned the first Christian martyr. Yet on the road to Damascus Paul was struck blind by the brilliance of Christ's image and immediately submitted without question to a truth he had previously denied with all his considerable intellectual resources. At that moment, drained of theology, he gave himself completely to the all-absorbing other-than-self. As I have already suggested, precisely the same thing happens to Stephen Dedalus.

Yet for Paul and for Stephen, the moment of ecstasy cannot be indefinitely prolonged, but the significance of the truth revealed is followed in both instances by exegesis, a process in which the reason analyzes and then synthesizes the meaning of the irrational revelation. Paul, after regaining his sight, begins to reflect on the life of Jesus and His reported words; and in his epistles (particularly in Romans) he spends much of his time quarreling with the old religion, in order to define the new. Yet as a Jew, trained by "the party of circumcision," his understanding of the new is articulated most often in the terms and rhetoric of the old.

And the same is true of Stephen Dedalus, whose exegesis is grounded in the theology of the faith he has rejected. "McAlister," he says, "would call my aesthetic theory applied Aquinas. So far as this side of aesthetic philosophy extends, Aquinas will carry me all along the line. When we come to the phenomena of artistic conception, artistic gestation and artistic reproduction, I require a new terminology and a new personal experience."[11] And so he should, for the two must, of necessity, go hand in hand. Yet the key word in this passage is "personal." Paul's revelation could by no means be termed a pure illumination of self. Indeed his ego was largely submerged in the image of Christ (though there are those who say it surfaces from time to time in a kind of fastidious priggery.) But with Stephen the expression of self is the ultimate devotional act. If there is any muse, it is *his* muse rather than *the* muse; and no one else may lay claim to her.

Thus in his arguments with the Pharisees of Ireland he insists on the ultimate supremacy of the so-called "creative act," which he believes must take place outside the community of family, church, and nation. As he puts it in one dogmatic statement to his foil Davin, "The soul is born first in the moments I told you of. It has a slow and dark birth, more mysterious than the birth of the body. When the soul of a man is born in this country there are nets flung at it to hold it back from flight. You talk to me of nationality, language, religion. I shall try to fly by those nets."

Again the image of flight with its echoes of the cuckoo tale, the Daedalus myth, the legend of Horus. But here the mystical experience of flying becomes a trope in discourse, the occasion for a programmatic statement on the creation as defined by the new orthodoxy. And so it goes with Stephen as he contends with adversary after adversary, vanquishing them with an ease that belies the complexity of the positions they advocate. (We might all wish for philosophical opponents so muddle-headed and inarticulate!)

Yet in his last encounter, he meets a formidable peer in his friend Cranly, who is able to teach him the limitations of his own arrogant intellect. The occasion of this final dialogue is initiated by Stephen himself, who, despite his frequent declarations of independence, is deeply troubled by a family quarrel.

—With your people? Cranly asked.
—With my mother.
—About religion?
—Yes, Stephen answered. After a pause Cranly asked:
—What age is your mother?
—Not old, Stephen said. She wishes me to make my easter duty.
—And will you?
—I will not, Stephen said.
—Why not? Cranly said.
—I will not serve, answered Stephen.
—That remark was made before, Cranly said calmly.
—It is made behind now, said Stephen hotly.[12]

Cranly immediately gains the upper hand in this initial segment of the conversation; for not only does he maintain his equanimity, but he also puts his finger precisely on the pressure point of Stephen's rebellious nature: "I will not serve" is the devil's line, and anyone who refuses to live within the constituted limitation of God's autonomy is by definition satanic. Cranly is calm in pointing out the truth because for him it is no shocking discovery: He already knows his friend well. But the interesting thing about the brief exchange is the manner in which Stephen reacts to Cranly's remark. Instead of being amused or coldly contemptuous, he is angered to the point of responding with a silly and ineffectual play on words. Why should the charge of diabolism so disturb him if he has rejected the Church and her dogma? Cranly pursues this question with Jesuitical skill, determining that Stephen neither believes nor disbelieves in the Eucharist and is unwilling to attempt a resolution of this crucial dilemma, largely because in his intellectual pride he is pleased with the new man he has become. The dishonesty of his position is apparent, particularly in light of the pain he causes his mother in refusing to make his communion. Cranly presses him on the issue, first testing him with a statement that Jesus may have been a charlatan, then noting Stephen's manifest shock and asking, "And why were you shocked if you feel sure that our religion is false and that Jesus was not the Son of God?" When Stephen equivocates, Cranly raises essentially the same question in a more sharply focused formulation: "And is that why you will not communicate, because you are not sure of that too, because you feel that the host too may be the body and blood of the son of God and not a wafer of bread? And because you fear that it may be?" "Yes," replied Stephen, "I feel that and I also fear it." "I see," says Cranly.[13]

**AND SO DO WE.** The rebellion, the rejection of the old faith, the mystical revelation, the carefully devised theology—they are all part of a fragile and tenuous system that might well fall to pieces under close and persistent scrutiny. "But does it matter," one is tempted to ask, "if Stephen is skeptical in regard to the Church and credulous in his dedication to the religion of art?" The answer to this question should be clear from Stephen's attitude toward his Easter duty and from his later replies to Cranly: His peculiar commitment to art is born of extravagant pride, pride in his own intellectual integrity; yet it is obviously impossible for any honest thinker to enthrone an ideal and absolute freedom in his heart without first disposing of the other question, the truth or falsity of Christian revelation. For if the Eucharist is the Body and Blood of Jesus Christ, then the artist cannot "recreate life out of life" or "refuse to serve." And an unwillingness to pursue this question is no more or less than a refusal to confront the ultimate lie of his life.

This attitude, of course, is typical of the gnostic, as Voegelin has pointed out:

> The gnostic thinker really does commit an intellectual swindle, and he knows it. One can distinguish three stages in the action of his spirit. On the surface lies the deception itself. It could be self-deception; and very often it is when the speculation of a creative thinker has culturally degenerated and become the dogma of a mass movement. But when the phenomenon is apprehended at its point of origin, deeper than the deception itself will be found

the awareness of it. The thinker does not lose control of himself: the *libido dominandi* turns on its own work and wishes to master the deception as well. This gnostic turning back on itself corresponds spiritually, as we have said, to the philosophical conversion, the *periagoge* in the Platonic sense. However, the gnostic movement of the spirit does not lead to the erotic opening of the soul, but rather to the deepest reach of persistence in the deception, whose revolt against God is revealed to be its motive and purpose.[14]

And, as if to prove Voegelin's thesis some 35 years before its publication in *Science, Politics and Gnosticism*, Stephen flees from Cranly back into the narrow and comfortable confines of his gnosis, betraying once again the deceitful nature of his flight: "I will not serve that in which I no longer believe whether it call itself my home, my fatherland, or my church: and I will try to express myself in some mode of life or art as freely as I can and as wholly as I can, using for my defense the only arms I allow myself to use—silence, exile, and cunning."[15]

No more perfect analogue to Satan could exist in a work of realistic fiction, and thus he retreats from the only discursive encounter of the novel in which the question of the constitution of being is placed squarely in the path of his perilous journey. Significantly, this combat is his last. Henceforth he will speak not to others but to himself, in a diary which epitomizes his struggle to sustain the self-illusion. And the last two entries signal his success as a practicing gnostic, whatever his occasional horror at the vision of damnation, an old man with "redrimmed horny eyes." In his valedictory he tells us that he will persist in worshiping the god of self and in recreating self out of self in order to devise some object for adoration: "Welcome, O life, I go to encounter for the millionth time the reality of experience and to forge in the smithy of my soul the uncreated conscience of my race . . . Old father, old artificer, stand me now and forever in good stead."[16]

WHO IS HE AT THE END OF THIS NOVEL? Is he Daedalus or Icarus? Is this narrative the portrait of the triumphant artist-as-hero, or is it the portrait of a damned soul? The critics who have best addressed themselves to this ultimate question, Walter Sullivan and Caroline Gordon, disagree on whether or not the author and the hero are to be equated, though both understand Stephen's story as rooted in impiety. Mr. Sullivan is firm and terse in his conclusion: "Stephen is Joyce." Miss Gordon, on the other hand, seems to say that Joyce's obvious contempt for Stephen continues throughout the narrative beginning with an ironic stance toward the child and ending with the final paragraphs in which the hero's damnation is rendered as deplorable and even tragic.[17] How, then, are we to resolve such an argument in the light of the novel's apparent gnostic implications?

In the first place, I would argue that if Miss Gordon is correct, then Joyce has misapplied his considerable talents as a rhetorician; for those passages which display the full range of his lyric prose are the ones which celebrate Stephen's aesthetic ecstasies, while, with the exception of the Cranly segment, he reserves his keenest irony for scenes in which he renders spokesmen for the old order.

But more importantly, Joyce's structuring of the action makes clear the meaning of his narrative. He spends too many pages of his novel in denigration of the spokesmen for family, Ireland, and Church to untie all his intricate knots with one scene featuring Cranly's well-executed attack. However Miss Gordon—all of us—might wish Joyce to be Daedalus, grieving for his fallen son but himself redeemed, we must finally conclude that at this stage of his career, like Stephen, he has mastered the finer techniques of gnostic self-deception and has been trapped by the artifice of his own creative imagination, the monumental achievement that both tells his life's story and intimates its inherent tragedy.

"Free. Soul free and fancy free. Let the dead bury the dead."[18] This is the new Christ speaking, Stephen/Joyce, the redeemer of self; and we the readers who are allowed into the *sanctum sanctorum* of his inner soul must listen to his voice in hushed adoration. For it is his spirit that has bridged the gap of years and informed the time in which we live. The rhetoric of freedom so prevalent in our decade is only in part the result of the political revolutions of the 18th century. The kind of freedom people speak of today is more likely than not the freedom of Stephen Dedalus and James Joyce, which is something more than emancipation from political tyranny. It is freedom from social custom, freedom from family, freedom from tradition, freedom from Church, freedom from the other-than-self, freedom from the created order, freedom from God. And if we as a generation believe passionately and absolutely in this beautiful, impalpable, imperishable illusion, we may in part thank James Joyce for our troubling faith.

# Notes

1 Eric Voegelin, *Science, Politics and Gnosticism* (Chicago: Henry Regnery Company, 1968), p. 9.

[2] James Joyce, *A Portrait of the Artist as a Young Man* (New York: The Viking Press, 1964), p. 7.

[3] See John Kelleher, "The Perceptions of James Joyce," *The Atlantic Monthly* (March 1958), p. 86.

[4] Joyce, p. 169.

[5] Voegelin, p. 169.

[6] Joyce, p. 170.

[7] *Ibid.*, p. 169.

[8] *Ibid.*, p. 171.

[9] *Ibid.*, pp. 171-72.

[10] Walter Sullivan, *Death by Melancholy: Essays on Modern Southern Fiction* (Baton Rouge: Louisiana State University Press, 1972), pp. 97-113.

[11] Joyce, p. 209.

[12] *Ibid.*, pp. 238-39.

[13] *Ibid.*, p. 243.

[14] Voegelin, pp. 32-33.

[15] Joyce, pp. 246-47.

[16] *Ibid.*, p. 253.

[17] Caroline Gordon, *How to Read a Novel* (New York: The Viking Press, 1957), pp. 210-14.

[18] Joyce, p. 248.

# Scarlet Sister Julia:
# The Rise and Fall of a Literary Reputation

TIME, WHICH CAN MAKE A DIAMOND or reduce bone to powder, dispos-
es of literary reputations with the same sovereign finality. Thus F. Scott
Fitzgerald, forgotten at the time of his death, is now remembered by millions, while the once-famous Sarah Josepha Hale is known only to meticulous literary scholars and their most submissive graduate students. In a few
years, of course the relative renown of these novelists may be altered—even
reversed. But somehow I doubt it. For what has made Fitzgerald's work
durable is not the veneer of polite "radicalism" which may have brought him
a portion of his initial readership in the 20's. Nor has Sarah Josepha Hale's
19th-century piety redeemed her from oblivion. The only thing that endures,
it seems, is a genuine artistic rendition of what is true in human nature; and
as much as critics like Lionel Trilling might protest the idea, I am convinced
that most readers of fiction are not primarily interested in moral postures,
social philosophy, or historical verisimilitude. They are interested in stories
and people. They do not read *Moby-Dick* as a catechism or as a chronicle of
the short-lived whaling industry, nor would they study *Uncle Tom's Cabin*
solely as a treatise on the evils of slavery if they had not been trained to do
so by confused English teachers. The critic who measures works of fiction
against the dogma of some regnant piety in order to determine their ultimate worth is bound to fail, just as a doctor is bound to fail who determines
the relative health of his patients exclusively on the basis of their views on
the current economy.

Obviously this truth is not as self-evident to others as it is to me. Indeed,
as vital evidence to the contrary, ideologues of all stripes, armed with their
own well-honed fragments of truth, continue to hack away at literary reputations, the great as well as the modest. Thus a commentator in *Partisan
Review* calls the narrator of *Moby-Dick* a white racist honky, while his opposite number in *National Review* convicts William Faulkner of being a "liberal" (the ultimate crime, I would conclude, in that particular court). And
poor Henry James, who writes of heroic self-sacrifice in the grand epic tradition, is condemned in both *National Review* and *Partisan Review* for being a
deviant of one sort or the other, a sinner against the discrete and contradic-
tory theologies that each faction defends against the onslaught of the infidel.

Melville, Faulkner, and James are obviously impervious to such attack, but the reputation of Julia Peterkin has suffered severely at the hands of ideological critics, both early and late. At the beginning of her career she was denounced by Old South apologists and fundamentalist preachers, to say nothing of cousins and aunts nervous for the preservation of family status. These adversaries seemed to believe that she was impious toward the local gods; and still unsure of her talent, she was shaken by their abuse, as her early letters reveal.

Fortunately, the initial response from literary circles was friendly, even laudatory, though conditioned to some extent by the social and cultural climate of the day. We must remember that in 1924, when *Green Thursday* was published, the revived Ku Klux Klan was a significant political power, particularly in the Midwest; Al Jolson was at the height of his Broadway career, performing in blackface as the happy, singing "good-old-white-folks' darky"; and Jim Crow, after two or three decades, had become the custom as well as the law throughout the South.

Needless to say, literary depictions of black characters were usually reflective of this general atmosphere, and as a consequence, Mrs. Peterkin's work was welcomed by self-styled liberals for what it was—an honest portrait of true-to-life blacks rather than some fictional recreation of Mr. Bones. Joel Spingarn, the scholarly president of the NAACP, wrote of *Green Thursday*, "Nothing so stark, taut, poignant, has come out of the white South in fifty years."[1] W.E.B. DuBois, reviewing the book in *Crisis* (the NAACP house organ), said of Mrs. Peterkin, "She is a Southern white woman but she has the eye and the ear to see beauty and know truth."[2] Charles Puckette, in the *Saturday Review of Literature*, wrote that *Black April* "must stand as the most genuinely successful attempt yet made to capture the soul of these people. This book is put down with the feeling that one stands nearer to truth than one has stood before, in a field of fiction the surface of which has been often scratched, and the rich depths seldom upturned. Other fiction of negro life seems false in the light of Mrs. Peterkin's achievement."[3] An anonymous reviewer in *The Nation* speculated that *Black April* was "the finest work produced thus far dealing with the American Negro."[4] Robert Merrick in *The New Republic* said approximately the same thing: "possibly the most convincing presentation of the Negro that has yet been made by a white person."[5]

I cite these passages not only to illustrate the unqualified praise with which her early works were greeted in so-called liberal circles, but to make a more important point. As favorable as these comments may seem to admirers of Mrs. Peterkin's fiction, they all derive from an assumption, either stated or unstated, that the importance of her achievement is to be measured by the relative verisimilitude with which she renders black characters. No one in this group bothers to distinguish between her virtues as a sociologist and her virtues as a novelist.

In 1924 the failure to make such a distinction proved harmless enough, and by 1929, after Mrs. Peterkin had won a Pulitzer Prize for *Scarlet Sister Mary*, her reputation as a significant American writer seemed to be permanently secured. Yet the political climate began to change rapidly during the 30's, and after World War II a new civil-rights movement rendered an earlier sociology obsolete. Without delving too deeply into the question, I would suggest that dramatic events in the 50's and 60's produced as a byproduct a rigid orthodoxy in "black fiction" which was designed to serve the specific objective of reordering society. The enveloping action of this fiction was, by prescription, a white-dominated community of economic and social exploitation. While important examples of such fiction had been published in an earlier era, the piety of the "New Revolution" would no longer tolerate a realism that did not serve as a means to political ends. Realism outside the framework of the power struggle was regarded as a form of reaction, and this attitude led to the swift erosion of the fragile ground upon which Mrs. Peterkin's reputation rested, for she was no longer a good sociologist, and no one had ever laid a foundation for her reputation as a literary artist. Thus at present she is largely ignored in the pages of critical and scholarly journals, even those primarily devoted to the study of Southern literature; and when she is mentioned, it is as a portrayer of blacks, and invariably she is dismissed with condescension or outright hostility. As examples of the current attitude toward her work, I would cite two passages, one from Willard Thorp's *American Writing in the Twentieth Century*, the other from John M. Bradbury's *Renaissance in the South*.

Mr. Thorp, in contrasting Mrs. Peterkin's work with that of DuBose Heyward, writes:

Heyward's pages are spotted with purple prose but Negro critics agree that his understanding of Negro life was remarkable. They are less enthusiastic about Julia Peterkin whose best-known work, *Scarlet Sister Mary* (1928), won a Pulitzer Prize. As the wife of a plantation manager, Mrs. Peterkin knew the Negroes of her region well, but in her later work she condescends to them and falls back on the legend of the happy, childlike Negro, content with a clean cabin and plenty of fat-back and pot-liquor.[6]

First, it is interesting to note the sharp contrast between Mr. Thorp's assessment of Mrs. Peterkin's work and the opinions voiced by her earlier critics. It is difficult to believe that he is discussing the same novelist. And who are the "Negro critics" whom he cites but will not name? What do these critics have to say about the unqualified approval of black activists such as DuBois, Walter White, and Paul Robeson? Were these commentators of the 1920's simply imperceptive or does truth live precariously in the shifting shadow of the left wing? Whatever the answers to these questions, I detect one area of agreement common to the two generations of critics: again, both view Mrs. Peterkin almost solely in terms of her sociological significance.

I AM PUZZLED, however, by Mr. Thorp's emphasis on her "later work" as exemplary of condescension. As a matter of fact, it is in *Bright Skin*, her last novel, that Mrs. Peterkin departs from her familiar pastoral mode to explore in detail the conflict between the stability of an old agrarian order and the lure of urban life. Cricket, the "bright skin" or mulatto of the title, is of all the author's major characters the farthest from being "content with a clean cabin and plenty of fat-back and pot-liquor." To the contrary, she is a rebel against the plantation community from the time she is a child. Her first lover is a stranger from the outside world, and his chief asset is an automobile, that basic symbol of change and modernity. Though her lover is murdered, Cricket is never again satisfied to remain among the plantation folk, whom she regards as her inferiors. In the climax of the novel she leaves them all behind and flees to New York with a lover and her black supremacist grandfather, the leader of a separatist movement in Harlem. Her first husband, Blue, who chooses to remain in the stable plantation community, is, throughout the novel, too troubled and love-stricken to find true contentment anywhere. And in addition to the major characters, Mrs. Peterkin introduces some new and disturbing elements into her familiar world, among them an old man whose keening lament for his lost childhood in Africa is among the most disturbing of all her scenes. In this novel no one is happy; no one spoons pot-liquor; no one's cabin is gratifyingly clean.

The same general assessment could be made of *Roll, Jordan, Roll*, Mrs. Peterkin's final work, which is a collection of early sketches, supplemented by a few tough-minded additions and several informal essays which touch on such matters as the degradation inherent in slavery, the hard discipline necessary for survival in the struggle with nature, and the customs and beliefs which govern the conduct of the blacks on Lang Syne plantation, a world Mrs. Peterkin knew better than any of her critics, early or late, black or white. With one or two minor lapses, I can think of no book less likely to fit Mr. Thorp's description than this hard-boiled vision of the spare but dignified life some blacks lead as a result of historical circumstance. Clearly he has read both of these books carelessly, if indeed he has read them at all.

Perhaps the more revealing of these later evaluations, however, is that of John M. Bradbury, which appeared in his exhaustive study of modern Southern literature published in 1963. Mr. Bradbury is frank in admitting that one of the purposes in writing his book is to "redress the critical imbalance" caused by the South's New Critics, who have ignored "a strong and wide-spread liberal wing," whose "problem novels," he says, "have proliferated." Presumably because of sheer bulk they deserve mentioning. Or is it because of their piety? Mr. Bradbury is unclear, but the tone of his comments on Mrs. Peterkin is unmistakably hostile:

> Mrs. Peterkin's novels, all of them Negro-bound, display an old Southern weakness, despite their basis in intimate observation; her Negroes are represented as curious phenomena with sensationally odd characters. The fundamental traits she exploits are moral irresponsibility and savage superstition. *Scarlet Sister Mary* gained wide popularity for its lurid mixture of sexual promiscuity, religion, and superstition, with authenticity guaranteed by its author's position as mistress of a large South Carolina plantation. But this novel in particular lacks conviction—*Black April* is perhaps her best. In none of her four books of fiction do basic economic and social problems figure, and white owners appear only as vague beneficent deities.[7]

This passage poses greater difficulties than Mr. Thorp's, in part because Mr. Bradbury's rhetoric is harsher, laced with contempt rather than with mild distaste. It is difficult to counter allegations concerning the reasons for the success of *Scarlet Sister Mary*, but perhaps one can go to the contemporary reviewers for the best insights on the question. Herschel Brickell, in *The Saturday Review of Literature*, said the book "firmly establishes its author as an interpreter of negro character; but more than this, it leaves no room for doubt that she is a novelist whose work has enduring quality."[8] Robert Herrick in *The New Republic* said that the book was "something more than a novel—the revelation of a race, which has lived with the whites for hundreds of years, without becoming known beneath the skin."[9] Ben Wasson, in *Outlook and Independent*, recognized Mrs. Peterkin's departure from the use of stereotypes. "Mrs. Peterkin escapes such things; she is above them. Her book is real because she realizes that people, be they black or white, are fundamentally alike."[10] And Joseph Warren Beach found the novel "entirely free

... from any flavoring of patronage, sentimentality, apology, defense."[11] Mr. Bradbury is entitled to his opinion, of course, but there is sufficient internal evidence in his commentary to suggest that he has an ax to grind.

His reference to *Scarlet Sister Mary*'s "lurid mixture of sexual promiscuity, religion, and superstition" provides us with some clues to the nature of his bias, particularly in his telling use of the coordinate conjunction. Obviously sexual promiscuity bothers him when linked with religion and superstition. He does not, for example, find anything "lurid" in the incestuous sexuality and suicide of *Lie Down in Darkness*. Nor is he bothered by what he describes as Charles Curtis Munz's "liberal indictment of white sharecropping practices." Note his tolerance when he writes, "Munz's novel does pile on its rapes and other violences, but it retains a fundamental integrity and rigidly excludes propagandistic author intrusions."[12] Presumably Mr. Munz has been careful to avoid mitigating his sexual assaults with any "lurid" concern for Christian redemption. Neither Mrs. Peterkin nor Dostoevsky is so prudent.

Indeed there is a striking resemblance between Mary Pinesett and Sonia Marmeladov of *Crime and Punishment*. Both out of a kind of necessity indulge in sexual intercourse—the former because of her naturally loving nature, the latter to feed her family. Mary takes on a series of lovers, one at a time, and no bedroom scenes exploit the occasions for Mrs. Peterkin's readership. Meanwhile, Mary is a force for good in the plantation community, muting the harsh Pharisaism of church deacons by teaching them, both by advice and by example, to be kind and forgiving to one another and to question the rigid application of church law in cases where penitent sinners are concerned. In the end Mary has a religious vision following the poignant death of her favorite child, and in a scene as "lurid" as anything found in *Elsie Dinsmore* she is rebaptized into the church, the comic heroine in her moment of reintegration.

Superstition does play some role in the narrative, just as it undoubtedly played a role in the black community of Lang Syne plantation. Would Mr. Bradbury have the novelist ignore fact or truth? He is happy enough when the ignorance and bigotry of white characters are held up to the light for examination, though to give him his due, he objects to outright diatribes. Can he not see the historical and sociological implications of superstition in the black community? Mrs. Peterkin is hard on both superstition and some aspects of religious primitivism. Why does Mr. Bradbury not understand the sympathetic burden of her fiction?

An answer to this question may be implicit in the structure of Mr. Bradbury's argument and in its last sentence. First, I note a similarity in organization between Mr. Thorp's paragraph and Mr. Bradbury's. Each begins with a reference to the portrayal of "Negro life"; each moves to a discussion of *Scarlet Sister Mary* and to the question of Mrs. Peterkin's authority as the mistress of a plantation; each ends with the suggestion that the author is exploiting old stereotypes, though Bradbury carries the matter further by writing, "In none of her four books of fiction do basic economic and social problems figure, and white owners appear only as vague beneficent deities."[13] Has Mr. Bradbury derived his opinion of Mrs. Peterkin from Mr. Thorp, or are both simply following a natural course in discussing Mrs. Peterkin's work from a retrospective point of view? Mr. Bradbury does not cite Mr. Thorp in his index, so perhaps the latter explanation of these similarities is more logical.

Yet one fact cannot be ignored: White owners do not appear in Mrs. Peterkin's four works of fiction as vague, beneficent deities. Indeed, they do not appear *at all*. The author deliberately excluded them from her works because, as she wrote to Emily Clark early in her career, she intended to avoid the pros and cons of racial controversy, refusing to subordinate the humanity of her characters to the "basic economic and social problems" that Mr. Bradbury demands. Is this attitude "an old Southern weakness"?

To ANSWER THAT QUESTION, let us turn to the two most successful black novelists of our time, Ralph Ellison and James Baldwin. Mr. Ellison maintains that the black experience in American fiction has been "distorted through the overemphasis of the sociological approach" and that those people who advocate or practice such a literature destroy the values in black culture "which are beyond any question of segregation, economics, or previous condition of servitude."[14] Mr. Baldwin makes essentially the same point when he writes that "The failure of the protest novel lies in its rejection of life, the human being, the denial of his beauty, dread, power, in its insistence that it is his categorization alone which is real and which cannot be transcended."[15]

I can think of no better paraphrase of what Mrs. Peterkin herself believed about the nature of such sociological fiction. But let us leave these commentators and turn to Mrs. Peterkin herself. For if interest in her work is to be revived—as I think it should be—then we must at least know what she was attempting to accomplish in her literary career.

We already see that she objects to what Mr. Baldwin calls "the protest novel." To this issue I would add only the observation that in her fiction she quietly transplanted her fictional Gullahs from Fort Motte to the Sea Islands, where there had long been a verifiable tradition of absentee landlords, thus making her imaginary world consistent with the facts of South Carolina history.  Had she wished to show the beneficence of white paternalism, she would surely have included idealized owners in her narratives.

But we have her own written opinion on the subject of such sentimental portraits.  In a review of Lyle Saxon's *Children of Strangers* she launches a more eloquent attack on old-fashioned stereotypes than either Mr. Thorp or Mr. Bradbury.  She classifies them into three types:

> The most popular one showed loyal, grateful slaves, or ex-slaves who were devoted to the families of their present owners and eager to sacrifice themselves for their white friends.  Another prized portrayal presented the Negro characters as amiable, carefree comic figures, full of easy laughter and always ready with a gay song or nimble dance step.  A third well-known presentation showed the Negro as a drinking, gambling, worthless creature who was such a menace to white civilization that he spent most of his days on the chain-gang until he was finally lynched by a mob of white citizens resolved to protect white society from injury at his hands.
>
> These patterns of Negro conduct were emphasized in literary productions so persistently that they were accepted as authentic.  And not until comparatively recent years have our dark-skinned neighbors been treated as individuals, as human beings whose position in the social scale is complicated by problems and difficulties not found in the lives of their white contemporaries.[16]

It was against such stylized and unimaginative portrayals of the Negro that Mrs. Peterkin was reacting when she began to write her own sketches in the early 1920's.  To a great extent it was her attempt to render the South Carolina Gullah in purely realistic terms that led to her fame as a novelist.  Indeed in Mrs. Peterkin's fiction the stereotypes are present only by implication, hovering on the brink of possibility like gray ghosts to provide a contrast with the colorful flesh-and-blood characters she creates.  April, with all his arrogance and nobility, is set in bold relief by the shade of Thomas Nelson Page's obsequious servant; Budda Ben's bitterness is grimmer because of the frantic good humor of Mr. Bones; and Scarlet Sister Mary's virtue is at least partially defined by antithesis in the inflammatory rhetoric of the revived Ku Klux Klan.  That Mr. Bradbury, Mr. Thorp, and others fail or refuse to recognize this truth seems a pity, for it is on their authority that present-day students of Southern literature have ignored Mrs. Peterkin's achievement.  I must admit it is difficult for me not to suspect that most of these latter-day critics have derived their opinions of her work from rumor and hearsay.

In order to revitalize Mrs. Peterkin's literary reputation, I would suggest that readers and critics approach her on her own terms, not as a portrayer of "The Black" (who, after all, does not exist in the real world), but as a serious artist who attempted to render those blacks she knew as human beings caught up in ancient struggles with the land, with others, and with themselves, their blackness only one individual characteristic that places them at a particular time and a particular moment and place in their unique witness to the timeless truth of the human condition.

Like Mr. Bradbury, I have some grave reservations about the limitations of the New Criticism, but I believe such an approach applied to Mrs. Peterkin's fiction would yield abundant fruit and begin to reclaim her from her present oblivion. There is enough conscious artistry in her work—enough irony, paradox, and allusion—to satisfy any incipient Cleanth Brooks who might care to choose her work as a major project for investigation. And the essential structure of such novels as *Black April* and *Scarlet Sister Mary* can be discussed in terms as sophisticated and "Aristotelian" as those used by Northrop Frye. Indeed, at this particular moment in the evolution of a criticism of Southern literature, there is more of value still to be said about her works than about those of Flannery O'Connor, concerning whom so much has been written.

Finally, it is too much to hope that literary critics will ever cease to be subverted from their proper task by ideological concerns. They never have, even in the best of times; and at present we live in an age that has been politicized to an almost intolerable degree. More and more, in our zeal for the abstraction, we are tempted to superimpose our opinions and will on being, as well as on the literary works that mirror, recreate, or define being. We must, however, try to do better, whatever our mode of approaching the word or the reality.

## Notes

[1] Letter from Joel Spingarn to Julia Peterkin, quoted in Emily Clark, *Innocence Abroad* (New York, 1931), p. 224.

[2] W.E.B. DuBois, "The Browsing Reader," *Crisis*, XXIX (December 1924), p. 81.

[3] Charles M. Puckette, "On a South Carolina Plantation," *The Saturday Review*

*of Literature*, III (March 19, 1927), p. 660.

[4] *The Nation*, CXXIV (June 8, 1927), p. 649.

[5] Robert Herrick, "A Study in Black," *The New Republic*, LVII (December 26, 1928), p. 172.

[6] Willard Thorp, *American Writing in the Twentieth Century* (Cambridge, 1960), p. 259.

[7] John M. Bradbury, *Renaissance in the South: A Critical History of the Literature, 1920-1960* (Chapel Hill, 1963), p. 83.

[8] Herschel Brickell, "A Pagan Heroine," *The Saturday Review of Literature*, V (November 3, 1928), p. 318.

[9] Herrick, *loc. cit.*

[10] Ben Wasson, *Outlook and Independent*, CL (November 21, 1928), p. 1212.

[11] Joseph Warren Beach, *The Twentieth Century Novel* (New York, 1932), p. 232.

[12] Bradbury, pp. 151, 152.

[13] Bradbury, p. 87.

[14] Ralph Ellison, "That Same Pain, That Same Pleasure: An Interview," *Shadow and Act* (New York, 1964), p. 23.

[15] James Baldwin, "Everybody's Protest Novel," *Partisan Review*, XVI (Spring 1949), p. 585.

[16] Julia Peterkin, "One Southern View-point," *North American Review*, CCXLIV (December 1937), pp. 397-98.

# Caroline Gordon: Two Essays

## The Short Fiction of Caroline Gordon

THE STRUCTURE OF THE NOVEL is large enough to accommodate almost any genuine talent, however undisciplined; and though the greatest novelists are skillful and learned as well as gifted, even a figure like Theodore Dreiser, whose works are sprawling and primitive like massive pueblos, has earned a permanent place in the history of American literature. But the short story demands a special piety, a studied devotion to the intricate technique of fiction; and consequently only the finest craftsmen can successfully practice this special art. For within its narrow confines one cannot play loose and free with point of view or bury a bad sentence; a writer may make up his own rules, but he must follow them to the letter or incur the scorn of the perceptive reader. For this reason, no more than a handful of modern writers have produced short stories which are both technically sound and rich in fictional values.

Such a writer is Caroline Gordon, whose artistic discipline has always been adequate to control the wide range of vision she brings to her fiction. Indeed she tends to crowd into her stories more than their formal limitations would seem to permit: the total experience of a region's history, the hero's archetypal struggle, the complexity of modern aesthetics. In every instance, however, she succeeds in bringing the broad scope of her narrative into focus and in creating the ideal fictional moment, when form and subject are at war and the outcome hangs forever in the balance.

Yet there is a classic simplicity in most of her short stories, an unusual economy of incident and detail which decorously masks their essential thematic complexity. Even the prose is, for the most part, spare in its diction and syntax, particularly in the first-person narratives, dominated by a tone that is quiet and conversational, the intimate language of the piazza on a warm summer evening.

And it is in this quality that one finds a clue to the origins of Miss Gordon's narrative virtue. For she is still in touch with the oral tradition which in her formative years was a vital element of family life. Like William Faulkner and Katherine Anne Porter, with whom she has much in common, her experience of the nature of being begins in the family, with its concrete relationships, its sense of wholeness, its collective memory. In fact, many of her stories are the artistic rendition of incidents involving her father, her brother, and more distant connections, events which formed a significant part of her earliest and most important understanding of the world. For Southern writers of her generation, the family was a natural symbol of the order of existence, the basic analogue for everything of importance; and therefore it provided a key to the meaning of community, history, politics, morality, the transcendent and timeless.

Thus to render the family was to come to terms with all of these larger considerations simultaneously and to do so as concretely and as unselfconsciously as possible in the post-Cartesian world, which is, after all, the world of fiction. For if anything survived of an earlier and more coherent order, it survived in a rural agrarian society which still held fast to some concept, however dimmed, of *pietas*, the tripartite virtue which informed Western civilization until the late Renaissance and undergirded the works of Homer, Virgil, Dante, and Shakespeare.

It was no problem, then, for Miss Gordon and her Southern contemporaries to move, say, from family history to regional history; for they were, after all, one and the same thing, the latter almost perfectly preserved in the former. And so the reader finds in her first volume of stories, *The Forest of the South* (1945), not only the Aleck Maury stories, based on the life of Miss Gordon's father, but also tales of the Civil War and Reconstruction, which undoubtedly originated in anecdotes that came to her by way of family reminiscences.

Indeed, every narrative in *The Forest of the South* and in *Old Red and Other Stories* (1963) has the unmistakable ingredients of life itself, those sharp and singular details that one immediately recognizes as containing truths beyond the province of the mere "angelic imagination." Thus Miss Gordon's fiction moves *toward* abstraction rather than proceeds from it, and is always symbolic rather than purely literal or purely allegorical. For this reason she never falsifies the world as, for example, Shirley Jackson does in order to serve the tyranny of intellect. Heart and head in Miss Gordon's work never come to blows; and neither betrays the steady, uncompromising senses, which are the primary means of fictional understanding. In other words, her artistic vision is whole and inviolable, which can be said of few modern writers.

This wholeness is something which is hers by inheritance, yet such a legacy does not automatically ensure the validity of fiction; and few Southerners have matched the achievement of Caroline Gordon, Katherine Anne Porter, and William Faulkner. What must be added is a certain technical

sophistication that can be earned only by hard work and critical speculation. To resort to an imperfect analogy, one could say that without some
technical mastery of his medium the painter cannot transfer his perception
of the subject to canvas. Only a thoroughly trained draftsman like Picas-
so could rearrange the features of the face to capture the essential counte-
nance of his model.

THE EVIDENCE OF MISS GORDON'S CONCERN for her craft is revealed not
only by its embodiment in her novels and in her short stories but by theory
and explication in two of the most important books in the canon of 20th-cen-
tury criticism, *The House of Fiction* (1950) and *How to Read a Novel* (1964).
The first of these, written with Allen Tate, is one of the best textbooks ever
published on the subject, and serves to instruct the writer as well as the reader. Particularly valuable is the appendix which contains, among other things,
the clearest analysis ever given of point of view, that unique element which
distinguishes fiction from all other literary compositions. In her analysis the
student is led to the heart of the problem that the novelist and the short-sto-
ry writer must face in coming to grips with an action; and, though Miss Gordon's discussion is as complex as the subject itself, she exposes with remarkable clarity the basic narrative methods available to the writer.

*How to Read a Novel* offers an advanced course on the subject and perhaps provides a more valuable insight into Miss Gordon's own body of work
than does *The House of Fiction*, since here she not only analyzes theme and
technique but advances aesthetic theory as well. In this collection of essays
one can see clearly the connection between the fiction writer's narrative
mode and his total vision, which for her is finally moral in essence. Thus the
technical failure of Andre Gide's *The Counterfeiters* is attributable to a lack of
artistic integrity, willingness on the part of the French novelist to submit to
the world's body and his consequent attempt to force life into the procruste-
an bed of his own innate perversity.

The Gide of Miss Gordon's essay sheds considerable light on her own
fiction, though her discussion is by no means intended to be self-serving.
Unlike Gide she is always submissive to the ambiguities of existence, and
therefore her technique is never used to distort or to oversimplify. Her first-
person narrators are invariably fallible, even when she intends them to be
normative, and so their humanity both qualifies and highlights their virtue.
But more to the point, she never takes unfair advantage of the great liber-
ties allowed by the central intelligence. This restraint, evidence of an artistic
submission to her heritage, is particularly significant in such stories as "To
Thy Chamber Window, Sweet" and "Old Red," where the action is rendered

in the consciousness of Aleck Maury, a character based on her own father. Mr. Maury is a compelling figure whose stubborn independence and total commitment to the ritual of the hunt are almost epic in their implications; yet Miss Gordon, in her fidelity to experience, also reveals the inevitable ambiguity of such unmitigated individualism, the price that others must pay for Mr. Maury's single-minded pursuit of his own will. In this respect such stories are akin to the "poetry of inclusion," where tension always serves to adjust the abstract vision to the concrete world of possibility. The result is an heroic mode that is closer to Homer and Dante than to Virgil, and Mr. Maury emerges as an admirable man rather than as an exemplum of goodness devoid of flesh and blood.

Yet despite her rendition of life's opposites Miss Gordon's irony is classical in tone rather than modern, the irony of high seriousness. Unlike most 20th-century writers, she tends to dignify her characters rather than to demean them in the eyes of the reader. In this regard it is instructive to compare her treatment of hopeless spinsterhood in "All Lovers Love the Spring" with James Joyce's analogous story "Clay." In the Joyce narrative—which despite its fine economy has been too highly praised—Maria, the unfortunate reject, is reduced in stature to a degree that finally threatens to compromise the reader's natural pity. Lacking beauty, intelligence, and even the vestige of feminine charm, she is alternately sentimentalized and ridiculed in a tone that earns for her a measure of contempt as well as sympathy. On the other hand, Miss Gordon's old maid has something to offer a man, and consequently her plight is more lamentable. Like Maria she is homely, a fact which her cousin Roger, whom she has secretly desired, is unable to overlook. But she is not stupid, nor is she totally devoid of womanly grace. Thus her wasted life, which is spent in service to an aged mother, is ironic on a level which suggests the tragic. And while Joyce closes his story with the maudlin remarks of a drunken young man, thereby lowering the plane of irony, Miss Gordon's ending is lyrical, a description of the sensuous beauty of spring as celebrated in the responsive heart of a woman who clearly deserves a better fate than the neglect of her shallow and insensitive cousin.

Of course the difference between the two stories can be explained by the vastly differing outlooks of their authors. Joyce rejected the notion of a traditional Ireland and had little sympathy for his Dubliners, the products of a society he regarded as tawdry and sterile. Miss Gordon, in contrast, viewed the South of her time as a vital community which could gather in, with a certain degree of love and charity, its misfits and eccentrics. In such a community the ironies of existence are as least partially reconcilable and hence protected from the unrestricted exercise of pride, Joyce's chief sin as a writer of fiction.

Caroline Gordon's short stories are such a substantial achievement that one is astonished to read her own comment on the subject: "I cannot bear to touch [to read] any of my short stories..." (*The Southern Review*, VII [Spring 1971], p. 450). Her attitude here is reminiscent of Alice, who, upon finding herself reduced to a fraction of her normal proportions, laments, "I never was as small as this before, never! And I declare it's too bad, that it is!" Yet like Alice, whose persistent identity at that size defies the laws of physics, Miss Gordon is herself even when her ample understanding of man, society, and history has been reduced to the dimensions of the short story. In this respect she ranks among the foremost writers of her time, and her art will endure.

\* \* \*

## Introduction to a new edition of *Green Centuries*

CAROLINE GORDON spent most of her adult life trying to steal time to write. Like many serious novelists, she taught in college creative-writing programs, where she read and criticized the work of students, attended innumerable faculty functions, and tried to avoid entangling campus politics. She once called poet Wallace Stevens "something of a monster," because he pursued a career as an insurance executive. Had she really understood the no-nonsense world of business, she might have found it less distracting and more conducive to writing than the academy.

In addition to her teaching, she had other pressing responsibilities. She was a wife and mother; and she devoted much of her creative energy to her husband, Allen Tate, and their daughter. Allen was a chore from the beginning. A charmingly self-indulgent man, he was always preoccupied with his own career, with the pursuit of his numerous literary friendships, and with other women. He was also hospitable to a fault. As a consequence, the Tate household was forever crowded with guests, including some destined to be among the most formidable literary figures of the age—Robert Lowell, Hart Crane, Mark Van Doren, Delmore Schwartz, Andrew Lytle, Malcolm Cowley, Arthur Mizener, and Robert Penn Warren, to name but a few.

With this succession of nonpaying boarders, the novelist was forever stretching meals, monitoring sleeping arrangements, and patching up quarrels (when she wasn't starting them herself). Small wonder that it took her some three years to write *Green Centuries*, which many critics believe is her finest novel. She started work on the book in 1938, when she and Allen were teaching at Greensboro, North Carolina, and she finished it at Princeton in 1941. During this period, she had to deal with the usual distractions:

house guests, Allen's writer's block, and academic society. She complained to Muriel Cowley:

> Must get back to my Indians. I plan to kill off twenty six of them today but alas, I will have to stop the bloody work at four o'clock to go and pour tea at a ladies' gathering. The faculty ladies here are all great organizers—and callers. If they know who you are they call on you because they like to call on writers. If they don't know who you are they call more than ever to console you for being so obscure.

*Green Centuries* was indeed about Indians in a time when they were less fashionable as literary subjects than they are today. To most Americans of the 1940's, "the only good Indian was a dead Indian," or else one attending a mission school on the reservation. Yet in her extensive research on frontier life, Miss Gordon discovered that the Cherokees of that period were more civilized than the white invaders and more refined in their sensibilities. She saw in their society, soon to be destroyed, a beautifully ordered world of ceremony and ritual in which the basic activities of life were given form and transcendent meaning. Miss Gordon grasped what few people of that period understood: that the civilization of the Cherokees was as finely structured and as sensitive to life as a spiderweb.

Against this highly sophisticated and orderly community, she juxtaposes the coarsening freedom of the white pioneers, who, as they moved westward, shed the vestiges of their Christian European heritage and reverted to their basic instincts for self-gratification. The principal white characters in *Green Centuries*, though by no means two-dimensional villains, find it difficult to maintain their full humanity as they confront the seductive freedom of the American frontier. Unlike the Cherokees, whose every action is invested with transcendent meaning by a traditional society, the frontier folk are often bestial in the pursuit of basic needs and self-centered in their relationships with one another. Theirs is a nightmare vision of liberty grown renegade and insatiable, a world in which the strongest ego prevails.

Though this summary may sound like a 1990's fictional stereotype of the historic confrontation between the noble Indian and the wicked European settler, Miss Gordon's narrative is considerably more complicated and infinitely more credible. In the first place, she does not regard white European civilization as rapacious and barbaric. Her white characters run into spiritual difficulty on the frontier because they lose sight of their religious and cultural heritage in the vast wilderness. Released from biblical and communal controls, they are less human than their Indian counterparts; but the culture from which they come is presented, however implicitly, as good rather than evil.

In the second place, the Cherokee nation is neither oversimplified nor sentimentalized. Miss Gordon's Indians are not noble savages, instinctively virtuous because they still remain in a state of nature. Like the white characters, the Cherokees are fallible creatures living in a fallen world. If they behave better than the European pioneers who threaten and eventually destroy them, it is not because they are innately good but because they act within the rigid confines of convention and tribal law. As human beings, they are no less cruel or lust-driven than their white counterparts. They simply deal in a more orderly fashion with their failings.

IN READING *GREEN CENTURIES*, one must remember that it was written at a time when the historical works of Frederick Jackson Turner and Henry Nash Smith were quite the rage among liberal intellectuals, who saw in the frontier experience "the crucible of democracy." In the wilderness of the New World, they argued, the white settlers found both freedom and equality. No one was judged by birth or riches but by the ability to survive and prevail. (You survived the rigors of nature, and you prevailed over the Indian.) And you were at liberty to become whatever you wished. In Absolute Nature, these social critics maintained, you found Absolute Freedom. (And that's how the New Deal began.)

Miss Gordon, who had probably read more of the primary documents from this early period than all but a handful of historians, believed that such a view was not only simplistic but wrongheaded. And her novel is based on an entirely different understanding of the early history of the nation—an essentially conservative Christian perspective.

In *Green Centuries* we see no awakening political consciousness, no Whitmanesque celebration of equality and self. Miss Gordon's protagonist, Orion Outlaw, cares less about democracy than he does about survival and appetite. He is so infatuated with his own independence that he rejects the very circumstances in which political activity must take place. Thus politics, which is by definition a communal preoccupation, is for him an entanglement to be avoided. In fact, he flees into the wilderness precisely because he does not want to accept the responsibilities of living in society.

It would be wrong, however, to suggest that *Green Centuries* is about history or political philosophy or anything so abstract. It is a novel rather than a romance, and it is about people rather than ideas. Orion Outlaw is a tragic figure who exemplifies great virtues and possesses great flaws. Like his classical namesake, he is the ultimate hunter, accompanied only by his dog, Sirius, forever pursuing the kill. Yet Orion is not the simple and unchanging character of myth, but a highly complicated man who comes to a tragic awareness of his flaws only after he has destroyed all possibility of leading the good life.

True to the name Outlaw, which is what the MacGregors called themselves after the failure of the Jacobite cause, he flees all authority to seek the wilderness, leaving behind a community where life is still reverenced, where customs and manners are still observed, where courtship is still ritualized in dances and games, and where marriage is still the norm. Orion takes with him Cassy, the daughter of an Anglican clergyman. They have already become lovers; and though the opportunity presents itself at a later time, they choose not to marry.

The relationship between Orion and Cassy is the primary focus of Miss Gordon's narrative—the initial joy of being together, the raising of a family, the prosperity that comes from hard work. Indeed, for a while it seems as if the frontier is fully capable of producing the kind of independence that Orion seeks and Cassy is content to accept.

However, their relationship cannot survive the rigors of the wilderness and Orion's desire to move ever westward. Daniel Boone, a friend and neighbor for a while, epitomizes the free spirit of the pioneer—Boone, who abandons his homestead and moves on when stability and order begin to trouble his spirit, fetching along his long-suffering but compliant wife. Far from presenting him as heroic, Miss Gordon renders Boone as a flawed man who represents the worst impulses of the age. Cassy tries to thwart Orion's desire to follow Boone's example; but eventually her efforts prove unsuccessful. The dangerous life they have chosen ends tragically in alienation and death.

IN CONTRAST TO ORION AND CASSY, Miss Gordon gives the reader Archy Outlaw, Orion's brother, and Archy's Cherokee wife, Monon. Though initially a far less formidable figure than Orion, Archy chooses a better path to follow and in the end achieves a peace and maturity that Orion never approaches. The victim of a hunting accident, Archy is discovered by Indian warriors, who take him back to their village and later initiate him into the tribe.

There he learns the customs and beliefs of the Cherokee nation and becomes a hunter, taking the name of Bear Killer. It is through Archy's eyes that we understand the orderly world of the Cherokees, where virtually every action is a ritual invested with religious significance, from the hunting of wild game to the sexual union of man and woman.

In tracing Archy's assimilation into the Cherokee nation, Miss Gordon is able to present dramatic contrasts between life in a traditional society and the life of the frontier. When Orion is tempted by the wife of a neighbor, his betrayal of Cassy is selfish and perfunctory, an act of pure lust unchecked by convention or conscience. On the other hand, in the Cherokee nation, on one night during a special harvest festival, women are permitted to choose any man for a sexual partner, regardless of marital status. One act is an exemplum of unchecked lust. The other is a controlled exercise of sexual desire.

Likewise, hunting and warfare are nothing more than brutal and dehumanizing slaughter to Orion and his fellow frontiersmen. One white man, Joe Hubbard, tells casually of ambushing a Cherokee brave, wounding him, dragging him three miles at the end of a rope, and then skinning him to make a saddle. To Hubbard, the Indian is no more than an animal. And to Orion they become something even lower in the order of nature. Miss Gordon describes him on a field after battle, surveying the corpses of slain Cherokees.

> He started running and suddenly it was like some day in summer,
> when going into the field, he would find a melon that had not
> been there the day before and then another and then another, and
> would run from row to row, counting the long, dark shapes. So
> now he ran over the field and the bodies he came on were to him
> like the fruit he had been used to number on that summer day.

In this beautifully crafted passage, Miss Gordon shows Orion's understanding of the slain warriors as no more than vegetables ripening in a field, the lowest form of living thing. As the scene closes, he stands in a puddle of blood, laughing. "We let it out of 'em, didn't we?" he cries. "We let it out of 'em!"

Among Archy Outlaw's Cherokees, however, a deep reverence for life informs the principal masculine pursuits of hunting and warfare. Both activities are governed by rigid rules that prescribe respect for prey and enemy. Hunters pay solemn tribute to the animals they have killed, and warriors treat their fallen adversaries with dignity. As Andrew Lytle has written of Miss Gordon's Indians, "Their warfare did not evince a destructive instinct. It was a religious rite, and therefore a social rite, which submerged the end of fighting which is death beneath the ritual practice of it."

It is important to remember that the contrast between frontier life and life among the Cherokees is revealed not through discursive passages or interior monologues, but through the action of the novel, which seems to develop naturally and inevitably, without suffering from thematic manipulation by the author. In fact, so skillfully did Miss Gordon disguise her thematic intent that an old friend, John Crowe Ransom, thought she had surrendered to naturalism.

*Green Centuries* may well be Caroline Gordon's masterpiece. Certainly it is one of the most well-wrought novels to emerge from the so-called Southern Renaissance. The intricate structure of parallel actions is handled with discipline and imagination. By the end of the novel, all the loose ends are tied up by invisible hands, and the meaning of the characters is fully realized without compromising their integrity as human beings. As a consequence, *Green Centuries* is both a good yarn and a book of genuine literary significance—the work of a master.

It is also worth noting that Miss Gordon's prose in this novel is more inventive and lyrical than in her earlier works. Rhetorically, she risks more and gains more, without ever falling into the trap of sacrificing her characters or action for a burst of self-conscious poetry. She knew the difference between a poem and a novel. She wrote novels.

These qualities make *Green Centuries* a valuable model for serious students of fiction to analyze and follow. Miss Gordon, a highly conscious artist, works with classical restraint, avoiding tricks and affectations; and for this reason her later works are lessons in how to tell a story simply and dramatically, while at the same time pushing the art of fiction beyond conventional boundaries.

OF COURSE, consummate artistry doesn't always please the public or pay the bills. The Tates had hoped to live for a while on the royalties from *Green Centuries*, and their expectations were by no means unrealistic. *None Shall Look Back*, an earlier novel with an historical setting, had sold more than 10,000 copies, enough to support the author and her family for a year. *Green Centuries*, in many ways a superior work, might well have done better. Unfortunately, it sold so poorly that royalties failed to pay back the publisher's advance.

Clearly, the period in which the action was set did not appeal to audiences in the early 1940's. *None Shall Look Back*, a contemporary of *Gone With the Wind*, was about the War Between the States—a perennially popular subject of fiction and history. The pioneer experience had already provided a number of novelists with romantic subject matter, but apparently the public was weary of the period, particularly when treated in realistic terms. In *Close Connections*, a recent biography of Miss Gordon, Ann Waldron reports that *Green Centuries* was rejected by at least one Hollywood producer because it belonged to "the coonskin cap group." Had she chosen to write about ladies and gentlemen in white wigs, she might have fared better. Indeed, Frederick Lewis Allen wrote to her about the book, expressing the snobbery of the current literati: "We can't get much interested in 'Hit war' people."

Miss Gordon was extremely depressed by the experience and wrote to a friend, "My book was a complete failure, financially, didn't even pay back its advance . . . It was poor timing, of course—people are tired of pioneer stories, and I think that in a way it is a hard book to read, but I had expected it to do better than it did."

Her disappointment turned to bitterness when she went into Scribner's bookstore, saw *Saratoga Trunk*, a popular potboiler, on prominent display, and looked in vain for her own novel. She wrote indignantly to Mark Van Doren: "I could not find my book anywhere so asked a clerk if he had a book called *Green Centuries*. He led me to a table, piled high with garden books and so help me God proffered me a herb manual."

More than 30 years later, when she was serving as professor of creative writing at the University of Dallas, she still lamented the failure of *Green Centuries* to receive the popular audience she felt it deserved. She saw a copy of the paperback in a Salvation Army thrift shop and came away haunted by the sight.

"I find it heartbreaking to see novels in second-hand bookstores," she said. "They're like old friends who have been abandoned by their families."

Yet *Green Centuries* has seldom been out of print for long; and critical articles increase with every passing year, assessments that are invariably laudatory. Though the novel was once rejected by the public, it now promises to have a longer life than the bestsellers of 1941, most of them written by people of lesser talent and integrity. Indeed, it is now recognized as one of the enduring works of the Southern Renaissance.

In a dry season, when novelists of literary merit are few and when critics no longer demand or even understand genuine craftsmanship, it is time to take a second look at Caroline Gordon's work in general, and *Green Centuries* in particular. She was a writer who understood the full potential of the novel and was able to break new ground, both in technique and in subject matter.

Yet, unlike some innovators, her narratives have always been available to the general reader. Though a literary figure of historical significance, she is primarily a first-rate storyteller and a shrewd student of the human heart. In addition, she touches on the immutable truths of human experience and reminds us of the perennial need for community, rituals, and a religious vision to give form and meaning to life. These truths remain essential to the survival of a people, whether in pioneer days, when Americans had yet to discover a national identity, or in the last decade of the 20th century, when we have all but forgotten who we once were. Caroline Gordon is one of a handful of writers who can help us remember, and for this reason alone it is important that she be read.

# Allen Tate

*Introduction to a new edition of*
Stonewall Jackson: The Good Soldier
*by Allen Tate*

ALLEN TATE WROTE *Stonewall Jackson: The Good Soldier* in 1927 when he was living in New York with his wife, Caroline Gordon, and their small daughter. An anti-romantic in literary theory and sensibilities, he was attempting to be that most romantic of all things—a man of letters who survives on what he writes. It was just as difficult a role to fulfill then as it is today, and Tate wrote quickly whatever brought in quick cash: book reviews and essays, and—only when he could allow himself the luxury—an occasional poem. (It must also be said that during this period, the Tates lived rent-free in their Greenwich Village apartment, in exchange for which the poet-essayist performed certain janitorial duties, including the firing of the furnace.)

During the 1920's, biographies sold well—better, on average, than novels—so Tate agreed to write a biography of Stonewall Jackson for Milton, Balch and Co. It is difficult to believe that the publishers knew what they were doing when they allowed him to choose his subject. In Northern literary circles, Tate was usually polite and circumspect about regional controversy. Writing for *The New Republic* and friendly with intellectuals of the Left, he could even be deprecating about the South in casual conversation—at least about obvious Southern peccadillos and affectations. But a careful listener might have caught the irony in his voice and wondered about the use of such phrases as "the War between the States." His editors did not listen carefully and ended up publishing a book that is still something of a literary scandal.

For by 1927, Tate—along with John Crowe Ransom, Donald Davidson, and Andrew Lytle—had begun to resent Northern attacks on the intelligence and integrity of their region and were in the process of planning a counterattack which would be published three years later as *I'll Take My Stand*. In a sense, Tate's biography of Stonewall Jackson (published in 1928) was the first assault in a war to regain Southern self-respect, the literary equivalent of the firing on Fort Sumter. It was bold, aggressive, and merciless—not unlike Stonewall Jackson himself, who ordered his men to fire at the bravest Yankee officers and to shoot Confederate stragglers.

165

In many ways Jackson epitomized what Tate and the Agrarians believed was virtuous and enduring about the South. In the first place, he was from a family of small farmers rather than a member of the privileged planter class. Tate, Ransom, Davidson, Lytle, and the other Agrarians (with the exception of Stark Young) never believed in the existence of a Southern "aristocracy"; and Tate says of the region in his own time that it was inhabited by "a whole people . . . sorely afflicted with the delusion of ancient grandeur." Jackson, not Pierre Gustave Toutant Beauregard or even Robert E. Lee, was the Good Soldier, a mountain man who was well mannered but unpretentious, loyal to his own kind but never proud. Tate and the others understood Jackson quite well. They had come from such people themselves.

Second, Stonewall Jackson never suffered a significant defeat. Like Nathan Bedford Forrest, whose biography Lytle would later write, Jackson was a consistent winner, largely because he knew how to move troops quickly, instinctively understood when and where to attack, and was calm and rational under fire. Of Jackson, Southerners could easily say, "Had he not been killed, we would have won the War." For Tate, in 1927, the War was still winnable.

Third, Jackson was a deeply religious man. A skeptic himself at this stage of his life, Tate nonetheless recognized the importance to society of a religious vision, a supernatural mythos to give order and meaning to life. He well understood the degree to which the South was informed by such a vision, and he was convinced that the North was committed to a radical materialism that threatened the survival of the Old Republic. Jackson was a man whose entire life, including his military career, was guided by religious conviction. He was utterly oblivious to danger because, like any good Calvinist, he believed he was as safe on the battlefield as in his own parlor, until his time came. Tate admired that certitude and probably envied it. After a long struggle with doubt, he would eventually become a Roman Catholic. In the meantime, he understood that it was the hard-shell beliefs of people like Jackson that gave the South its essentially sacramental understanding of nature, history, and society.

These qualities combined to make Jackson the perfect Southern paradigm, the ideal figure for the region to commit to memory. Radcliffe Squires, in his otherwise excellent literary biography, reproves Tate for not capturing the tragedy of the War. But Squires fails to understand that, in Tate's narrative, Jackson is not intended to be tragic but epic, a hero of the past—writ large to teach latter-day Southerners who they were and how they should behave. Tate didn't want to be Seneca. He wanted to be Vergil. Squires, who understood everything else about Tate, failed to understand his Southern sensibilities, which were very finely honed in 1927, in part because of the ridicule of the South growing out of the Scopes Trial, in part because Tate had been living in New York City for several years and was tired of being patronized. (During those years he was known by his Northern acquaintances as a man who used his courtly manners as an aggressive weapon.)

Squires might have examined more carefully the proportions of Tate's chronicle, which was not the story of a man's life so much as the account of his deeds in battle. Tate tells us as little about Jackson's life as he can. There is virtually nothing about his loss of one wife and the all-too-hasty courtship of another; his bumbling, pedestrian career as a teacher; his personal idiosyncrasies; his chronic indigestion. These are the ingredients of a man. Tate gives us the portrait of a hero, because he believed that was what the South required at a moment when it was beginning to forget its past.

As for his chronicling of battles, Tate also follows epic rules rather than the rules of conventional biography or modern fiction. We see battles as grand strategies rather than vignettes of personal experience, rendered through interior monologue. It is the action that is important rather than the thought and sensibilities of the participants. The book is closer to the *Iliad* than it is to *The Red Badge of Courage*.

But Tate departs from the pure epic mode in one significant respect: He devotes several long passages to the political background of the War, its causes, the beliefs and ideals that fueled it. Such passages were necessary by the late 1920's, because, even with a handful of veterans still alive, the world in which the War was fought was rapidly disappearing, inevitably destroyed by the triumph of raw industrial might and a new American pragmatism. Tate felt he had to instruct a late generation of Southerners concerning the society of their grandparents, if only to counteract the simplistic version of 19th-century history they were reading in their high-school textbooks.

His own account of the circumstances surrounding secession constituted the chief scandal of the volume. He stood the conventional explanation on its head. According to this version:

> The Yankee industrial society had its own form of slavery: "This [the Northern] atmosphere was beginning to be charged with commerce and industry. Commerce and industry required a different kind of slave. He would be a better slave; he would have the illusion of freedom."

> The North rather than the South bred the real rebels against the United States and their Constitution: "The Northern

revolutionists chose to interpret the Constitution through some mystical sense that had no exact correspondence with the letter of that document. 'The spirit' (because it is irresponsible) 'killeth; the letter giveth life.' They interpreted it by abstract right. The South interpreted it historically, literally."

The North declared war on the Union: "On the 15th Lincoln called for 75,000 volunteers to put down the 'rebellion.' No one need be deceived by the word. A revolution is not started by the party that fires the first shot; a revolution is a question of ideas.

"It was now a living fact that the North was trying to destroy the social and political structure of the United States by force of arms."

To Northerners of the late 1920's, these ideas seemed either blasphemous or hopelessly eccentric. Today they probably appear so to most (if not all) Southerners. Yet they were the accepted version of the War to many Southerners of Tate's generation—and probably to virtually all who lived in the South before the turn of the century. Only after several generations of textbooks published in Boston and New York did the War take on the simplistic look it has today—a crusade to free the slaves from cruel and rapacious masters.

Aware of the Yankee myth and its growing acceptance, even among Southerners, Tate decided to disturb the pure narrative texture of his epic to remind his readers that the South had its own version of the "irrepressible conflict" and that the heroism of a man like Stonewall Jackson could only be understood in terms of a commitment to that political view. Jackson, after all, believed that slavery was immoral, owned no slaves, and had little in common with the rich planters who did. If you wanted to understand why he was willing to fight and die for the Confederacy, you had to see the war in terms other than those defined by the victor.

Had Tate written this epic account even 30 years later, he might have presented his arguments in more detail—and with corroborating evidence from the letters and memoirs of 19th-century Southerners. Certainly he would have adopted a more moderate tone. For the narrative is full of insolent asides calculated to quicken the pulse of sympathetic readers and drive up the blood pressure of nearly everybody else. It is unabashedly partisan, and for some, unbearably so.

Yet this total quality, like the political commentary, was calculated to accomplish a specific purpose with a chosen audience. It was apodictic rhetoric, the kind of language used in preaching to the choir. We still hear it employed by keynote speakers at political conventions. Its intent is not to convince or to instruct but to excite and unite in common cause. If you are a Democrat at a Republican convention, you find such language tiresome at best, blood-boiling at worst; but when you go to your own convention, the same kind of rhetoric magically acquires meaning and immediacy and power.

Tate was writing *Stonewall Jackson: The Good Soldier* for a mystical convention of Southerners in his generation—an audience of far-flung delegates who had the capacity to make common cause against an enemy they still confronted, still saw as hostile. Southern politicians of that day routinely referred to carpetbaggers, scalawags, the Republican Party in terms of contempt; and they still gathered at cemeteries on Confederate Memorial Day, though in diminishing numbers. As late as 1948, candidates for office in the 11 states of the Confederacy could wrap themselves in the Stars and Bars and win a lot of votes. Tate understood the public uses of such rhetoric and chose it for his epic narrative because, during that era, it was the language instinctively adopted in talking about that War, those heroes. If it seems strident and reckless today, it is because we have lost the context in which it was first cast. In 65 years, the current accounts of the civil-rights struggles will probably seem just as quaintly partisan.

IN THE FINAL ANALYSIS, however, *Stonewall Jackson: The Good Soldier* is still a first-rate piece of work by a first-rate literary artist. The same year Tate also published *Mr. Pope and Other Poems*, a volume that contained some of his standard anthology pieces, like the title poem and "Ode to the Confederate Dead." A year earlier he had published "Poetry and the Absolute," his first important critical essay. He was in the process of establishing a formidable literary reputation. And while the attitudes he struck in this volume were not calculated to ingratiate him with the New York crowd, the book did add breadth to his reputation as a man of letters. It showed that he could manage narrative prose and that he knew politics and history as well as literary theory.

It must be said, however, that for all its narrative virtues—its spare, serviceable prose; its lack of irrelevant lore; its attention to the dramatics of a good tale—*Stonewall Jackson: The Good Soldier* was a young man's book. It was recklessly conceived. It was halfheartedly researched. It was impudent to the point of being foolhardy. In his choice and treatment of his subject matter, Tate was throwing down the gauntlet to the Yankee scholars who thought they had laid the Southern cause to rest.

However, in a literary world that was "liberal" but less "politically correct" than our own, he was able to survive and prosper because he was a modernist in his aesthetics and because being aggressively Southern was considered quainter and less wicked than it is today. No one was ostracized for flying the battle flag, and the Lost Cause was treated with some respect on the stage and in films.

However, it is doubtful that Tate would have undertaken the same project 20 years later or that he would have treated it in the same cavalier way. The mature Tate would have been more prudent and more arch. He would have been less epic and more discursive. And his irony would have been shaved more finely—so finely, in fact, that those who read the book might not have recognized it at all. Twenty years later Tate was no longer regarded as a "Neoconfederate" but as a cosmopolite, a citizen of the Republic of Letters, that international community of artists that has no geographical or linguistic boundaries.

Soon Tate would be quarreling with Donald Davidson over the latter's "Lee in the Mountains," saying that the emotions expressed in that poem were extraliterary, that no one could or should make a poem that had as its purpose the fostering of regional piety. It was essentially an aesthetic rather than an historical argument, but it provides us with some insight into Tate's literary persona as it developed in later years. As far as the Republic of Letters was concerned, he was no longer Stonewall Jackson; he was a Frenchman, observing American regional conflict from his studio with a critical detachment, a latter-day Marcus Aurelius (who in his *Meditations* thanked a mentor for teaching him not to care whether the blue team or the green was victorious).

At least, to the literary world this is what Tate seemed to be.

To those Southerners who knew him in later years, he was someone quite different. A cynical partisan might have said he was a sutler, one of the mercenary traders who came to the battlefield before and after a great conflict and sold goods to both sides. For Tate was the modern man of letters when he was in the North and still an unregenerate, if somewhat politic, Confederate when he was among his old friends in the South.

But cynics notwithstanding, he was actually something better than a sutler. He was more like a spy, who lived among his enemies, adopting their ways and rhetoric while still retaining a loyalty to his own country. In this role Tate was able to define the essential complexity of his region and its history—and to be listened to by some of the most influential people of the time. And when he was at home with people who understood all these matters, he could speak more freely—and not always without risk.

**ONE EXAMPLE SHOULD SUFFICE.** In the early 1970's, when he came to the University of Texas at Arlington to address a literary gathering, he was frail and aging. He had to ask the younger men who met him at the airport to walk more slowly, because he had difficulty catching his breath. (The disease that would eventually kill him was beginning to take charge.) As the group entered the Robert E. Lee Room where Tate was scheduled to speak, one of the local faculty members mentioned that the school had just banned the Confederate battle flag from the campus, despite the fact that the city had been named for the Lee-Custis house and the school athletic teams had always been known as "The Rebels."

"As a matter of fact," he said, "the battle flag hung in the blank space on that wall until only yesterday."

Tate's eyes flashed quickly, but his expression didn't change. He seemed to listen to the information with no more than perfunctory interest.

"Everyone is still boiling over the matter," said the faculty member. "The university's president sided with the small band of protesters. Caved in at the first sign of trouble."

At the ensuing luncheon Tate found himself seated next to that same president, a fussy little man who didn't quite know how to respond to the famous poet's distant and precise courtesy. Finally, after the meal, Tate was introduced and rose to speak.

"As some of you may understand, I feel very much at home here in the Robert E. Lee Room," he said. "It's nice to know that at least in this place, the South's heroes are still remembered."

The silence deepened and all eyes turned to the president, sitting beside Tate, beginning to shift in his chair.

"But there is something missing," Tate said. "There's a huge white space on the wall back there."

He looked down at the president with a cold eye and pointed.

"I would hope to see a large Confederate flag hanging right there." The assembled students gasped, then burst into applause.

It was not just a jest or a random impulse that caused Allen Tate, near the end of his life, to stand up once more for the old Cause. He had been reared in an era when the memory of Lee and Jackson and a hundred other heroes was still alive in a society not yet defeated by progress and uniformity and Yankee practicality. His generation, as he himself wrote, was the last that could turn backward toward the past and see the South as it once was—and at the same time look forward to see what modern ideologues were urging it to become. He had lived, he said, in a "moment of self-consciousness," and out of that moment had come the enduring vision of the South—preserved in poems, novels, criticism, and narrative history—the greatest literary out-pouring in modern America. And it was that enduring South to which he paid tribute in his brief but deliberate breach of propriety. The man of letters and the Southerner were at peace with each other for a moment in a darkening twilight where he had a few friends close at hand.

It was that man—frail, fighting for breath, but with a hard glint in his eye—who, almost a half-century earlier, had given this extraordinary gift to his people: this epic account of their great military hero.

# The Future of the Southern Renascence

*A lecture for the Intercollegiate Studies Institute, 1974*

*Dr. Landess was introduced by Dr. M.E. Bradford: "My work tonight is
simple pleasure, for I am here to present to you my friend. Tom Landess is
a native of Florida, educated at Vanderbilt and the University of South Carolina.
Thus he has been ostensibly protected by both nurture and ancestry from most of
the isms of which it is my business to complain. I cannot tell you how well I know Tom,
but he remains a continuous surprise after years of association, as poet, critic, teacher,
and as sometime politician. . . . Tonight he has chosen to examine for our instruction
. . . literary historiography. I know of no American scholar who comes to grips so quickly
with the terms of a question or is more gifted or more persuasive in devising his answers."*

I HAD INTENDED TO USE what Dr. Bradford always calls the rhetoric of
assumed modesty, but he has pretty much preempted the possibility for
that. I do wish he had told you that what I say here tonight is not supposed
to be taken as seriously as what some of the other people have said, but he
did say I was a poet, so I suppose that covers the matter.

Like anything else, the literature of the South may be scrutinized from
as many perspectives as there are viewers. Yet, in fact, critics of Southern
literature have obviously tended to influence one another, to build on previous insights and speculations, and, finally, to attempt certain well-articu-
lated theses concerning the nature and origins of the so-called Renascence.

At this stage the difference between theory and immutable law occasionally becomes blurred. Now among the theories that might be called generic,
at least two seem to dominate scholarship in the field. Though each of these
theories might be tortuously traced back to ancient Greece or some other
suitably archaic source, I would like to suggest that they have been associated in their recent incarnations with two Southern universities, each of
which has produced an extraordinary number of scholars in the field. The
first of these is the University of North Carolina at Chapel Hill, where for
many years the eminent sociologist Howard W. Odum focused the attention
of colleagues and students on Southern culture and all of its manifestations,
literary and otherwise.

I think, without oversimplifying the matter, that Chapel Hill critics have tended by and large to emphasize the sociological aspects of literature more than have their counterparts from Vanderbilt. Many have been self-styled liberals who have severely condemned antebellum society as cruel and exploitative and have advocated most of those economic and social programs fostered by successive national administrations. These critics are, for the most part, progressives in their view of history, in their hope for the future. During the period between World War I and World War II, they advocated rapid industrialization as a primary solution to the region's social and economic ills.

The Vanderbilt critics, on the other hand, have tended to emphasize formal criticism at the expense of the sociological. Their mentors have been those Fugitive-Agrarians who helped to popularize the New Criticism: John Crowe Ransom, Allen Tate, Donald Davidson, the early Robert Penn Warren. In contrast to Chapel Hill's school, the Vanderbilt critics are often self-styled conservatives who have seen in the Old South a flawed but basically normative civilization that was a New World continuation of the classical Christian cultures of Western Europe.

As a consequence, the Vanderbilt scholars have frequently fought political and social programs designed to bring the region into step with the rest of the nation. Their view of history is more melancholy, at times apocalyptic. Specifically, they have viewed industrialism as the wooden horse brought into their Troy by persons too idealistic or greedy to realize the consequences of their actions.

At present, Vanderbilt critics may feel more sympathetic to industry than they once did, but not much. These descriptions are fragile to be sure. But the contrasts are real and deeply felt by members of both parties.

It would be an exaggeration to suggest that these two factions continue to fight the Civil War well into the second half of the 20th century, with Vanderbilt wearing the gray, Chapel Hill the blue, and Louis Rubin, like some indefatigable sutler, running his wagonload of wares back and forth between the opposing forces. As a member of the Vanderbilt party, I would have to admit that the analogy is self-serving; therefore, I will reject it with the utmost contempt. Perhaps the Trojan War will serve us better after all, with Vanderbilt defending the ancient walls and Chapel Hill attacking.

In this brief summary I have emphasized differences in philosophies rather than in critical method, because philosophical differences are perhaps more relevant to the theories of nature and origin than are differences in the manner of criticizing a specific author's work, though the two are related.

Now, to the question: Why in the world did all of those Southerners suddenly begin to write poetry and fiction during the 1920's? Predictably, there are Chapel Hill accounts and Vanderbilt accounts, as well as brilliant accounts by such neutrals as Lewis Simpson.  But the two versions I would like to focus on tonight are to be found in *Three Modes of Southern Fiction* by C. Hugh Holman and "The New Provincialism," a well-known essay by Allen Tate.  I choose these particular examples not so much because they are the most typical or the most comprehensive, but because they best suit my own purposes, which will surface a little later, no doubt to the surprise and delight of all.

I WILL BEGIN WITH MR. HOLMAN'S THESIS, which at first glance appears to be simple and easy to dispose of.  Yet Mr. Holman demands a greater measure of respect than one might initially wish to accord him.  For one thing, his arguments are not only graceful but gracious as well, for he treats those with whom he disagrees with courtesy if not absolute generosity.  In writing of the Fugitive-Agrarians, he does so with only a trace of irony as he praises their criticism of Faulkner.  And when the time comes to be more severe with them, he gallantly steps aside and allows the ghost of Thomas Wolfe to administer the beating.  And in addition to his genteel charm, Mr. Holman is seemingly diffident in his style, carefully stating at the outset that all generalizations tend to strip from concrete realities, actualities, their individual characteristics.

Thus, he continues, there is no real South except as a high-level abstraction within which land, language, race, climate, mountain and plain, pine and palm are mixed together in a common conception.  He admits the usefulness of the term, however, but argues for a more limited and modest set of categories: three Souths or subregions that he designates as the Tidewater South, the Piedmont South, and the Deep South.  In further defining these categories he borrows the schematic designs of two oft-cited authorities: literary historian H.A. Taine and social critic W.J. Cash.

From Taine he takes the tripod classification of "sources which combine to produce an elementary moral state"—race, surroundings, and epoch. [Hippolyte Alphonse Taine (1828-93) put forth a well-known critical formula—*race, milieu, et moment.*]  From Cash he borrows typical descriptions of Tidewater, Piedmont, and Deep South.  Finally, to each of the three regional subdivisions he assigns a novelist who he says reveals the impact of these three diverse cultures: Ellen Glasgow for the Tidewater; William Faulkner for the Deep South; and Thomas Wolfe for the Piedmont.

Thus to summarize, we have three abstract categories, each of which is tricotimized, typically described, and specifically illustrated.  It is indeed a tidy feature, set forth with seeming modesty, well documented and methodically argued, and to anyone who may still resist the beauty of the symmetry, Mr. Holman appeals to universal experience. He writes:

> Only one who has failed to note the differences in the reactions of these sub-regions to the 1954 Supreme Court decision can assume that the South has been uniform in its pattern of response. And those who think they can see a [George] Wallace or [Ross] Barnett in Atlanta or North Carolina simply have overlooked the historical racial and social differentia of those three regions.

Here, I believe, Mr. Holman has made a strategic error. He might have, by the sheer beauty of abstract design, persuaded us to accept without question his thesis, had he not in a rash moment invited us to look at the real world. To be sure, in 1965 North Carolina had no George Wallace serving in high office. But by 1972 the Alabama governor had captured a large majority of Democratic delegates in that state, many if not most in the piedmont and mountain counties like the one Thomas Wolfe came from.

And after Mr. Holman penned this essay, Charlotte, the largest metroplex between Atlanta and Washington, D.C., became the most violent and bloody of all major Southern cities in its response to racial desegregation. A possible rival for this title would be the Nashville of nearly a decade earlier. But like Charlotte, Nashville, Tennessee, is, alas, in Mr. Holman's Piedmont section.

As to the people's response to *Brown* v. *Board of Education*, Mr. Holman's statement is chronological. Of course, those who failed to see any differences would assume the uniformity in the South's pattern of response. But, no, I will not even let that truism stand unchallenged, designed as it is to compliment his subregion. For I lived on the North Carolina-South Carolina border for a number of years, watching two television channels in each state—simultaneously.

To be sure, the editorial comments from Asheville, Wolfe's hometown, and Charlotte sounded as serenely moderate as does Mr. Holman, while the commentators from Spartanburg and Greenville occasionally showed red galluses under their dark suits. But an even more dramatic contrast is to be found in the news they reported. In North Carolina, racial crime seemed to abound. In addition to the bombings in Charlotte, I recall the kidnapping of a civil-rights leader.

To be sure, the University of North Carolina complied early and without significant incident, though perhaps not quite so smoothly as did Clemson University, the first desegregated institution of higher learning in South Carolina, upon the campus of which stands the plantation home of John C.

Calhoun. National commentators seemed surprised, given the conservative nature of the South Carolina leadership, especially if contrasted with such North Carolina liberals as Terry Sanford. Had they but clearly known the mind and authority of conservative state senator Edgar Brown, they might have been less astonished with South Carolina—though in a different way more profoundly shocked than they had hoped to be.

As I turn over those years in my unbiased memory, I can even recall a distinct difference in the conduct of the North and South Carolina Ku Klux Klans. In the hills of North Carolina klaverns inundated the landscape with ugly incidents. On the other hand, in South Carolina, where the Klan was strong only in the piedmont section, a genial group under the Dragonship of Booster Bob Scoglin was spreading sunshine—passing out Christmas baskets among the poor of the black community and distributing membership applications with a cover letter that began, "If you want your neighbor beaten or your wife flogged don't join the Ku Klux Klan."

But I have too long dwelt on this contrast, in part, perhaps, because I enjoy doing it, and, in part, you will recall, because Mr. Holman invited me to consider the point. In truth, I think his choice of a test is a poor one, and I fear too prematurely self-congratulatory for a North Carolinian who is admirably proud of his state. While some communities did behave better than others, Mr. Holman cannot demonstrate that so-called Piedmont sections did better than Tidewater sections or Deep South sections—or Eastern or Midwestern sections, for that matter. For time is in the process of revealing an awful truth to many Americans about their regions and localities, and in the process people are beginning to acknowledge publicly that what they formerly thought was merely Down Yonder is in fact next door and everywhere—race, surroundings, and epoch notwithstanding.

So Mr. Holman's sociological distinctions do not hold up to the one test of experience he proposes, at least not to some of us who lived on the South Carolina side of the Piedmont border during the 60's. Yet not only does he insist on the objective validity of these distinctions, but he extends their literary implications so absolutely that he must again be challenged. And this is a long quote:

> When the South becomes, as it has in our time, the subject of important literary work, each of its sub-regions provides a different subject matter to the novelist. The combinations of subject matter, the author's talents, and their personal relationships to their region result in distinctive fictional modes. Taine's race, surroundings, and epoch differ markedly in each sub-region, and the

result is a radical though not always recognized difference in the works of fiction shaped by the various sub-regions. This distinctiveness is pervasive and almost total, for the Southern novelists of the 20th century have not shared the historians' and the critics' limited view.

I am astonished at Mr. Holman's last sentence. It appears at a glance self-contradictory. After insisting that use of the subregions provides a different subject matter to the novelist, that the result is a radical difference in the works of fiction, and that this distinctiveness is pervasive and almost total, he seems suicidal in concluding that "Southern novelists of the 20th century have not shared the historians' and the critics' limited view." But of course he is right, if you use H.A. Taine and W.J. Cash as your historians and Mr. Holman as your critic. Besides, no subject, even Southern fiction, as simplistic as he tries to make it, can be as simplistic as its own schematic description. If I am not mistaken, he is merely saying: No house is as two dimensional as its blueprint.

LET NOW US NOW EXAMINE his authority for all this systematic reductionism. First, W.J. Cash, author of *The Mind of the South*, produced a portrait of the region by brushing in the numbered areas with bright primary colors. Stand back, squint your eyes, and you may be able to pretend that you are looking at a creditable painting, but you can never believe you see a Southern landscape.

Cash would be recognized for the narrow-minded ideologue he really is if he did not have a marvelous rhetorical genius for the typical description that makes people believe they are actually studying flesh-and-blood reality instead of abstractions dressed up in wigs. Mr. Holman, incidentally, understands that Cash is unreliable and says as much in his appendix on sources. But he seems determined to use him anyway, almost as a demonstration of faith, the way a pietistic family might trot out an idiot uncle to greet their dinner guests.

Taine, whose book first appeared in 1864, is, in devising these categories, slicing the Gordian knot of existence into three parts. The American source of such schemata is Puritan New England and, more specifically, the logic of Petrus Ramus as translated by John Milton, which provided the subject matter for the first theses at Harvard University.

As Perry Miller points out in *The New England Mind*, philosophy among sages of that region was at the beginning dominated by Ramus, and, indeed, in his book, Miller even reproduces the French logician's diagram of existence, which looks like a genealogical chart with abstract Latin nouns in place of the names of Grandma and Grandpa. Take any phenomenon, says Ramus, divide it into two parts, occasionally three, subdivide it again as may be necessary, and finally you will understand all there is to know about the subject.

People, for example, can be so classified. And no matter how you begin you always end up with us and them, right and wrong, good and evil. Such thinking, as you can imagine, made it easy to burn your neighbors as witches once you had distinguished them from your own species. Such thinking can also make it easy for you to secede from the South if you are from North Carolina and feel superior to Alabama or Mississippi.

Let us now look at Mr. Taine's categories and see what validity they really have as applied to Southern literature. As for "race," I am not going to wander into that dismal swamp, even with a genealogical chart to guide me. I am surprised to see Mr. Holman out there waving me in with a cheerful smile, up to his hips in it. Such distinctions as Taine uses them seem to me to exist, if anywhere, in Jung's collective unconscious.

I cannot believe it is important that Faulkner wrote *The Sound and the Fury* because, as Mr. Cash tells us, the Deep South was settled by the half-wild Scotch and Irish clansmen of the 17th and 18th centuries. "Epoch," the times in which an author lives, may be the most important influence on his artistic sensibilities, but Mr. Holman pays comparatively little attention to this crucial concern in setting up his charts and tables. He can't be said to bear down hard on surroundings, environment, the social setting. For him something imprecisely and politely Marxist unintentionally enters the arena—a dark, sharply defined shadow surrounded by the penumbra of an unattractive class consciousness.

He refers to the Mississippi Delta as characterized by a capitalistic system in a world with no previous sense of ownership, the Indians having lived under a simple code of communal property. One would only read Eugene Genovese's *The World the Slaveholders Made* or Lewis M. Dabney's *The Indians of Yonapatawpha* to learn just how imprecise and useless this description is. But enough. In Mr. Holman's studies we find Ramus's machinery, fueled by a kind of error-ridden economic determinism that no one has ever believed in, despite protests to the contrary. And a whole unwieldy contraption has been cranked up to attack Southern literature—a rusty engine squeaking and honking into the dark forest to slay the dragons.

The resultant critical essays should be at least as bad as, say, Maxwell Geismar's book on Henry James, but such is not the case. In truth, Mr. Holman, after all his heavy framework in the first chapter, has written surprisingly well on Ellen Glasgow, William Faulkner, and Thomas Wolfe. I cannot agree with every one of his observations, but some of them seem incisive, true, and original. Furthermore, I am impressed at times by his logic, his sensitivity, and his willingness to grant strengths or weaknesses where he would rather not find them. These are rare qualities, and they mark him as a man who is liberal in the best sense of that much-abused term. Why, then, one must ask, do good critics feel tempted, even compelled, to construct such systems, all the while apologizing for them, as Mr. Holman does for both Cash and Taine?

It is a good question, a crucial one. But I think I will now ask you to direct your attention away from the moderate Mr. Holman and turn your eyes to the immoderate Mr. Tate. I say "immoderate" not only because Mr. Tate's political opinions have been regarded as scandalous ever since he contributed his chapter to I'll Take My Stand, but because the tone he takes in "The New Provincialism" can only be described as oracular, as if each word has been writ by the providential finger in a tablet of stone. No modest demurrers here, no citation of ancient authority, no bibliographical appendices. One footnote to an earlier essay of his own, from which he quotes no doubt in order to avoid saying again what has already been said perfectly. Nor does he, like Mr. Cash, deceive us into believing that he has plundered whole libraries of primary sources and that what we are reading is therefore a series of well-ordered facts.

To the contrary, Mr. Tate's tone suggests precisely what he was doing, which was expressing his own opinion on some extremely important social and literary matters. He does not bow down to the Baal of objective scholarship because he knows that such a god does not exist. He simply builds his own sacrifice of wood and then waits confidently for the flame to descend, and, as far as I'm concerned, it does, at least 99 percent of the time.

IN "A NEW PROVINCIALISM," first published in 1945, Mr. Tate is addressing himself to the question of what is to become of regionalism and its literature in an intellectual community preoccupied with "One World" and "Four Freedoms," and, more specifically, what will become of Southern literature. He asks, will the new literature of the South or the United States as a whole be different from anything that we knew before the war? Will American literature be more alike over the country and more like the literature of the world?

Mr. Holman's Thomas Wolfe would answer "yes" in a lyric outburst of innumerable words later to be assembled and edited by Maxwell Perkins. But Mr. Tate, also from Mr. Holman's Piedmont South, says something slightly more disturbing. First, he makes an important distinction between regionalism and provincialism, a distinction that reveals a philosophical point of view diametrically opposed to Mr. Holman's. For Mr. Tate's idea of region is not as qualifying for a limiting set of specific circumstances, but as a matrix of what he describes as certain patterns of thought and conduct handed down to its inhabitants by their ancestors.

Regionalism, he concludes, is thus limited in space but not in time. He clarifies his statement in a way that is almost embarrassing to quote after discussing Mr. Holman, but I must do so: "When the regional man and his ignorance of the world extends his own immediate necessities into the world and assumes that the present moment is unique, he becomes the provincial man." What Mr. Holman wants to make of Ellen Glasgow, Thomas Wolfe, and William Faulkner, then, is a group of provincial rather than regional writers, products of their own unique place and moment who can do no more than define that uniqueness and comment on it.

But regionalism, said Mr. Tate, at least in America, has tended to preserve what Christopher Dawson has described as a balance of the Hellenic world and a Christian otherworldliness, the ideals of which have been handed down in time by a Western European civilization that was created out of the conquest and ordering of Rome, and sustained in America often with great difficulty by such regional sensibilities as those found in the South and elsewhere.

The "Four Freedoms," abstractions dreamed up by the Big Four at Dumbarton Oaks, cannot replace the transcendental view of Christianity because they are secular, rooted in materialism which holds that the physical welfare of man is the ultimate end of the political and social order. Technology becomes barbaric without Christianity, he says, and Christianity will disappear in the flood of a new nationalism that, along with the myth of science, has undermined regional economies, and which in 1945, because of the international situation, is creating a world economy.

Let me pause to say a word of praise for Mr. Tate's courage in speaking out against the "Four Freedoms" at this particular moment in history. This may not mean anything to you younger people, but I can think of no public utterance in our time that could possibly seem as blasphemous to the public orthodoxy, because today we do not respond as a nation the way we did during World War II. I am surprised that Mr. Tate was not set upon and murdered by the Boy Scouts. Freedom of Thought, Freedom of Religion, Freedom From Want, Freedom From Fear. I remember the Norman Rockwell illustrations.

Tate, the regional man, understood the foolishness of such rhetoric even as the new provincials were praising it, and the hollow echo of those forgotten phrases mock our present pretensions, our slogans of the day. Tate, the regional man, attacked internationalism because he was interested in the preservation of a cultural tradition. [George] McGovern, the provincial man, attacked the same policies because he was interested in withdrawing our economic resources from one set of temporal problems and reassigning them to another set more immediate and pressing.

The economic turn of Mr. Tate's argument is fruitful because he insists on the superiority of smaller regional economies. They make the independence of a community that could still hold the image of a classical Christian heritage. World culture without the end of preserving a higher civilization becomes world province. He is not optimistic, however, given the impulse behind the Four Freedoms. As he puts it, industrial capitalism has given us the provincialism without regionalism, and we are committed to cant solutions of problems that seem unique because we have forgotten the nature of man.

But what does this kind of speculation have to do with Southern literature? Here is the revealed word in a few sentences: "First, with the war of 1914-1918, the South re-entered the world but gave a backward glance as it stepped over the border. That backward glance gave us the Southern Renascence, a literature conscious of the past and the present." In this passage, Mr. Tate says a great deal in a single sentence about a complex question. First, he tells us that the South during the relatively short span of four years re-entered the world.

Putting aside for a moment the precise pinpointing of time, we must try to understand what he meant by the spatial image he presents. When we remember that he has spoken earlier of a peculiar balance of Greek culture and Christian otherworldliness, the meaning of the passage comes into focus and the appropriateness of the image he creates for us is apparent. Time is limited in terms of fate. The South during an earlier period is gifted in the territory of the traditional consciousness, where it was upheld that, as he puts it, honor, truth, imagination, human dignity, and limited acquisitiveness alone justify a social order.

Considering the fact that Mr. Tate is contrasting a New Provincialism that is limited in time but not in space with an older regionalism that is limited in space but not in time, this final metaphor defining the Southern Renascence is not only apt but brilliant, the kind of performance one would expect from a consummate poet. But there is one part of the figure that I find disturbing: the insistent emphasis on that border. We all understand what a border is, and we know that such imaginary lines are calculated by surveyors with extraordinary accuracy. People are so certain about the existence of borders that they are willing to die for them, sometimes by the hundreds or thousands.

To be sure, a certain amount of latitude must be permitted in a poetic statement, but here Mr. Tate is helpful, because he defines for us the tenure that corresponds to the borders. It is the four-year span between 1914 and 1918, the time of World War I. He does not specify the reason for choosing this period, but the lengthy discussion I have already summarized gives us the necessary clues, and with some basic knowledge of political and literary history his implication can be easily deduced. World War I was the first event following the Civil War that happened to the entire nation, and the consequence for the South was not only the rebirth of some small national consciousness but increased industrialism.

And, as we have seen, industrialization has led to the dehumanization of man until bereft of his spiritual nature and purpose. Thus did the South in this brief era come to a point when it began to lose its regional character. At that moment came the backward glance, followed by the Southern Renascence. It is difficult to tell how long after that backward glance the Southern Renascence occurred, but in thinking about that border one must conclude that only those writers who were alive during the period between 1914 and 1918 could be said to have strategically been in the Renascence. These would be the writers of Mr. Tate's own generation.

Then, indeed, he names those he deems to be the most enduring, all of whom he must have known personally. So far, so good, I am tempted to say, largely (I suspect) because of my admiration for Mr. Tate's poetry, his literary criticism, and his fine reading of history and modern politics. Certainly I must agree with his distinction between regionalism and provincialism and with his concurrent remarks on the state of the world in 1945. But we have treated Mr. Holman too badly to go easy on Mr. Tate. For we must, if we are thoughtful, ask the question, "Are you saying that a backward glance can be made only as one crosses the border, that present-day writers by the mere accident of birth are incapable of writing a comparably enduring fiction or poetry?"

Mr. Tate, who has briefly addressed himself to this question at the beginning of his essay, reiterates his answer at the end, saying:

> In an earlier essay, I said: "From the peculiarly historical consciousness of the Southern writer has come good work of a special order, but the focus of this consciousness is quite temporary. This has made possible the curious burst of intelligence that we get at a crossing of the ways, not unlike on an infinitesimal scale the outburst of poetic genius at the end of the 16th century when

commercial England had already began to crush feudal England."
I see no reason to change that view.

Spellbound by the glow of our own splendidly paved path, we can miss
the terrible implications of this frozen package, which has the sharp keen
of certitude in it, as if the author had been there and seen the fiery chariot
ascending, for the mantle fits securely and easily on his shoulders: There shall
be no more harps in Israel. But he is no more like that. Instead, in this one
passage, I believe, he is just another economic determinist. And regardless of
his expressed admiration for the classical Christian tradition, he has learned
a great deal, perhaps too much, from modern behaviorists, the mad alche-
mists of rationalism, the sorcerers of the probability code. We would much
rather he had gone to Delphi. There at least the answers were ambiguous.

LET US EXAMINE HIS ARGUMENT MORE CLOSELY, however painful the process may prove. What he is saying is that a certain kind of culture, one based
on the traditional virtues of Greeks, Romans, and Christians, produces a people who have a sense of the timeless and therefore resent the false proposition that their particular moment is unique with its own radically peculiar
set of historical circumstances. This generation, he says, crossed that border
between the otherworldliness of Regionalism and the worldliness of Provincialism, and they alone were able to see both forward and backward in time.
Their particular moment then, when compared with our own or all future
moments, seems to be unique with its own radically peculiar set of historical circumstances.

As for those Southern writers who come after the fortune-favored Renascence generation, because industrialism has changed the economy of the
region and therefore destroyed its independence, these later poets and novelists can no longer experience that sense of timelessness, of continuity with
the past, that was once a part of Southern life. Hence, their achievement will
be less than that of their predecessors necessarily, as if on a certain day, one
factory too many was built in Bessemer, Alabama, and the moment the ribbon was cut half the typewriters in the region stopped, and the other half
started to turn out an inferior product.

I exaggerate in order to point out the true nature of this argument, first
published in 1935, repeated in 1945, and echoed since by dozens of critics
who do not seriously question what they are saying. Mr. Tate, who was an
admitted skeptic at the time, though one who believed in the necessity of
faith, knew full well what he was about. In the same essay he writes: "This
is a catastrophic view. I suppose it cannot be wholly true." In these honest

sentiments, Mr. Tate is neither as immoderate as he seems to be elsewhere in the essay nor as certain of the concept he advances. He knows better. He gives us his system anyway. So, said Eric Voegelin, do all gnostics. In *Science, Politics, and Gnosticism*, Voegelin writes that the gnostic seeks "dominion over being in order to seize control of being. The gnostic constructs his system. The building of systems is a gnostic form of reasoning, not a philosophical one."

One can immediately see the application of this description in Mr. Holman's work, though Mr. Tate is partly philosophic, only covertly systematic, and therefore somewhat more elusive. But let us proceed with Voegelin further. A gnostic thinker really does commit an intellectual swindle, and he knows it. After he constructs his system, the thinker becomes aware of the untruth of his assertion or speculation but persists in it in spite of his knowledge. Notice how this part of the description fits not only Mr. Holman's admission but Mr. Tate's as well. And we can see these protests as not merely dissidence but an old gnostic pattern. Tate's confession almost redeems him, but not quite, for in the end his rationalistic impulses overpower him, and he invokes a system to conjure up the future.

Later, after many essays that would contradict this position, he was to write of this period in his life: "As I look back upon my own verse, written over more than twenty-five years, I see plainly that its main theme is man suffering from unbelief; and I cannot for a moment suppose that this man is some other than myself."

What, then, is to be said for theories of the Southern Renascence? Do I mean to suggest that they are all gnostic and therefore worse than useless? First let me say that there is an important difference between talking about what happened and what had to happen. The past and present are knowable, even if only imperfectly, through reason and faith. Until those times foretold in the Book of Revelation, a decidedly unsystematic work, the future is to a great extent mysterious and, more important, alterable. No one, not even the poet, is permitted the luxury of behaving as if the outcome were a foregone conclusion.

It is therefore prudent, even necessary, to try to find in literary history certain truths about the relationship between the artist and his world, a relationship that is undeniably modified and highlighted by the times and community in which he lived. If a student wants to learn something about how one group of Southerners came to write the kind of poetry they did, then you could read Louise Cowan's chronicle of the Fugitives. In her Preface she writes that her narrative is a kind of parable demonstrating the operations of poetry like the operations of grace among mortal men—and so it is. But a proper parable, which embraces the full complexity of life in addition to emphasizing certain truths about the mimetic imagination. She does not try to systematize, neither does she write monstrous overdrafts on the literary bank accounts of future Southern poets. For Southern poetry did not end with the Fugitives, nor did Southern fiction languish at the hands of novelists born after, say, 1910.

Is Mrs. Cowan correct in defining the quality of *pietas* as a natural ingredient of most Southern poetry? Then, James Dickey has carried on the tradition with a skill equal to the early masters, many of them, and a power greater than most. Perhaps because the Fugitives had prepared his audience for him, Dickey is able to write openly and with feeling of love for family, God, and his native region. As for fiction, I believe, among many others, Madison Jones's body of work has begun to challenge that of many of the earlier figures, if you want to look at the imaginative acts in the same light as you would view competitions at a county fair. And Jones' novel *A Cry of Absence*, which I urge you to read, is, in my judgment—which is unerring in these matters (we all talk that way, you see)—a finer single work than anything done by Robert Penn Warren. And Jones is not alone.

The feeling that fiction has declined can be explained in part by the loss of Faulkner. Mr. Tate, Mr. Davidson, and others always see the earlier period of Southern literature as analogous to the 16th century, with Faulkner and Shakespeare as the dominant figures. The analogy is a good one. Remove Shakespeare from the 16th century, and how does that era measure up to the 17th century? Are we then prepared to talk about a great falling off with Donne and the Metaphysicals, Jonson and the Sons of Ben, Dryden, Milton? There is evidence then that the creative moment can prolong itself when it is nurtured in good faith. I will grant that the evidence is open to contrary opinion, but I would submit that to construct a usable future out of the frail substance of reason is to expose yourself to the huff and puff of the Big Bad Wolf. Such systematizing is philosophical error because it denies both the limitations and the free will of men. It is theological error because it is a sin against the doctrine of grace, for it presumes to bind God's hand to Heaven. God can reach into time and mess up history whenever He sees fit, and those who imply He can't, no matter how pious their reasons, are committing the ultimate act of impiety.

FINALLY, AND WITH SOME TREPIDATION, I will leave you with a parable of my own. Once upon a time there was a society that was ruled by an old aristocracy, whose traditions and fortunes came from the land. But gradually times changed, the old ways were challenged by the new, and in a moment of self-consciousness they produced great artists and one master. But the moment of self-consciousness passed; economic conditions altered. The landed gentry lost their voice of authority, and the society was taken over completely by the merchant class—bankers, capitalists—whose power derived from their manipulation of money.

The ultimate victor in this economic war, a bourgeois of the first order, finally became dictator. Now, everyone said, there will be no more artists. But there were, because that dictator was Cosimo de' Medici, and he was a man as well as a banker, just as the artists, critics, politicians, and even grand dragons I have been discussing are first and foremost men. And because Cosimo chose to patronize the arts, a new birth of creativity swept over Florence after the artists and the one great master, Dante, had all died, and this creativity spread to other parts of Europe. While in Italy this imaginative activity manifested itself primarily in painting and sculpture, those works were in fact often narratives by implication, with members of the Medici family represented in traditional themes in Christian and classical mythology.

The timelessness of the present was emphasized by its association with the eternal, as in Botticelli's *Adoration of the Magi*, which is both a religious panorama and the portrait of a wise family in the service of Christ. In addition to Botticelli, this brief period produced in Florence alone Bernini, Giorgione, the Palazzo Vecchio, Andrea del Sarto, Verrocchio, Ghiberti, Perugino, Leonardo da Vinci, Filippino Lippi, Raphael, Tintoretto, Michelangelo, and many, many others. Who can say the hand of God did not reach down and touch Cosimo de' Medici? Who can say His hand is not always reaching down to every place and every time?

# Madison Jones

*Introduction to a new edition of* The Innocent *by Madison Jones*

THE FACT THAT MADISON JONES has not been as popular with a mass readership as have Sidney Sheldon and Danielle Steel says more about the current state of American letters than it does about Jones's fiction. He is a writer in the Great Tradition at a time when too many readers are unwilling or unable to appreciate a novel that requires them to pay attention to language and thematic nuances as well as to plot and character. Madison Jones writes fiction that demands the careful scrutiny of words as well as thoughtful consideration of their meaning. No one can read and fully comprehend a book like *The Innocent* or *A Cry of Absence* while sitting in the dentist's office. The sound of a distant drill shatters the concentration necessary to appreciate the subtleties of the text before the reader's nervous eyes. Most Americans read novels in waiting rooms or between television shows—and they do so to forget pain. Hence the limited audience for which Jones has always written.

To make this observation is not to suggest that Jones's novels are dull or doggedly "literary." They are neither. Their plots are crammed with exciting action: serial murders, sex, revenge, racial conflict, perversion—all the amenities our age has come to expect of its fiction. Indeed, Jones uses many of the same raw materials that the writers of bestsellers use; but he treats both his subject matter and his readership with respect and infinite care—perhaps a self-destructive strategy among a people whose attention span, as a consequence of television viewing, has narrowed to that of a housecat.

As a consequence, Jones's eight published volumes of fiction are intensely enjoyed by the few and unappreciated by the many, something that can also be said of the novels of Jane Austen, Henry James, and Joseph Conrad. Such works may attract a handful of readers in any given age, but they survive the ignorance and laziness of the popular marketplace and eventually are read by millions. Jones will surely join this company.

Madison Jones was born in Nashville in 1925 and earned a B.A. at Vanderbilt University, where he studied under Fugitive-Agrarian Donald Davidson. With Davidson's encouragement, he enrolled in Andrew Lytle's creative-writing program at the University of Florida, where he studied his craft and earned his M.A. Lytle remembers him as a student who learned every lesson quickly and almost perfectly: "You just told Madison what he had to do, and he would do it. You didn't even have to tell him how."

After earning his M.A., Jones taught freshman English at Miami of Ohio and then moved to Auburn University, where he served on the faculty until retirement. During those years he published a body of work that won him significant critical acclaim and only occasional public recognition. His shortest novel, *An Exile*, became a Hollywood movie entitled *I Walk the Line*, though the film version contained little of the depth and tragic irony of Jones's work. His novel about racial conflict in the South, *A Cry of Absence*, received wider attention than his other works because of its subject matter; but it mirrored so many of the complexities of the civil-rights era that it angered Southern apologists and Eastern liberals alike, both of whom found their own stark and uncompromising portraits all but unbearable. Jones's other novels have escaped the attention of the mass media, though they are all lively tales that might well be translated to the screen—however, not without risking the integrity of the original.

THOUGH HE HAS BEEN COMPARED to Robert Penn Warren, Jones's fiction is quite different from that of his Southern contemporaries. However, to some degree he can be understood as a Southern Thomas Hardy, a writer whose grim narratives chronicle rural traditionalism locked in mortal struggle with a superficial and pitiless modernity. Like Hardy, Jones sees the dangers in a religion of progress, one that invites its adherents to reject the past and believe in the abstract creed of a bigger, finer tomorrow.

Unlike Hardy, Jones harbors no stubborn illusions about the virtues of those who struggle to redeem tradition. They, too, fall prey to troubling abstractions, already victims of the disease they seek to prevent. And there is another difference. In Hardy's novels, characters like Michael Henchard and Tess Durbeyfield are mowed down by the forces of change like hapless stalks of wheat. By contrast, Jones's characters are not caught in the grips of a stark, mindless fate but manage their own destruction quite nicely with nothing more than old-fashioned pride. If they are not recognizably Christian in their exercise of free will, they are more complicated than the Greek tragic heroes and heroines of Aeschylus and Sophocles, whose punishment is both a product of their own hybris and the engineering of Fate.

Jones has more in common with Thomas Hardy than similarities in the development of character and theme. Both writers exhibit an enviable capacity to create a scene so vivid that it remains in memory long after the reader has forgotten the entire corpus of other, more acclaimed writers. Hardy opens *The Mayor of Casterbridge* with a scene at a country fair in which the protagonist, drunk and disconsolate, sells his wife to an itinerant sailor. *The Innocent* likewise opens at a country fair, and the action begins so matter-of-factly that the reader settles in for a segment of unremarkable exposition, only to encounter, in a few tough-minded pages, a scene of raw horror, one that sets the tone for the ensuing action, and, at the same time, points up its underlying meaning.

Similar scenes mark Jones's other works: in *A Cry of Absence*, the son who awakes from a drunken stupor to discover his mother is about to murder him; in *A Buried Land*, when the casket of a beautiful girl is unearthed and her face, exposed to fresh air after decades of interment, suddenly disintegrates before the eyes of horrified viewers; in *Forest of the Night*, when a woman dies while in the throes of childbirth in the middle of a vast wilderness.

Such scenes in Hardy are sometimes nothing more than fictional theatrics. (He did, after all, regard his novels as "potboilers.") In Jones's works, however, the most dramatic moments in the narratives are also among the most thematically significant.

In addition, Jones outstrips Hardy, and virtually all his contemporaries, in at least one respect—his ability to create characters that are the very incarnation of evil. Alec D'Urberville is perhaps Hardy's most repulsive villain, but in the final analysis he is nothing more than a spoiled and selfish pseudo-aristocrat who deserves to be horsewhipped rather than hanged. Jones's villains are invariably wicked to the core, yet in a way that is as fascinating to the reader as to the unfortunate protagonist. It is difficult to think of a contemporary novelist who is able to generate so much animosity for his characters. Hollis Handley and the Harpes have their equals only in such 19th-century fictional creations as Roger Chillingworth, Bill Sikes, and Uriah Heep.

It is the presence of these characters that reveals Jones's belief in the concrete reality of spiritual evil, as opposed to the broader and hazier social evil Hardy is willing to recognize. In the final analysis, Jones's works of fiction suggest that there are genuinely wicked people in the world, motivated by a gratuitous hatred that can neither be destroyed nor mitigated by social change. In this respect, Jones allies himself with the best writers of the past rather than with his contemporaries, most of whom, like Hardy, are preoccupied with the transient dogmas of psychology and sociology. It is Jones's genuine belief in the reality of evil, coupled with a carefully honed craftsmanship, that makes *The Innocent* one of the most formidable first novels of our time.

In its overall plot and thematic implications, *The Innocent* bears an inescapable resemblance to *The Return of the Native*. In both novels the main character is a man who has lived in a sophisticated urban world and then returned to his rural birthplace, expecting to rediscover the simplicity, purity, and peace he believes have always existed there. Both Jones's Duncan Welsh and Hardy's Clym Yeobright are refugees from modernity. They rightly see Progress as a false god who wins souls through bribery and deceit. But both characters, while fully understanding the nature of the enemy, fail to recognize the flawed humanity of those they idealize—the rural "primitives," all of whom are not so pure in heart or so simple as Welsh and Yeobright think. As a consequence, both men are doomed to tragic failure, though the resolutions in the two novels are quite different.

Like Clym Yeobright, Duncan Welsh finds that, despite his sympathy for rural life, he is a stranger to his own family, an outsider in his native community. The years in the city have altered his perception, blunted his sensibilities, changed him irrevocably. As much as he longs to do so, he cannot pick up his life where he left off.

At the same time, the people to whom he has returned have also changed. His father has become withdrawn and uncommunicative. He doesn't understand why his son has come back any more than he understands why he left. In addition, the years of hard work and gradual defeat have taken their toll. He is a broken man preparing to die.

Duncan's sister, Margaret Mary, also fails to live up to the idealized portrait of the country girl. She is hoping to marry Hiram Garner, a Methodist clergyman who preaches the social gospel and sees the old ways as obstacles to be overcome, enemies to be destroyed. Garner is also a native of the town, but from a family of plain people who during his childhood struggled to put food on the table. Beneath his righteous indictment of social ills burns an abiding resentment of past indignities, an envy of his social betters. Margaret Mary recognized the roots of Garner's moral arrogance and is willing to settle for him all the same, since she seems to have no other prospects. In so doing, she knowingly cuts herself off from her father and brother, fully aware of their opposition to the marriage.

In addition to Garner, Duncan must contend with the Jordan brothers, who come from a background not unlike Garner's but who have prospered extravagantly in the years Duncan has been away, mostly at the expense of their neighbors, small farmers whom they have reduced to near servitude. Dicky, the younger Jordan, is immediately hostile to Duncan. A swaggerer, he exemplifies the worst qualities of the new rich; and he and Duncan instinctively understand from their first encounter that they are natural enemies.

While Duncan sees Garner and Dicky as his chief adversaries, his greatest danger lies in another direction: from Aaron McKool, easily one of the most menacing characters in modern fiction. McKool, a squatter who lives deep in the woods on the Welsh property, first repels, then fascinates Duncan. A moonshiner, he is by turns sullen and ingratiating, a mad dog that occasionally wags its tail. Low-born and ignorant, he nonetheless exhibits a shrewd insight that enables him to fathom Duncan's darkest thoughts and to manipulate them to his own advantage.

Yet McKool is not merely self-serving. There is something gratuitously evil about his behavior. He harbors a malevolence that defies easy explanation. Garner and Dicky behave as they do because of their upbringing and their heady success. McKool seems to be a man who removes himself from society because he hates everyone else in the human race. In Duncan's spoiled paradise, it is McKool who speaks for the Serpent.

Yet there are moments in the novel when the reader finds McKool's twisted friendship with Duncan almost touching, as if, in an unguarded moment, the Devil himself were to heave a heartrending sigh. The relationship between these two constitutes the soul of the novel, and Duncan's most pressing moral problem is not how he will fight the apostles of modernity, but whether or not he can resist McKool's sly invitations to disaster. Jones manages the relationship brilliantly. It is the first evidence that his is a unique talent, one that asserts itself boldly, even in a first novel.

If McKool is the snake, then Nettie Roundtree is a Southern Eve. Like her prototype, she seems to possess no steady purpose or will of her own. Bland and submissive, she is no more than a fleeting image of the feminine presence so lacking in the lives of both Duncan and his father. She seems stylized and two-dimensional, not because Jones is unable to give her flesh and blood, but because the reader sees her through the eyes of Duncan, who never regards her as fully human. For this reason, he finds it impossible to understand or forgive her frailties, even though he himself has taken advantage of them.

More vivid and memorable is Aunt Virgy, the ancient black woman who was once a Welsh slave and who has outlived her masters and their children. Aware that black people must play an important role in his idealized South, Duncan makes it a point to see Aunt Virgy soon after he returns home. However, as the action progresses, his sense of noblesse oblige is dulled by coarsening experience and by the growing recognition that this old woman will not submit to stereotyping, that she will assert her will over his and tell him unpleasant truths about himself and those whom he believes he loves.

As a commentary on the growing harshness of their relationship, Aunt Virgy carries on an ongoing battle with a crow, who for a while is her best companion, and then her bitterest enemy. In the grisly resolution of this relationship, Jones reveals his enormous capacity for fictional invention. Aunt Virgy and the crow are worth half a dozen novels by more popular writers.

There are other black characters as well, sharply drawn, neatly juxtaposed against the blacks of Duncan's flawed memory. For example, Logan, the Faithful Hand, stands as a constant reproof to Duncan, whose growing alienation is more obvious to the blacks on the place than to Duncan's own family.

All of these figures play important roles in the action, but they also serve to give the reader insights into Duncan's character and to reveal his relationship to the overarching theme of the novel, which is finally more complicated than anything found in the works of Thomas Hardy. While an oppressive environment and the changing times are themselves Hardy's thematic preoccupation, they merely form the enveloping action of *The Innocent* and give the novel added historical dimension. Jones's narrative is really about what happens to the human heart when, in pride, it withdraws from family and community and lives in self-indulgent isolation. In this respect, Jones's vision is tragic while Hardy's, for all its rugged power, is merely pathetic.

MOST FIRST NOVELS do little more than hint at better works to come. Faulkner and Hemingway began brilliant literary careers with derivative novels. *This Side of Paradise* revealed a substantial measure of Scott Fitzgerald's talent but was poorly constructed—a brilliant and attractive failure. *The Innocent* is the real thing, a work substantial and well wrought, one that stands up against Jones's more mature works, which deal with the same painful conflicts and exhibit the same careful rendering of all the fictional elements. Where others discover their true voice in the course of an evolving career, Jones begins with a mature and characteristic novel, one that is easily recognizable as his own—and no one else's.

Of course, he learned a great deal as he continued to write. His handling of point of view became subtler and more innovative. In later works his prose is just a little better. (In *The Innocent* there are a few sentences he probably would like to take back.) But the difference is not important enough to consign this novel to a lesser place in the body of his works. It holds its own with *A Cry of Absence, Passage Through Gehenna*, and *A Buried Land*.

Indeed, *The Innocent* must rank among the very best works of fiction written during this period—and that would include the short stories of Flannery O'Connor and the novels of Eudora Welty. There is a high seriousness about this narrative that commends it to posterity for special attention. It is a work that belies the claim that the Southern Renascence ended with the death of William Faulkner and the decision of poets John Crowe Ransom and

Allen Tate to turn their attention to literary criticism. In writing *The Innocent*, Madison Jones has proved all over again not only the creative vitality of his region but the ancient truth that a masterpiece can be written in virtually any era, assuming of course that there is a genuine master to write it. Madison Jones is such a master, as this novel clearly demonstrates.

# Richard Weaver and the Old Rhetoric

*A lecture for the 2010 Philadelphia Society program on*
*"Ethics and Rhetoric in a Digital Age"*

**R**ICHARD WEAVER in his "The Spaciousness of the Old Rhetoric" can't provide all the answers to the question of why 19th-century Americans were moved by this language. To do so would be to explain a whole host of related questions. For example, why 19th-century readers loved novels overloaded with inert description like the works of Walter Scott, while we admire the tightly controlled narratives of Flaubert and James Joyce. Or why so much of 19th-century theater seems like mere recitation rather than the firing of the gun on Hedda Gabler's wall.

Early in the essay Weaver acknowledges that the problem can be explained in part by the loss of a national consensus: "It's now a truism that the homogeneity of belief which obtained three generations ago has largely disappeared. Such belief was, in a manner of conceiving it, the old orator's capital." I would like to elaborate on that statement in an effort to add a small measure of understanding to Weaver's ambitious essay, which ultimately touches on the destiny of America. I would suggest that the old rhetoric was characterized by three traits.

First, that it intended to address a much smaller audience than is first apparent. Second, that this audience, after recognizing the style and tone of the speech, would accept virtually anything that the speaker said as truth. And third, that it melded the religious and secular orders to lend the authority of the former to the latter.

Among other things, the old rhetoric was rooted in the unquestioned assumption that virtue was a thing as palpable and knowable as Newton's apple, and that it existed not only in individuals but in peoples as well and in nations. Speech after 19th-century speech affirmed that America's spectacular rise was God's reward for its exceptional goodness. Thus patriotic orators dignified and exulted the subject through the language of Scripture, allusions to biblical narratives, references to God, Our Lord, the Almighty, Providence, or, in George Washington's quaint phrase, "the benign parent of the human race." (Clearly Washington didn't believe in the Big Bang Theory.) Most who delivered these speeches, I think, believed unquestioningly that such rhetoric didn't merely adorn the subject like colored balls on a Christmas tree but probed its essential nature and defined its position in the created order. Such usage inevitably invested political discourse with religious overtones—the aura of prophecy authenticated by the blessing of God.

Small wonder the most important literary influence on American political oratory from the 17th century well into the 20th century was surely the King James Bible, translation of which began in 1607 and was completed in 1611. The English language available to the translators of this Bible was perhaps the richest and most versatile in linguistic history. For one thing, English had more words than other languages. More than 500 years earlier, the Norman Conquest had brought with it the French language, which with its polysyllabic Latin diction became the polite and proper alternative to a blunt, often monosyllabic Anglo-Saxon. By the early 17th century the two languages had become one.

Tough and earthy, grand and eloquent, no other language had quite the same capacity for Weaver's spaciousness as did 17th-century English, and no language was more familiar to 19th-century Americans. Most of them heard it in church on Sunday, both read and quoted from the pulpit, where sometimes sermons ran as long as three hours, what with no NFL games starting at noon and no shiny mall to shop. People read their Bibles during the week and went to Wednesday night prayer meeting, and when a traveling preacher set up his tent just outside of town we went to hear him preach the gospel night after night. I read somewhere that the Gay 90's song "There Will Be a Hot Time in the Old Town Tonight" originally referred not to an orgy, as I had always thought, but to the advent of an itinerant preacher.

In discussing the spaciousness of the old rhetoric, Weaver chose obscure examples, perhaps so he could discuss the phenomenon without reference to political controversy that might spill over into the 21st century. To make a couple of slightly different points, I would like to examine speeches by Daniel Webster, Abraham Lincoln, and Jefferson Davis.

ONE OF WEBSTER'S GREATEST SPEECHES was delivered at Plymouth Rock on December 22, 1820, in the kind of nasty New England weather that they seem to thrive on up there. As Webster said, it was at this time of year that the Pilgrims landed at that very spot, which he proceeded to consecrate with his rhetoric:

> There is a local feeling connected with this occasion too strong to
> be resisted, a sort of genius of the place which inspires and awes us.
> We feel that we are on the spot where the first scene of our history

was laid, where the hearths and altars of New England were first placed, where Christianity and civilized letters made their first lodgment in a vast extent of country covered with a wilderness and peopled by roving barbarians. We are here at the season of the year at which the event took place. The imagination irresistibly and rapidly draws around us the principal features and the leading characters in the original scene. We cast our eyes abroad on the ocean and we see where the little bark with the interesting group upon its deck made its slow progress to the shore . . .

And it goes on and on. Note Webster's commitment to the single place and its unique people. This is a speech for New Englanders, not for the rest of the nation, not for Andrew Jackson, not for Daniel Boone, not even for the dandies of New York City saluting each other with their gold-headed canes as they stroll down Fifth Avenue. Knowing that only New Englanders would come out on a day like this, he was free to expand on the myth that had already become a part of the region's heritage. Here I use the word *myth* not to mean a lie, but a commonly held belief of a people that helps them define themselves to themselves. Listening to Webster we almost forget that the Pilgrims who arrived in 1620 were not the first Europeans to land on these shores, not the first to introduce Christianity, not even the first to celebrate Thanksgiving. In fact, the Pilgrims were seeking to join the already established colony at Jamestown, founded in 1607, and were blown off their course; but who cares about dates when you are shivering on a gray beach trying to light the fires of ancient piety in subzero weather.

Webster's version has much in common with the other creation myths of tribes and nations around the world, which teach a specific community that they are the first people. Obviously Webster's myth has been exported to the entire nation. A majority now believe that the Plymouth Pilgrims were the very first European settlers to land on these shores and that they invented Thanksgiving. Poor old Jamestown. Occasionally someone down here lodges a complaint. A while back an unreconstructed South Carolinian said, "I don't want my children taught that their country was brought up by a boatload of lost Yankees."

NO ONE UNDERSTOOD the proper and effective use of the old language better than Abraham Lincoln, who could engage in the rawbone give and take of partisan debate staged for the boys at Springfield and then craft and deliver the Gettysburg Address, a splendid example of 19th-century rhetoric, though more compact than most. First, let's look at the two discussions of

the five words in the Declaration of Independence Lincoln most admired—
"All men are created equal." In an 1857 speech on the Dred Scott decision,
he challenges Stephen Douglas's contention that the phrase meant all peoples are created equal—that is, the American people *en masse* were equal to
the British people.

Note the lack of any spacious rhetoric in this:

> I think the authors of that notable instrument intended to include
> all men but they did not intend to declare all men equal in all re-
> spects. They did not mean to say all were equal in color, size, in-
> tellect, moral development, or social capacity. They defined with
> tolerable distinctness in what respects they did consider all men
> created equal—in certain inalienable rights, among which are life,
> liberty, and the pursuit of happiness. This they said and this they
> meant.

At the dedication of the Gettysburg battlefield, however, the place, the
occasion, and the audience demanded a different kind of rhetoric, one that
lifted the hearts of those present, some of whom had lost husbands, sons,
and fathers at this very battle. A rhetoric that dignified the heroic dead and
placed their sacrifice in the context of a larger, more enduring truth. He did
not, as Julia Ward Howe did, say that it was the army of the Lord. He began
with an opening phrase, "Four score and seven years ago," not the kind of language you would use in conversation at the dinner table. These first words
were a signal to his audience: What follows will be a language more to be
savored and then pondered over, an appeal to heart rather than head.

As the speech develops it becomes the liturgy of a secular communion,
one that Lincoln and his audience share with each other and with the dead.
Of this speech Weaver wrote: "At Gettysburg Lincoln spoke in terms so
generic that it is almost impossible to show that the speech is not as much a
eulogy of the men in the gray as the men in blue, inasmuch as both made up
those that struggled here." I can't buy that. I'll skip the discussion of it but
to say that Lincoln concludes by saying that this war settled the question of
whether or not we would continue to have government of the people, by the
people, and for the people. The Confederacy certainly didn't want to abolish that form of government. There could have been an argument there, on
both sides—but in this group, at this particular time, no argument.

Jefferson Davis, had he been standing on the fringe of that sun-drenched
crowd, might have pursed his lips and looked around, and raised eyebrows.
I'm sure he would not have broken the decorum of the occasion by shouting

out "You lie," but he could have engaged in serious debate on the proposition. Jefferson Davis in his inaugural address talks about the Declaration of Independence as well, and he uses it as a reason for secession, with the American Revolution as his example.

I WANT TO CLOSE by showing you what happened to the old rhetoric. It degenerated into bathos and pomposity, and I have found the best example. This is one of my favorite passages in all of American literature. Gov. Bob Taylor used to speak around the country using this old rhetoric when it was long since out of style. He was governor at the time when Tennessee had its centennial celebration, so he had to greet a lot of people, some of whom were the traveling salesmen called drummers, and so he welcomes them with this statement:

> If I were a sculptor, I would chisel from the marble my ideal of a man—I would make it the figure of a drummer with his grip. If I were a painter I would paint a picture of Jacob's ladder and a drummer upon its rungs. I would paint the angelic form of a drummer ascending and descending with the best line of harps on the market to sell to the inhabitants of the celestial world. God bless the Drummers—they are the personification of Christian endeavor and all they need is pink tights and gauzed wings to make them equal to the cherubim and seraphim. Who could imagine a vision more sublime than innumerable drummers flying through the air with their grip sacks in their hands, diving and sporting among the clouds like porpoises in midsea oceans?

At the end he burst into song. I know the tune, but I'm not going to sing it. If this kind of rhetoric, with its florid goodness, has long ago disappeared from the public arena, we still have speeches that use the same extravagant language infused by the same vague emotional fervor and that even invoke the Almighty—speeches that offer a darker vision of America. I have several examples, but I will read just one:

> The government gives them drugs, builds bigger prisons, passes a three-strike law, and then wants us to sing "God Bless America." No, No, No! God Damn America—that's in the Bible—for killing people. God Damn America for treating our citizens as less than human. God Damn America for as long as she acts like she is God and she is supreme.

How did we evolve from the land of Webster and Lincoln to the land of the Rev. Jeremiah Wright? More to the point, what can we do about it in the digital age? I'm not sure that sea changes of this magnitude are subject to conscious correction. It takes millions and millions of slovenly people to let a great nation fall into careless disregard of its own spiritual well-being. The virtue of America is not something you can address independently of all its 300 million people. It's a question Persia, Athens, and Rome must have asked themselves—and history. And the reply for them came back cold and merciless. Whatever your virtues may have been, they were only human virtues, and therefore you always lived in the shadow of God's closing hands.

# LINCOLN

# Abraham Lincoln and the Rhetoric of Love

*Recently I left the academic community and moved to an island off the coast of South
Carolina, where I am running a business under an assumed name, known only to me and
the state and federal tax services. My house is paid for, and I have enough money left to send
my children through school and to pay my health insurance. As for surviving in the event
that my business fails, the waters of the Atlantic Ocean are still full of crabs, fish, and shrimp,
and there are kindly farmers living nearby who will supply us with vegetables and fruit.
It is only in the light of this newfound independence that I am publishing the following
essay on Abraham Lincoln. I confess that it is only a small part of a study which
I have been writing over the past few years—mostly late at night with the shades
drawn and the doors locked. There are, after all, Lincoln lovers everywhere; and
as my friend and former colleague M.E. Bradford found out, they are full of fierce,
vindictive hatred for anyone who speaks ill of the Great Emancipator. As you will
soon see, I have given up all hope of federal preferment. My will is written.
I need only add that the following is an excerpt and does no more than
foreshadow a more explicitly political analysis of Lincoln's rhetoric, though
the reader might be able to deduce the direction in which I am moving.*

A S RICHARD WEAVER HAS DEMONSTRATED in *The Ethics of Rhetoric*,
the lover and the rhetor have much in common. Indeed, when a young
man calls on a young woman he is customarily both; for tradition requires
that the language of love be artful as well as ardent, imaginative as well as earnest, free of trickery and deceit and designed to move the beloved to respond
to the soul in addition to the body. Furthermore, in the best times the false
rhetorician is deplored as much in matters of the heart as he is in matters of
state, for integrity is the quality most sought after in both.

Lincoln clearly believed, as did his age, that the manner in which he
conducted himself as a suitor had communal as well as private implications.
Neither he nor the public he so frequently courted would have recognized a
moral climate in which a politician's romantic or sexual indiscretions were
ignored as irrelevant to his candidacy for office. His language in correspondence with women indicates, as we will soon see, a fervent desire to be understood as behaving within the boundaries of a very strict code of honor, one
that clearly derives from a tradition which was already complicated and well
formed in the time of Chaucer.

What also seems clear in examining these letters is the degree to which some historians have exaggerated the "natural" and "democratic" character of manners on the Illinois frontier. It is probably more accurate to suggest that manners in our own time are far less formal and aristocratic in their implications than they were in Lincoln's Sangamon County. To be sure there were wild spirits in 19th-century Illinois who lived as if they dwelt among the animals, but we must remember that the frontier was always striving to become a civilized community; and if the first priority of the men was the establishment of businesses and trade routes, the priority of the women was the reestablishment of all the social amenities that they had left behind. Chief among these, of course, were the rituals and niceties surrounding courtship, for women in 19th-century America still found themselves defined in terms of marriage and motherhood. If they had to shoot Indians, chop firewood, hoe beans, and jump over a broom as a prelude to cohabitation, it was not by choice that they did so but out of cruel necessity. There are few records of women who, like Daniel Boone, moved westward as soon as the space around the cabin was cleared to the length of a large tree.

There might be greater evidence to support the argument that at times the newer communities were nervously punctilious about affairs of the heart; because, without the protection of a stabler social order, women were more vulnerable to the triflings of men. Not that they could afford to be *too* punctilious, for life was hard, opportunities were few, and social lines were blurred. Yet Lincoln's own words indicate that he knew he was involved in an ancient game; that the rules were strict; that women, by and large, served as the referees; and that if he played falsely or left himself open to such a charge, his fierce ambition might be irremediably compromised.

In evaluating Lincoln's role as the rhetor of love, we are to some degree hampered by legend and by the well-meaning apologists who have fostered it, for we must first come to terms with the bittersweet image of Ann Rutledge, about whom such figures as Carl Sandburg and Edgar Lee Masters have written with lyric intensity. No American love story is more cherished and none more connotative of the Edenic myth of the old frontier where life was pristine and perilous. And no one ever rendered it with greater cunning than Carl Sandburg, who found Lincoln a subject matter more suited to his robust talents than even the slaughterhouses of Chicago.

> Back to New Salem he came in the spring of 1835, and there was refuge for Ann Rutledge, with her hand in a long-fingered hand whose bones told of understanding and a quiet security. . . . In the fall she was to go to a young ladies' academy in Jacksonville;

206

and Abraham Lincoln, poor in goods and deep in debts, was to get from under his poverty; and they were to marry. They would believe in the days to come; for the present time they had understanding and security.

The cry and answer of one yellowhammer to another, the wing flash of one bluejay on a home flight to another, the drowsy dreaming of grass and grain coming up with its early green over the moist rolling prairie, these were to be felt that spring together, with the whisper, "Always together."

He was twenty-six, she was twenty-two; the earth was their footstool; the sky was a sheaf of blue dreams; the rise of the blood-gold rim of a full moon in the evening was almost too much to live, see, and remember. . . .

August of that summer came. Corn and grass, fed by rich rains in May and June, stood up stunted of growth, for want of more rain. The red berries on the honeysuckles refused to be glad. The swallows and martins came fewer.

To the homes of the settlers came chills and fever of malaria. Lincoln had been down and up, down again with aching bones, taking large spoons of Peruvian bark, boneset tea, jalap, and calomel. One and another of his friends had died; for some he had helped nail together the burial boxes.

Ann Rutledge lay fever-burned. Days passed; help arrived and was helpless. Moans came from her for the one man of her thoughts. They sent for him. He rode out from New Salem to the Sand Ridge farm. They let him in; they left the two together and alone a last hour in the log house, with the slants of light on her face from an open clapboard door. It was two days later that death came.

This passage deserves momentary attention, if only as an example of the manner in which Sandburg assembled his monumental study of Lincoln, a work which is too often admired for the wrong reasons. A close examination of the episode reveals that the poet says more about the birds than about Lincoln and Ann Rutledge. The bare outline of their story is hardly a lean paragraph's worth of news: They knew one another; they were engaged; she caught the fever and died. As a matter of fact, Herndon's original account of this "love affair" is a little more complicated, involving a rival suitor and some hint of consequent difficulties; but Sandburg is not interested in complexities but in the poetic evocation of bittersweet memories, not only of his great epic hero but of the American frontier in all its simple glory, where love as well as politics was pure and untainted by the rise of an industrial class system.

All of the same images might be conjured up in rendering the love life of John Wilkes Booth, for whom the sky might also have been a sheaf of blue dreams; but any reader would have spotted and resented such a sentimental ploy. Not so with the reader of a Lincoln biography. Sandburg had license from a whole generation of Americans to "sweeten the image," to make of this spare tale a romance as fat and fleshy as anything written by Fanny Hurst or Frances Parkinson Keyes. Had he written such an account of George Washington's early loves he might well have been hooted off the front page of the *Times Literary Supplement*. After all, can we permit him that image of "the slants of light on her face from an open clapboard door?" Is there such a thing as a "clapboard door?" How do we know Ann Rutledge lived in a clapboard house? How do we know her bed was directly in the path of the door? But there is no need to go on with such nitpicking. Sandburg's purposes and techniques are all too clear.

Besides, a more important point needs to be made: There is no contemporary evidence that such a tender relationship ever existed. As Benjamin Thomas notes, "In the face of affirmative reminiscences, Lincoln students can scarcely declare with certainty that no such romance took place. But most of them regard it as improbable, and reject utterly its supposed enduring influence upon Lincoln."

The history of the Ann Rutledge legend is interesting, though a little too complex to detail. David Donald attributes its magnification to William Herndon's perennial quarrel with Mrs. Lincoln and his desire to inflict as much pain as possible on that already unhappy woman. Donald suggests that the creation of this tragic romance also helped Herndon to explain those long periods of melancholy that fell upon Lincoln from time to time. For Sandburg, it is an occasion for poeticisms and also coloration for the portrait of "Lincoln, the Man of Sorrows."

**UNFORTUNATELY FOR 20TH-CENTURY READERS,** the long shadow of Ann Rutledge obscures the details of a courtship that can be documented by letters and by written accounts of those people directly involved. Herndon's story of Ann Rutledge was based on a reminiscence of a man speaking almost 30 years after the death of Ann Rutledge, whom he does not name in his published version, though he does say that all the facts are available to any would-be investigator. The details of young Abe's relationship with Mary Owens are recorded in surviving letters, many of which are signed "Lincoln."

Though interpreters may disagree on their implications, the facts surrounding Lincoln's relationship with Mary Owens are fairly well documented in letters, in contemporary accounts, and in Herndon's correspondence with the lady herself after Lincoln's death. Like Lincoln, Mary was from Kentucky, but from a family of some means and gentility. The young Lincoln met her first when she was in New Salem visiting Mrs. Bennett Abell, her sister; and three years later when Mrs. Abell was in Kentucky, she persuaded Mary to return to New Salem, where she and Lincoln became involved in a relationship that eventually proved painful to both of them. From his letters and from her later recollections we can deduce that they had at least talked about marriage. Indeed Lincoln apparently told Mrs. Abell that if she would bring her sister back from Kentucky he would marry her, though authorities disagree as to how serious his remark was intended or received. Perhaps Lincoln spoke in jest. Probably so. Whatever: The question of marriage was broached; the "lovers" entered into a period of courtship; the relationship was terminated on a discordant note; and both went on to marry others and to lead separate lives.

Not an unusual story, to be sure. Almost everyone experiences an early abortive romance—a near triumph or a narrow escape. What is important, however, is the manner in which one behaves under such circumstances. It is satisfying and provocative for historians to moon romantically over the possibly apocryphal story of Ann Rutledge, but Mary Owens did exist and was in fact courted by Abraham Lincoln. We have several accounts of the affair (including his own), and we can make some significant assessment of the man's character during this period of his life by examining this relationship, which was important to him at precisely the time he was beginning his political career.

Herndon, whose later life was devoted to research concerning the exploits of his old partner, wrote Mary Owens first for the letters, and later for her own explanation of what they meant. Her recollections of the relationship are obviously colored, and her words shed uncertain light on the portrait of two lovers:

> You say you have heard why our acquaintance terminated as it
> did. I too have heard the same bit of gossip; but I never used the
> remarks that Dame Rumor says I did to Mr. Lincoln. I think I did
> on one occasion say to my sister, who was very anxious for us to
> be married, that I thought Mr. Lincoln was deficient in those little
> links which make up the chain of a woman's happiness—at least
> it was so in my case. Not that I believed that it proceeded from a

lack of goodness of heart; but his training had been different from mine; hence there was not that congeniality which would otherwise have existed. From his own showing you perceive that his heart and hand were at my disposal; and I suppose that my feelings were sufficiently enlisted to have the matter consummated. At the beginning of the year 1838 I left Illinois, at which time our acquaintance and correspondence ceased, without ever again being renewed. My father, who resided in Green County, Kentucky, was a gentleman of considerable means; and I am persuaded that few persons placed a higher estimate on education than he did.

Edgar Lee Masters sees this account as corroborating Lincoln's own narrative in his April Fool's letter to Mrs. Browning. Masters' version of the affair, though unflattering to Lincoln, presents him as a thwarted lover whose egotism "killed any chances he ever had with her." But the relationship was surely subtler than Masters is willing to grant, as even this brief passage reveals. Had Mary simply rejected a suitor she thought unworthy, her remarks might have been gentler and more complimentary. But there is in them a keen edge that reveals her long-cherished resentment. She was made of finer clay than he. Her father, she will have Herndon know, was "a gentleman" and "of considerable means," a believer in education. How could anyone think that such a one as Lincoln could have aspired to so great a prize?

Yet she saved his three letters all of the years, during the time when he was no more than a country lawyer, through his many defeats in the political arena, finally producing them only after he had been elected president, served a term, and been assassinated. In regarding them one cannot find the slightest trace of literary merit. There are no imaginative turns of phrase, no poetry, not even some extravagant praise for her charms that might have inspired a less than beautiful woman of some gentility to preserve just these crude words against the oncoming of age and forgetfulness. Surely she kept the letters because of the deep feelings she harbored for their writer, feelings not without their darker aspect.

And in her third exchange of correspondence with Herndon she reveals even more of her rancor. She recalls the time when Lincoln failed to assist her in crossing a stream, an event which she juxtaposes against his gallant rescue of a hog mired in mud. And then, with her bitterness showing, she recalls the jocular message that Lincoln sent her by way of Mrs. Abell years later: "Tell your sister that I think she was a great fool because she did not stay here and marry me." Her comment to Herndon was terse and revealing—"Characteristic of the man!"

Masters believes that she refers here to the "egotistical manner" which so offended her that she rejected Lincoln's proposal. All of the evidence together suggests that it was a subtler insult to which she refers. In order to define the nature of that insult, let us examine Lincoln's own letters relating to the subject.

The first of these is dated December 13, 1836, and suggests that the relationship between the two has progressed to the point where he can express some dissatisfaction at being apart from her, but most of his commentary is not personal but political, a report on doings at the state capital, full of references to specific issues and punctuated with comments on his own poor health and low spirits. In closing he apologizes for the letter, which he calls "so dry and stupid that I am ashamed to send it," suggesting, perhaps, that he is acutely aware of his ineptitude in the writing of *billets doux*.

Apparently by May 7, 1837 (the date on the next surviving letter), the relationship had progressed to the point where the two have talked of marriage, for Lincoln writes:

> I am often thinking about what we said of your coming to live
> at Springfield. I am afraid you would not be satisfied. There is
> a great deal of flourishing about in carriages here, which would
> be your doom to see without sharing in it. You would have to be
> poor without the means of hiding your poverty. Do you believe
> you could bear that patiently? Whatever woman may cast her lot
> with mine, should any ever do so, it is my intention to do all in
> my power to make her happy and contented: and there is nothing
> I can imagine, that would make me more unhappy than to fail in
> the effort. I know I should be much happier with you than the
> way I am, provided I saw no signs of discontent in you. What you
> have said to me may have been in jest, or I may have misunder-
> stood it. If so, then let it be forgotten; if otherwise, I much wish
> you would think seriously before you decide. For my part I have
> already decided. What I have said I will most positively abide by,
> provided you wish it. My opinion is that you had better not do it.
> You have not been accustomed to hardship, and it may be more
> severe than you now imagine. I know you are capable of thinking
> correctly on any subject; and if you deliberate maturely upon this,
> before you decide, then I am willing to abide by your decision.

In this letter Lincoln is at best curiously ambivalent toward the woman whom he addresses as "Friend Mary," wanting her to share his life but warning her over and over that if she chooses to do so she will probably be miserable. Since we do not know the precise nature of their conversation about her "coming to live at Springfield," we cannot say with any certitude how Lincoln intended his letter to be received, though Mary's response to Lincoln's initial overtures seems to have been a good deal more positive than either she or Herndon would indicate some 30 years later.

It is possible, of course, that he was, as he suggested, so overcome by a desire to see her happy that he felt constrained to discourage her from "casting her lot with his." Such unselfish sentiments occasionally surface in romantic attachments, though we must suspect something less than complete altruism in one who constantly reminds his beloved that he is willing to make such a sacrifice. In the better fictional examples the hero will not allow his beloved to know he is "doing what is best for her." Having been so informed, no woman could help but consider the possibility that she was being jilted.

Then again, we could place the most cynical construction on Lincoln's letter and argue that he wished to disengage himself from a sexual alliance which, once consummated, was no longer attractive to him, and from which he wished to extricate himself while at the same time enjoying the lady's continued affection. In short, we might contend that he wanted to string her along without having to marry her, as he had told her he would.

However, a third interpretation seems more likely. Beginning to weary of a half-hearted courtship from which he had hoped to derive more in the way of romantic satisfaction, he was looking for a way out—and one which would not only leave him with his honor intact but also divest him of any legal risk. For in the 19th century, breach of promise suits were more of a threat to the treacherous lover than they are in the latter half of the 20th century.

Notice that nowhere does he mention the word "marriage"; instead he writes of "your coming to live at Springfield." A cagey phrase, particularly when juxtaposed with his later "whatever woman may cast her lot with mine, should any ever do so . . . "

**AMBIGUOUS THOUGH THIS LETTER MAY SEEM**, however, it is the soul of clarity and directness when compared with the following, which we reproduce *in toto*, lest the full impact of its subtlety be lost in mere paraphrase.

Springfield Aug. 16th 1837

Friend Mary,

You will, no doubt, think it rather strange, that I should write
you a letter on the same day on which we parted; and I can only

account for it by supposing, that seeing you lately makes me think of you more than usual, while at our late meeting we had but few expressions of thoughts. You must know that I cannot see you, or think of you, with entire indifference; and yet it may be, that you, are mistaken in regards to what my real feelings towards you are. If I knew you were not, I should not trouble you with this letter. Perhaps any other man would know enough without further information; but I consider it *my* particular right to plead ignorance, and your bounden duty to allow the plea. I want in all cases to do right, and most particularly so, in all cases with women. I want, at this particular time, more than anything else, to do right with you, and if I *knew* it would be doing right, as I rather suspect it would, to let you alone, I would do it. And for the purpose of making the matter as plain as possible, I now say, that you can now drop the subject, dismiss your thoughts (if you ever had any) from me forever, and leave this letter unanswered, without calling forth one accusing murmur from me. And I will even go further, and say, that if it will add anything to your comfort, or peace of mind, to do so, it is my sincere wish that you should. Do not understand by this I wish to cut your acquaintance. I mean no such thing. What I do wish is, that our further acquaintance shall depend upon yourself. If such further acquaintance would contribute nothing to your happiness, I am sure it would not to mine. If you feel yourself in any degree bound to me, I am now willing to release you, provided you wish it; while, on the other hand, I am willing, and even anxious to bind you faster, if I can be convinced that it will, in any considerable degree, add to your happiness. This, indeed, is the whole question with me. Nothing would make me more miserable than to make you miserable— nothing more happy, than to know you were so.

In what I have said, I think I cannot be misunderstood; and to make myself understood, is the only object of this letter.

If it suits you best to not answer this—farewell—a long life and a merry one attend you. But if you conclude to write back, speak as plainly as I do. There can be neither harm nor danger, in saying to me, any thing you think, just in the manner you think it.

My respects to your sister.

Your friend
LINCOLN

Benjamin Thomas, who is among the fairest and most objective interpreters of Lincoln's life, writes of this extraordinary document: "Evident-
ly Lincoln wished to escape gracefully from a romance now gone stale. If
so, the lady obliged him. She ignored his letter, and they never met again."

And small wonder!

Undoubtedly Mary must have concluded at this point—if not earlier—
that she was not only weary of indifference but also of a man who could not
bring himself to speak honestly and openly of his feelings. Yet again we find
more than merely the confused country swain in Lincoln's tortuous rhetoric. The legal mind is at work here, weighing every phrase against statute and
precedents, careful lest any statement, however bland, be open to miscon-
struction by a third party. "You must know that I cannot see you, or think
of you, with entire indifference."

One would hope that every human being could make that statement of
every other human being. Indeed the sentiment must have seemed disagree-
ably fatuous from a man who was to write only a few sentences later: "Nothing would make me more miserable than to believe you miserable—nothing more happy, than to know you were so."

And yet: "I cannot see you, or think of you, with entire indifference."
This limpid denial of disinterest is not the poetic understatement of an ardent
swain paying an old compliment in a new way. Instead it suggests the tip-
toeing of a wary bachelor who has, while groping down the dark boarding-
house corridor, inadvertently blundered into the old maid's bedroom.

Indeed he follows this disavowal with a qualification: Even though he
does not feel "entire indifference," "yet [YET!] it may be, that you, are mistak-
en in regard to what my real feelings towards you are." How could she possibly have any doubts after the earlier letters, the months of devoted attention
to her (as well as to the mired hog), the moments of manly forthrightness
that one would expect from the Lincoln of myth, whose blunt words on the
stump so impressed the likes of the rough-hewn Clary's Grove boys? Yet if
she were at this point still in doubt about his feelings—why, he would immediately clarify them for her. Or so he would seem to suggest. But, except for
insisting his happiness is dependent on hers, he makes no further mention
of his feelings. Instead he lapses into a rhetoric which is manifestly legalistic:
"but I consider it *my* particular right to plead ignorance, and your bound-
en duty to allow the plea. I want in all cases to do right, and most particularly so, in all cases with women."

Did the lawyer take over unawares here, or did Lincoln write while holding a candle first over his letter and then over a well-thumbed copy of Black-
stone? Either way the passage is a tricky transition in which the lawyer-lover

neatly brushes aside his own feelings, still undefined, and focuses instead on the lady's sentiments, which he cautiously circles, advances on, pokes, and then jumps back from as if they were a dying rattlesnake.

"I'm just an ol' country boy," he says, "so you've got to spell it out for me. Because, shucks, if I only knew what would make you happy I would do it. It's all up to you. If you don't want to answer this letter (in effect, if you want to end our relationship), then I'll understand. In fact, if such a course of action will make you happy, then by golly I hope you do it. But wait a minute! Don't try to blame me for the breakup, because I'm not suggesting *that* at all. No ma'am! But I am willing to release you from any promise you might feel you've made, *provided you want to be released*, though I'm willing to make the relationship even more binding if such a bond would make you happy (which it probably wouldn't)."

And after his circumlocutious flirtation with meaning, Lincoln writes, "In what I have said, I think I cannot be misunderstood; and to make myself understood, is the only object of this letter."

Can anyone doubt the sly truth of this statement? Surely no one could have made his intentions clearer to a woman who was both educated and of refined sensibilities, while at the same time protecting himself from the literalist who, missing an outright disavowal of his earlier pledge, would conclude that such a pledge had never been offered. But Mary got the message, and saving what pride she still retained, she did what he hoped she would do—she never replied to his letter.

THE LATTER-DAY READER can see in this well-honed document the incipient politician flexing his rhetorical muscles, and it might be profitable to pursue this line of thought to hint at its full ramifications. Let us regard Lincoln not as the lover but as political rhetor and Friend Mary not as some poor fat girl about to be jilted but as the public, struggling to understand the principles that motivate the public man speaking to them. Let us assume that he wants their good will, at the very least that they not be active in opposing him; but he realizes, even as he is about to speak, that should he completely reveal himself he would be vulnerable to attack, would be despised for his self-serving infidelity. Yet he must move his audience in a certain direction in order to satisfy these very passions that he dare not expose.

So the first thing that he establishes is the mask of that virtue in which he is most deficient. If he is greedy, he will begin by asserting that he has no desire for gain. If he lusts for power, he will pretend he has no designs on public office. If he is secretly bellicose, he will protest that he hates war. "I come to bury Caesar, not to praise him," says Antony, and then launches into an encomium that turns the crowd into his deadly instrument of revenge.

Politicians and lovers have always accomplished their desired ends through the heightened use of rhetoric—sometimes honestly, sometimes dishonestly—and if Lincoln the lover deliberately puts on a mask of candor while at the same time practicing the fine art of malicious pussyfooting, then what about the lofty language of his later speeches? Can we not see in his letter to Friend Mary an early example of rhetoric used to urge an audience toward one course of action while protesting that he is doing nothing of the sort?

"But, my God!" one might exclaim. "You can't use a young man's early amatory misadventures to discredit him in his later public life!" And to be sure there are obvious limitations to the use of the above analogy. For one thing, no political constituency could bear to be told so equivocally that it was held in high esteem. The politician who addressed the voters as Lincoln addressed Mary S. Owens would be rejected just as Lincoln had hoped to be rejected, despite his assurances to the contrary.

But the art of saying one thing when you mean its opposite informs this private document; and that same art is practiced again and again in Lincoln's important public utterances, as could be demonstrated, for example, in his speeches on the prospects of war immediately after his election.

# With Malice Toward Many:
# Washington, Lincoln, and God

**M**OST AMERICANS in the 18th, 19th, and early 20th centuries believed in the public expression of religious sentiments as surely as they believed in publicly proclaiming their patriotism. Such expression wasn't merely their right. It was their duty. Indeed, religious faith was part of the "given" of any political debate, the common ground upon which all candidates stood when they rose to disagree with one another. Even in the late 19th century—when great oratory had given way to high-flown platitudes—politicians could still, in all sincerity, invoke the Almighty at the slightest provocation.

Among the most common acknowledgments of religious faith were those delivered at ceremonial occasions where there were no votes on the table, no veterans or preachers to enlist, no pragmatic reason to haul out the colors of rhetoric. One such occasion was the inauguration of a president. At that moment, with the election over, the nation's new chief executive and head of state speaks to the people for the first time. It was probably a much more significant occasion in earlier times than it is today, after so many televised debates, so many interviews, so many 60-second spots. But even in the 21st century the significance of the moment remains.

George Washington set the precedent in his First Inaugural Address by expressing his own submission to God and then the submission of the nation as a whole. He understood the special significance of this occasion. It was the first inauguration of an American president—first in what he expected to be an unbroken chain stretching into the future as far as the eye of imagination could see. He therefore had a special obligation to establish a precedent for succeeding presidents to recognize and follow. Note the wording and length of the following statement:

> Such being the impressions under which I have, in obedience to the public summons, repaired to the present station, it would be peculiarly improper to omit in this first official act my fervent supplications to that Almighty Being who rules over the universe, who presides in the councils of nations, and whose providential aids can supply every human defect, that His benediction may consecrate to the liberties and happiness of the people of the

United States a Government instituted by themselves for these essential purposes, and may enable every instrument employed in its administration to execute with success the functions allotted to his charge. In tendering this homage to the Great Author of every public and private good, I assure myself that it expresses your sentiments not less than my own, nor those of my fellow-citizens at large less than either. No people can be bound to acknowledge and adore the Invisible Hand which conducts the affairs of men more than those of the United States. Every step by which they have advanced to the character of an independent nation seems to have been distinguished by some token of providential agency; and in the important revolution just accomplished in the system of their united government the tranquil deliberations and voluntary consent of so many distinct communities from which the event has resulted can not be compared with the means by which most governments have been established without some return of pious gratitude, along with an humble anticipation of the future blessings which the past seem to presage. These reflections, arising out of the present crisis, have forced themselves too strongly on my mind to be suppressed. You will join with me, I trust, in thinking that there are none under the influence of which the proceedings of a new and free government can more auspiciously commence.

This statement occupied a substantial and preemptive place in his text, preceding his discussion of more pragmatic matters of state. Indeed, the passage was longer than his entire Second Inaugural Address. Here he said in so many words that, on such an occasion, propriety required the acknowledgment of God's role in the destiny of the United States. For the first time a president of the United States affirmed the belief that this nation had been especially blessed by God, Who looked with favor on its history and people. Succeeding presidents would echo these sentiments.

Washington, a faithful communicant of the Episcopal Church, specifically referred to the piety that all Americans shared at that moment when he said: "In tendering this homage to the Great Author of every public and private good, I assure myself that it expresses your sentiments not less than my own." "This is something about which we all agree," he was telling the new nation, "but it needs to be said all the same at public occasions such as this one."

He even closed this paradigmatic inaugural address by again invoking

God's blessing:

> Having thus imparted to you my sentiments as they have been awakened by the occasion which brings us together, I shall take my present leave; but not without resorting once more to the benign Parent of the Human Race in humble supplication that, since He has been pleased to favor the American people with opportunities for deliberating in perfect tranquility, and dispositions for deciding with unparalleled unanimity on a form of government for the security of their union and the advancement of their happiness, so His divine blessing may be equally conspicuous in the enlarged views, the temperate consultations, and the wise measures on which the success of this Government must depend.

Succeeding presidents followed Washington's example. Thus Thomas Jefferson, poster boy of People for the American Way, paid homage to the God of the Holy Bible: "I shall need, too, the favor of that Being in whose hands we are, who led our forefathers, as Israel of old, from their native land, and planted them in a country flowing with all the necessaries and comforts of life."

**FOLLOWING WASHINGTON'S EXAMPLE**, every president, including George W. Bush, has mentioned God in his inaugural address (or addresses) to the nation, a fact highly significant, since even in our own time—with the ACLU poised to pounce on every scurrying, squealing mention of the "G" word—newly elected presidents have invariably chosen to reaffirm the nation's belief that the United States remains a nation under God.

To be sure, many of these allusions to the Almighty were postponed until the final paragraph and in their brevity said little if anything about God's specific role in the nation's affairs. However, with one exception they clearly appealed to a benign and gracious Creator and Preserver. In that one address, He is presented as the angry scourge of the nation, a God who rained death and destruction on the American people as punishment for sin. Such a God is described in the Second Inaugural Address of our 16th president.

At his first inauguration, Abraham Lincoln's position as president was the very opposite of George Washington's. Washington had won a war that had united his people and established a new nation. He was known to virtually every American and wildly popular, certainly the inevitable choice to be the nation's first president. By contrast, Lincoln, relatively unknown and supported by a minority of the voters, was a polarizing figure, whose very election triggered secession. He was facing the prospect of a war that threatened to undo the nation Washington's victories had established.

So how could Lincoln hope to avoid what later generations would call "the irrepressible conflict"? On what common ground could the two sides stand to engage in civil discourse? Lincoln knew that politicians North and South, as well as the people they served, were overwhelmingly Christian and that he was expected to appeal to the same God that Washington confidently invoked at the beginning of the nation. But Lincoln's own belief—or unbelief—placed him outside the Christian community.

The best evidence shows that Lincoln didn't believe Christ died to take away the sins of the world or that He was the Son of God. On rare occasions, he accompanied Mrs. Lincoln to the Presbyterian church; but, in an era where membership in a Christian denomination was *de rigeur* for politicians, he never joined. The people who knew him best said he was a free thinker, a scoffer, a man who looked on the New Testament as a crazy collection of stories and homilies that at best bewildered him.

Whether sincere or insincere, Lincoln, in his First Inaugural Address, said merely: "Intelligence, patriotism, Christianity, and a firm reliance on Him who has never yet forsaken this favored land are still competent to adjust in the best way all our present difficulty."

Note that Lincoln first cited "intelligence," then "patriotism," both of which he addressed in the body of his speech. As for "Christianity," he allowed the word to lie in its crib—unfed, unloved. It carried almost no rhetorical weight in this single sentence, which itself is no more than 30 words pasted near the end of a 3,633-word text. Like other presidents, he was following Washington's prescription for an inaugural address, but he didn't waste more than a single word on a religion for which he had little use, either as a practicing politician or as a man.

He spent most of the other 3,603 words appealing to "intelligence"—reasoning with those Southerners who had left the Union and those who were poised to do so. In these passages, he mustered his evidence like the good lawyer he was. First, he stated in clear, unambiguous language his position on the future of slavery, by quoting from one of his earlier speeches: "I have no purpose, directly or indirectly, to interfere with the institution of slavery in the States where it exists. I believe I have no lawful right to do so, and I have no inclination to do so."

As for the so-called "fugitive-slave" controversy, he quoted the very passage in the Constitution that mandated return of escaped slaves, said the Constitution must be obeyed, and pointed out that "all members of Congress swear their support to the whole Constitution—to this provision as much as to any other."

Having attempted to reassure Southerners that he was not to be confused with New England abolitionists, he told them in lawyerly language that the Union was a contract entered into by all parties and could not be rescinded unilaterally: "No State upon its own mere motion can lawfully get out of the Union; that resolves and ordinances to that effect are legally void, and that acts of violence within any State or States against the authority of the United States are insurrectionary or revolutionary, according to circumstances."

In his two-paragraph peroration, he appealed, not to God or to the Southerners' Christian beliefs, but to their patriotism.

> I am loath to close. We are not enemies, but friends. We must not be enemies. Though passion may have strained it must not break our bonds of affection. The mystic chords of memory, stretching from every battlefield and patriot grave to every living heart and hearthstone all over this broad land, will yet swell the chorus of the Union, when again touched, as surely they will be, by the better angels of our nature.

It is an eloquent conclusion to a well-reasoned argument obviously crafted to persuade Southerners rather than to inflame Northerners. One has to understand the highly complicated circumstances surrounding secession not to wonder why it didn't motivate at least some Southern politicians to patch up the quarrel and remain in the Union.

FOUR YEARS LATER—after hundreds of thousands of men had been killed on both sides (more Northern troops than Southern troops), Lincoln had won another election without gaining a majority, and antiwar sentiment had boiled over in New York City and elsewhere. When Lincoln composed his Second Inaugural Address, he had seen his hope of a quick victory turn to ashes and his tenuous popularity turn to widespread animosity.

Unlike his perfunctory nod to Christianity and the "Him" in his First Inaugural, Lincoln relied heavily on biblical language in his Second Inaugural, quoting from the Bible, rhetorically clenching his teeth and pounding the pulpit like an Old Testament prophet, wagging a reproving finger at the sins of an entire nation, while specifically directing his fury (and God's) at the people of the South.

He begins this sermonic address by reminding his audience of an ironic fact: Both sides in the War worshiped the same God, with each asking for help to prevail against the other. But he left no doubt as to which side had earned God's wrath. The slaveholding South was unworthy to ask *anything* from God: "It may seem strange that any men should dare to ask a just God's assistance in wringing their bread from the sweat of other men's faces . . . "

Was he talking about Northern factory owners as well as Southern slave-holders? And about those who were living off dividends from industrial stocks? They too profited from the product of other people's manual labor. However, as he developed his jeremiad, he made it clear: He was talking only about slavery. The ensuing paraphrase of words spoken by Jesus (Matthew 7:1): "but let us judge not, that we be not judged" was ironically, unintentionally self-mocking, since Lincoln had already passed severe judgment in the front part of the very same sentence.

Then—in a cleverly wrought passage that discussed God's role in merely hypothetical terms—he suggested that the War, brought on by slavery, was the Divine Will intervening in history to punish the nation for the South's sin.

> The Almighty has His own purposes. "Woe unto the world because of offenses; for it must needs be that offenses come, but woe to that man by whom the offense cometh." If we shall suppose that American slavery is one of those offenses which, in the providence of God, must needs come, but which, having continued through His appointed time, He now wills to remove, and that He gives to both North and South this terrible war as the woe due to those by whom the offense came, shall we discern therein any departure from those divine attributes which the believers in a living God always ascribe to Him? Fondly do we hope, fervently do we pray, that this mighty scourge of war may speedily pass away.

This is a curious passage. In it, Lincoln spoke of the "Almighty" having "His own purposes." Yet the quotation was taken from the words of Jesus, in a speech to His disciples (Matthew 18:7). Why not come right out and use the "J" word? To be sure, orthodox Christians believed, then as now, that Jesus is God. But Lincoln didn't. It's barely possible that he saw the quote somewhere and didn't verify its source. However it is highly likely that he used "Almighty" because it sounded more like the Old Testament God, who was forever visiting disaster on those who disobeyed His commands, rather than Jesus, who tended to stress mercy and forgiveness. It was certainly a good quote for what Lincoln wished to say: that North and South alike had suffered because of the sin of slavery, but that the South ("by whom the offense cometh") had incurred the greater punishment.

Yet, if God wills that it continue until all the wealth piled by the
bondsman's two hundred and fifty years of unrequited toil shall
be sunk, and until every drop of blood drawn with the lash shall
be paid by another drawn with the sword, as was said three thousand years ago, so still it must be said "the judgments of the Lord
are true and righteous altogether."

This address was delivered on March 4, 1865. In just over a month, Lee
would surrender at Appomattox. The War was all but over, and Lincoln well
knew the price Southerners had already paid for their attempt to leave the
Union. Sherman and Sheridan—with Lincoln's approval—had made war
against civilians; burned their houses and crops; slaughtered their animals;
and ordered troops to shoot men, women, and children at random. Yet in
the Second Inaugural, Lincoln suggested that these war crimes were somehow ordained by the providence of God.

AS THE GETTYSBURG ADDRESS ILLUSTRATES, Lincoln knew how to use
biblical rhetoric to justify his own political choices and their catastrophic
consequences. For a man who thought as little of Jesus as Lincoln did, in this
address he made mighty good use of the red-letter sections of the Bible—
to curse his enemies and to picture himself as the instrument of God's true
and righteous judgment. In so doing, he stood Washington's precedent on its
head and once again revealed himself as the master manipulator of rhetoric.

Yet his ultimate affront to religious sensibilities occurred in his peroration, when—after using Scripture to scourge his enemies—he donned a cas-
sock and became, in that white space between paragraphs, the benevolent
dispenser of Christian grace, the peacemaker, the nurse of the nation that
God had so sorely afflicted.

With malice toward none, with charity for all, with firmness in
the right as God gives us to see the right, let us strive on to finish
the work we are in, to bind up the nation's wounds, to care for
him who shall have borne the battle and for his widow and his
orphan, to do all which may achieve and cherish a just and lasting peace among ourselves and with all nations.

Small wonder he is regarded as our greatest president. You can fool most
of the people all of the time.

# The Education of Mel Bradford:
# The Vanderbilt Years

I FIRST MET MEL BRADFORD on the stairway of Old Central, the building that for a time housed the Vanderbilt English department. The year was 1959. He'd just begun his doctoral studies there, and he was already a disciple of Donald Davidson, as was I. I remember him standing on the stairway, bending down to shake my hand—tall and underfed, with enormous blue eyes. He'd come there from the University of Oklahoma, where he'd majored in philosophy and was something of a neo-Hegelian. By the time he'd completed his doctoral work, there was none of that left.

During Mel's Vanderbilt years, the English department was among the most influential in the region. Its Ph.D.'s chaired departments at several universities and numerous smaller colleges. Even with a master's, Vanderbilt students could teach at prestigious institutions in virtually every Southern state, though in few north of Kentucky. (When three of us left Converse College in 1965, we had offers to move together to state universities in Georgia, Mississippi, and Alabama.)

In part this mobility was the result of a good-old-boy network that no longer exists. Vanderbilt people took care of their own. But we were also in demand because of the graduate education we received—a broad and intense discipline that prepared us to teach almost any course in any English department. So by the time he left Vanderbilt, Mel Bradford not only had covered the entire spectrum of English and American literature, but had mastered several approaches to the subject matter. Before Mel had finished his teaching career, he had taught Anglo-Saxon literature, Chaucer, the medieval lyric, the 16th century, Shakespeare, the 17th century, the 18th century, the English novel, Romanticism, Victorian poetry and prose, American literature, and modern literature—and he had published scholarly and critical articles in virtually every one of these areas.

Such scope and versatility was, in some measure, a tribute to his extraordinary mind, which retained almost every hard fact and abstract principle he ever learned. Many who were astonished at his detailed knowledge of history and political philosophy never realized that these were mere sidelines with him, that his grasp of literary history and criticism was even more terrifyingly comprehensive.

In addition to Bradford's prodigious intelligence, the Vanderbilt English department deserves a portion of the credit for his achievement. Both the graduate curriculum he pursued and the professors who taught him contributed significantly to the breadth of his learning. In addition, they helped to shape his attitude toward literature, history, and society.

From what he told me, Mel Bradford left Norman, Oklahoma, in some intellectual confusion. In Nashville, everything began to make sense. He had strong family ties rooted in the land—not only in Texas, where he was born, but in Tennessee, where Bradfords still lived and farmed. His father, Eustace, was a cattleman. Mel loved and revered him above all men. Every teacher he studied under at Vanderbilt would have understood and admired his father. Yet each one had a different lore to teach, a different vision of literature—and each one taught him something that was useful in political and social commentary as well as in literary studies. It is impossible to understand Bradford's remarkable achievement without knowing who these teachers were and what they had to teach.

FOREMOST WAS DONALD DAVIDSON, the sole Fugitive-Agrarian left at Vanderbilt, the only one who stayed until the end. Davidson regarded himself primarily as a poet. Because his traditional sensibilities were imperfectly attuned to the Modernist movement, his poetic reputation never matched that of fellow Fugitives John Crowe Ransom, Allen Tate, and Robert Penn Warren, who won numerous literary prizes during their distinguished careers and were usually included in standard anthologies of modern poetry from 1935 to 1960.

As an Agrarian, however, Davidson was among the most faithful and militant. The Fugitives, so named because of a magazine for which they wrote in the 1920's, were pure poets characterized by modernist irony and obscurity rather than by their political or social attitudes. The Agrarians, whose first symposium, *I'll Take My Stand*, was published in 1930, were antimodernist social critics who saw industrialism as a dangerous ideology. They did not, as a group, idealize the Old South, nor did they want to return to the past. They were neither utopian nor hopelessly nostalgic.

They wanted the nation, as well as the region, to maintain the then-precarious balance between agriculture and industrialism. If that balance were upset, they said, the cities would eventually fall into decay, urban crime would be rampant, nature would be desecrated, the family would fall into pieces, and romantic love would degenerate into mere lust. For 40 years they were laughed at by the liberal intellectual community. Over the next 25, the laughter died.

In the 1950's, Donald Davidson was still publishing social criticism that echoed the Agrarian warnings of the 1930's. And, after decades of silence, Davidson began writing and publishing poetry again. His poems, free of the crabbed modernisms so foreign to his nature, were open and forthright, some reminiscent of the later Yeats, others picking up a native strain that runs through English and American poetry from the medieval lyric to Ben Jonson to Robert Burns to Thomas Hardy.

He was not an impressive-looking man. He had thin, no-colored hair, narrow shoulders on a slight frame, and he walked slowly and deliberately, like someone with a bad back. When lecturing, he spoke in a quiet, matter-of-fact voice, with a pleasant Middle Tennessee accent. Occasionally he would display his wit, but his delivery was always low-key. Sometimes only a portion of the class would catch the joke.

He was neither eloquent nor hortatory, and he never, never used his class to promote his social or political views. If you wanted to know where he stood on the issues of the day, you could extrapolate his positions from his commentary on matters literary. When he lamented the loss of the oral tradition in lyric poetry, you could guess that he regretted what happened at Gettysburg and Shiloh. But only when you read his poems or essays could you confirm that deduction. Like all the other professors in the department, he believed it was unethical to use the classroom as a pulpit or a political podium.

When lecturing, Davidson approached literature as a New Critic—that is, an explicator of texts rather than a biographer, philosopher, or polemicist. Perhaps his best course was "The English Lyric"—concentrating on the medieval and Renaissance periods. He taught "The Ballad" as well, beginning with the English and ending with the American. He also taught "Modern Poetry," concentrating on T.S. Eliot and William Butler Yeats, and "The Modern Novel," a course that included, among other writers, James Joyce, D.H. Lawrence, and Joseph Conrad.

The first order of business in any Davidson course was examining the text itself: the words and images and tropes—their denotations, their connotations, their ambiguities. A typical written assignment in "The Lyric" was to choose a poem and simply tell what and how it meant. Davidson supplied you with no critical apparatus and no specialized vocabulary. You were expected to use your head and whatever language you had at your disposal. He was gentle in his commentary and charitable if not generous in his grading. Bright students got the hang of explication before the semester was over.

Explication was only the first step in the critical lesson Davidson offered. There was another dimension to his literary criticism—one that less gifted students never fully mastered. He shed additional light on the text of the poem by exploring the relationship between the spirit of the age in which the poem was written and the response of the poet to that spirit. Why, he would ask, is the medieval lyric so direct and simple, while the sonnet is so intellectualized? Or, why did Eliot have to turn *The Waste Land* into an intellectual puzzle, and what do the formal properties of this landmark poem tell us about 20th-century society and sensibilities?

Davidson wasn't the only person asking these questions in the 1950's, but the answers he was offering—and evoking from his better students—were the stuff of an intellectual counterrevolution, a revolt against current fashion that, by the late 1960's, had helped to transform the nature of 20th-century poetry and fiction and turn the tables on modernism. Neither Davidson nor his students made this happen, but they perceived the need for such change decades before it actually came to pass.

Mel emerged from Donald Davidson's classes with a healthy respect for the discrete integrity of the poem or work of fiction—and a belief that it could best be understood in the context of the age and society in which it was written, that the historical literary work was accessible to later readers only if viewed as having formal properties peculiar to its own time and place— which is quite different from saying that a poem or novel reflects the ideas of a particular era. It is easy enough to see that Matthew Arnold's "Dover Beach" is a poem about the loss of religious faith in the wake of Darwin and the Higher Criticism of the Bible. It is a little harder to grasp the concept that the metaphysical conceit is the result of the wedding of the poem to the printed page—or the collapse of the Ptolemaic view of the cosmos.

Donald Davidson cultivated that kind of literary sensibility in his students, and it is easy to see how a gifted political thinker like Mel Bradford could make use of this training in confronting, say, the Constitution and the Declaration of Independence. As in his analysis of poetry, he saw these documents as exhibiting formal properties mysteriously wrought by the age in which they were written and tempered by the deeper historical sensibilities of those who wrote them.

Had he not studied under Donald Davidson, I doubt that he would have seen the Declaration of Independence as a conservative document or understood so well the Constitution as crafted by a group of orthodox Christians concerned with the limitations of human reason and the continuity of their experience as traditional Englishmen.

IN SHARP CONTRAST TO DONALD DAVIDSON was Claude Lee Finney, who had a Harvard Ph.D. and a philosophical mind. Whereas Davidson concentrated on the text, Finney never really got around to it. He was a thin, white-haired man with a slight stoop who spent much of his time in class at the blackboard, drawing trilevel diagrams of neoplatonic emanations. When he lectured, his eyes glowed, as if he were enraptured by the rediscovery of the ancient truths he was reciting.

He began every course he taught—Shakespeare, Milton, Spenser, the Romantics—with the Ionian physicists, those precursors of Plato and Aristotle who talked about the nature of being in terms of primordial elements. While students took copious notes, more out of faith than understanding, he traced neoplatonism down through the Dark Ages, the Middle Ages, and into the Renaissance. Bemused Ph.D. candidates made reports on Proclus, Plotinus, Ficino, and Petrus Ramus, after which Finney would leap to the blackboard and rapidly sketch a chalk diagram that looked something like one of those instruments country grocers use to grab cereal boxes off a high shelf—a series of triangles that descended through the order of being, starting with God and ending up with a rock.

At the beginning of the first semester, no one understood what neoplatonic emanations were. By the end of the semester, they were as familiar and comprehensible as traffic signals. But there was no Shakespeare or Spenser, Milton or Keats on the final examination, because the class hadn't worked its way to that point in history.

The second semester began with more philosophers, the neoplatonists of the Protestant Reformation. Then, and only then, could anyone begin to understand the text itself, which Finney presented as a formal embodiment of the trilevel view of being that had filtered down through the centuries from Plato's original insights on the subject.

It was a beautifully systematic approach to literature, one the scholar could apply to a wide range of literary figures and periods. The less imaginative students concluded that Finney was himself a neoplatonist, a man so entranced by the schemata of ancient philosophy that he could barely live in the real world.

There were stories to support this theory, some of them offered by Finney himself. He once told me that years earlier, in a receiving line, he had failed to introduce his fiancée to Massachusetts Gov. Calvin Coolidge because he forgot her name. As a consequence, the young woman broke off their engagement.

He also grew orchids in a greenhouse; if his family forgot to call him, he would continue to work with his plants around the clock, oblivious to meals or bedtime. And a fellow student of mine carried Finney's books to the parking lot one day and saw a huge sign affixed to the dashboard: PICK UP GRANDMA!!!

But Finney, no pagan, knew what he was doing in the classroom. He was giving every Vanderbilt graduate student a complete history of mainstream Western philosophy. The blackboard in Bradford's classes often contained these same diagrams, as did the blackboards in other regional classrooms taught by Vanderbilt Ph.D.'s. But of equal importance, perhaps, was Bradford's less obvious use of this approach in coming to terms with American historical documents, which he understood as having been shaped by the same flow of Platonic and Aristotelian thought as the plays of Shakespeare.

**EDGAR HILL DUNCAN** taught Chaucer and Victorian literature. A kind and thoughtful man, he conducted his classes as if they were study groups composed of colleagues rather than students. The proud ones—those anxious to display their skills of explication in the classroom—sometimes found Duncan's classes frustrating. They consisted almost exclusively of reports given by students on a wide range of articles and books. Indeed, by the end of the year some felt as if they had learned more about the scholarship than they needed to know, since—after all—they were competent and highly original critics themselves.

First among equals, Duncan assigned the reports, because he already knew the scholarship. Otherwise, he was an intent listener like the rest of us. When a student would miss the main point of an article or omit an important fact, Duncan might ask a question or fill in the gap himself. But for the most part, his classes were taught by the students themselves. In this manner, he made certain that they knew medieval and late 19th-century literary scholarship—all of it—and had some taste of some classroom teaching.

If this experience was broadening, it was also humbling. Duncan forced students to submit to the body of scholarship in their chosen field, to tell themselves, "Before I can be certain my own critical perceptions are original, or even tenable, I must first see what all my predecessors have said on the subject."

Not only did this attitude prompt Mel Bradford to read extensively in the commentary of the past, it also reinforced his growing belief in the crucial importance of tradition—in this case, the scholarly tradition. Duncan helped to teach him what Faulkner once wrote, that the past isn't dead; it isn't even past. The extraordinary humility that Bradford displayed in his attitude toward his own work was something he owed, at least in part, to Edgar Hill Duncan, who taught us all, in the gentlest manner possible, that we were merely one among many, and not necessarily the most important one.

**ROB ROY PURDY** offered a course in Anglo-Saxon poetry—teaching the language during the first semester and encouraging students during the second semester to explicate *Beowulf, The Wanderer, The Seafarer,* and other Anglo-Saxon poems as if they were written by modern poets. He also taught one semester of the Chaucer course, where he also encouraged, without prescribing, contemporary critical treatments of *The Canterbury Tales* and other works.

Purdy's chief contribution to his graduate students was a latitude rarely found in Early and Middle English studies—the opportunity, after a semester of surveying the medieval scholarship under Duncan, to exercise their critical imaginations. His classes may well have produced some of the most original criticism in the graduate school, largely unpublishable at the time because the learned journals in that particular field were less than receptive to anything but analysis grounded in original scholarship of the most pedantic kind.

Purdy gave you release from the strictures the others in the department imposed. His course was like a holiday in the middle of Lent. It helped you return to a more stringent discipline with a hopeful heart.

Despite the fact that Duncan and Purdy were on less than friendly terms as a consequence of a departmental squabble many years earlier, their courses complemented each other perfectly. Each had a special grace to bestow. Purdy's grace was more easily received than Duncan's, but in the long run somewhat less redemptive.

JOHN ADEN came to Vanderbilt only a few years before Bradford. A tall, lanky man with sunken cheeks, he wielded an urbane wit that was entertaining and dangerous—perfectly suited to the teaching of 18th-century literature. Like the others, he was a Southerner by birth, and spoke with an elegant accent. His lectures were brilliant, laced with humor and fine irony.

Of all the professors teaching in the graduate school, Jack Aden was the most feared. He demanded near perfection from his students, and he piled assignments on their heads like a gravedigger shoveling dirt. Those who took his classes often complained that they had no time to take care of the basic necessities, much less do the work required in other courses.

He expected his students not only to master the most significant scholarship in the field, but also to know and understand everything written in the 18th century. Even the diligent scholar entered Aden's exam in a state of high anxiety, knowing that it would demand the most arcane knowledge as well as the most agile and disciplined mind. And Aden did not grade on the curve. He would have flunked an entire class with a wry smile on his face if his students hadn't measured up to his high expectations.

Mel learned some of the same lessons from Aden that he learned from the others—a respect for the text and the body of criticism, the necessity of knowing history, and a submission to his masters. But he also learned the work ethic of the genuine scholar in a way that he might not have learned quite as well from anyone else.

Over the years, Bradford turned out a prodigious amount of work: books, and articles and papers that became books. His bibliography was eventually so long that it would have wrapped around an elderly redwood tree. And he wrote everything by hand, sitting at his dining-room table, often until two or three in the morning, poring over books, then drafting a single paragraph or sentence, followed by a footnote that might cover an entire page.

Young men don't acquire that peculiar kind of discipline genetically. It is a virtue that must be instilled, like housebreaking a dog. Mel Bradford would often shake his head in wonder that he ever survived Jack Aden's class, but the greatest lesson Aden taught remained with Bradford until the end of his life. From the time he left Vanderbilt, he was never without scholarly commitments that required more of his time than he had to offer—and he always met those commitments.

WALTER SULLIVAN was primarily an explicator of texts, a teacher who seldom assigned scholarship and spent virtually all of his class time exploring meaning and highlighting technique. He specialized in fiction, and his courses were designed primarily for advanced undergraduate study; but graduate students who took them received inside information about the way in which a novel was put together. A successful novelist himself, Sullivan had a way of discussing a work of fiction as the author's solution to a narrative problem rather than as a work that appeared, fully developed, on the fall book list.

In a way, Sullivan reinforced Davidson's approach to literature; but he also brought his own unique sensibility to the text. And he was, with the possible exception of Jack Aden, the most entertaining lecturer in the department. His discussion of a Henry James novel like *The Spoils of Poynton* was punctuated by hilarious paraphrase that did affectionate violence to the original, while, at the same time, highlighting James's subtle layers of meaning. Mel used the same technique in his own classes and in lectures he delivered around the country.

Because each of these teachers taught literature in a different way, Mel learned a variety of approaches to his subject matter, whether in confronting literary studies or in the examination of historical and political documents. His versatility was in some measure a reflection of the variety found in the Vanderbilt English department.

However, it is important to realize that this department was by no means composed of individualists who struck out in different directions without so much as a friendly word to one another. In the most important ways it was utterly homogeneous, a department filled with Southern conservatives. You could prosper there if you were a liberal, because politics and social philosophy never reared their heads in the classroom. But, if you came with a conservative background, you felt immediately at home.

During the years the South was under attack for Jim Crow and other social policies, these men defended the region and its people in private conversation and sometimes in public statements. From the beginning, Mel found himself among sympathetic compatriots, if not outright confederates. With such teachers, he didn't have to waste time defending his convictions against the assaults of ideological adversaries. The English department was on his side, which meant he could talk openly and freely.

It is possible that Bradford might have acquired the same critical and scholarly discipline from some other institution, but I doubt it, given his temperament and the natural affinity he felt for these teachers. Nor is it likely he could have taught himself everything he learned in graduate school. Self-educated people are usually eccentric and misguided. A young mind, even a brilliant one, needs mature guidance.

When he struck out for Texas to begin his teaching duties at Abilene Christian College, Mel Bradford had all the intellectual weaponry he needed to take on the adversaries he was spoiling to debate—beginning with literary critics of the left who, in his opinion, had misread the works of William Faulkner, and proceeding to the historians and political theorists who were offering revisionist accounts of the founding and secession in order to serve a compulsive contemporary ideology.

With the exception of Walter Sullivan, Bradford's teachers are all dead now, and the last students who studied under them are nearing retirement or have already retired. Universities have changed radically in the past 40 years, and Vanderbilt is no exception. The moment for such broad and diverse scholarly training has passed, and perhaps with it the possibility of producing another Mel Bradford—at least in the foreseeable future.

Meanwhile, in a time when feeling passes for thought and invective for argument, teachers like Davidson, Finney, Duncan, Purdy, Aden, and Sullivan seem larger and wiser with every passing year, at least to those of us who studied under them. Long before he died, Bradford privately acknowledged his debt to them. His public testimonial can be found in a substantial body of work that seems to grow in significance with each passing year.

# Mel Bradford as Literary Critic

**M**EL BRADFORD was not really a political philosopher or historian. He was a literary critic, and in the beginning he did these other things on the side, the way Churchill built brick walls. Late in his short life he neglected his primary calling and devoted his creative energies to political and historical essays, but these works were more a product of his literary training than of any formal instruction in the world's great political thinkers or the history of the American Republic

I would stress that it was a very special literary training, one available for a time in a few universities, now fast disappearing from the landscape, like corn cribs and snuff cans. Bradford received a version of this literary education at Vanderbilt University, during the Indian summer of the Fugitive Agrarians, when the English department there was staffed by former students of this group, and where one—Donald Davidson—was still in residence. If you want to understand Mel Bradford's political commentary, you must begin there.

The Agrarian influence on Mel Bradford's work should be obvious—assuming, of course, you've read *I'll Take My Stand* and not merely the substantial body of wrongheaded commentary on that work. But the Fugitive influence is perhaps more elusive, in part because it is rooted in method rather than in ideas. The Fugitives were a coterie of Nashville poets, mostly from Vanderbilt, who met off-campus to discuss what Yeats called "the supreme theme of art and song." At some point, they began to write poetry and to criticize each other's work. They picked and pried at every word of every line, and at times, they even raised basic questions of rhetorical strategy: "Can you write a serious poem about God in the year 1922?" If so, how? The method they developed for dissecting poetry eventually became known as the New Criticism—an approach that focused almost exclusively on the text rather than on extraneous considerations.

The history of literary criticism for the previous century had been one movement after another carefully designed to distract the reader from the work itself. Even today, most professors of English don't know what literature is, don't like it, and would rather talk about something else. And that's precisely what they've been doing ever since courses in English and American literature were introduced into the standard curriculum. That's what deconstructionism is all about—a way of not talking about works of art.

A century ago, scholars were looking for "sources and analogues." Thus, when students opened their books to *The Canterbury Tales*, their professor would tell them to forget Chaucer's General Prologue and direct their attention to Boccaccio or the author of *Arabian Nights*, who used a similar device to introduce a collection of stories. (Anyone who wanted to learn about Chaucer would have to take a course in Boccaccio.)

Then there were biographical scholars, who were interested in the poet's life rather than the poem. Thus, instead of considering Keats's "Ode on a Grecian Urn," the professor would spend the class period telling students where Keats was living when he wrote the poem and what kind of marmalade he preferred on his toast.

Also, there were scholars who would examine in intricate detail the intellectual climate in which the writer lived and wrote. This approach brought the teacher closer to the text—but only a little closer, like a dog circling round and round a rattlesnake, afraid that the live and singing thing at the center of the circle might bite him.

It is that live and singing thing that the New Critics wanted to confront: the poem or novel or play itself—or rather its text, because the two are not necessarily the same thing. If sources and analogues, or biographical data, or arcane lore wanted to come to the party, that was all well and good. Each in its turn could dance with the text—provided they let the text lead.

JOHN CROWE RANSOM was the first to call it "the New Criticism," but actually it was a method of approaching texts that was quite old—indeed a practice rooted in primal literary perception. Ancient Jewish, Greek, and Latin scholars were "New Critics," because they paid attention to the text itself—to the words of the Torah or the psalm or the ode or the epic—and not to extraneous considerations urged upon them by a horde of assistant professors hustling for tenure.

Now, there were two obvious dangers inherent in the New Criticism. Like Apollo's chariot in the hands of a proud and headstrong boy, it could scorch the earth or leave it icebound.

The first of these dangers was "Humpty Dumptyism"—the idea that the work of literature could be molded into whatever shape the critic chose, like the Pillsbury Doughboy. You may remember that in *Through the Looking Glass*, Humpty Dumpty tells Alice: "When I use a word . . . it means just what I mean it to mean—neither more nor less." Humpty Dumpty the New Critic would say, "The work of literature means just what I choose it to mean, neither more nor less."

Thus, in the hands of Maxwell Geismar, a "sort of" New Critic with a Marxist bias, Henry James's works—witty and intricate dramas of moral consciousness—became the stylized exempla of class warfare. (As if any grubby prole would be allowed in the kitchen of a Henry James novel!) On the other hand, New Critics with a Christian perspective loved to baptize Homer and Hemingway.

Humpty Dumpty the New Critic saw the literary work as a thing to be exploited—a reflection of his own personality, an illustration of his own ideology, a weapon to be wielded in the battle of ideas. Perched precariously on that wall, he ordered the text about the way a retired general moves toy soldiers on a play battlefield.

The second danger of the New Criticism was the tendency of some practitioners to decree that time and place were no longer relevant to an understanding of the work of literature, that all poems and novels were written in Cloud Cuckooland. You didn't have to know anything about Elizabethan England to come to a perfect understanding of Shakespeare. Why, he lived just down the street from you. He used to deliver your morning paper, and when he went to college, he was in the same fraternity as your cousin Fred. So you know exactly what he was talking about, what he really meant to say, despite all those "thees" and "thous" and "forsooths." Ultimately, in plays like *Macbeth* and *The Tempest* and *As You Like It*, he was telling everybody to support liberal democracy and vote either Democratic or moderate Republican. For after all, he was a fine fellow, so how could he believe otherwise?

Bradford learned at Vanderbilt to avoid both of these dangers, while mastering the valuable techniques of textual explication. First, Davidson passed along to his students a belief in the absolute integrity of the work itself, its essential inviolability. Like a human being, a poem or novel was protected by its own Bill of Rights that allowed it freedom of speech, protection from unreasonable search and seizure, and the right to bear arms. In obedience to that Bill of Rights, Davidson never tried to conscript, say, James Joyce into his Agrarian army, nor would he permit any of his disciples to do so.

Second, while studying under Davidson and others in the English department, Bradford learned what he probably knew already in his bones—that poems and novels have their origins in time and place, a social and historical context that must be understood before the text itself is manageable. These were matters that could not be ignored.

But wasn't this approach—with its attention to historical and intellectual data—simply a return to the biographical emphasis and arcane knowledge of previous scholars? Not the way Donald Davidson taught his students to look at literary texts. Indeed, the uses Davidson made of intellectual and social history were the very opposite of old-fashioned historical or intellectual scholarship. He began with the text rather than its external trappings and asked the question: "What peculiarities in the formal properties of this work reveal its cultural and temporal context?" Or, to put it more precisely, "What techniques did the poet or novelist employ in order to meet the demands of a contemporary audience?" John Donne used "metaphysical conceits" because the old neoplatonic conventions were no longer vital by the 17th century. Yeats used a private mythology in his later works because there was no longer a viable public myth. T.S. Eliot used irony and deliberate obscurity in *The Waste Land* because a modern pragmatic society had abandoned the traditional belief in the poet's wisdom. Such historical considerations were not merely an irrelevant parade of academic erudition; they helped the critic to understand the inner dynamic of the literary work; indeed, they spoke to the question of its mysterious origins.

This, then, is a bare-bones description of the modified New Criticism that Mel Bradford learned from Donald Davidson. It is, by necessity, a simplistic account of what Davidson had to offer his students. A quiet, matter-of-fact lecturer, he looked like a small-town banker or lawyer. When in class, he talked only about the formal properties of literature, avoided at all costs the subject of contemporary politics, and never asked his students to join the lonely parapet he manned as the last, sad Confederate soldier. He would have considered it a breach of academic ethics to do so. Yet somehow the boldest and most perceptive of his students enlisted in his army. Among us all, Mel Bradford was the best.

MEL WROTE HIS FIRST PUBLISHABLE ARTICLES while still taking graduate courses. Like Davidson, he was by nature combative, and sought to engage the enemy at the first opportunity. There were plenty of battlefields then, but one of the most ill defended was the fiction of William Faulkner. Since the 1930's, the critics of the left, in typical Humpty Dumpty fashion, had insisted that Faulkner was a social satirist whose works were written to expose the depravity of the South in general, and Mississippi in particular—that most depraved of all places.

Both as a New Critic and a neo-Agrarian, Bradford knew better. Yoknapatawpha County—Faulkner's fictional world—was inhabited by idiots who committed acts of bestiality and old ladies who slept with the corpses of their dead lovers, but in that respect it was no different from Cook County, Illinois, or Orange County, California. What made Faulkner's works a permanent part of the literary landscape was his depiction of traditional virtue in conflict with vice, beauty in the clutches of time. Critics of the left viewed

Faulker's work instrumentally, as a means to a political end. Even as a graduate student, Mel set out to challenge this enormous critical error.

In 1962, he took up the case of "The Bear," a segment of Faulkner's *Go Down, Moses* that the left admired inordinately because its hero, Ike McCaslin, gives up the land he inherited from his slave-owning forebears, believing it has been tainted by the peculiar institution. Ike is convinced that he has absolved himself of all guilt because he has given the land back to everybody, black and white, in what Faulkner calls "the communal anonymity of brotherhood." Such a sacrifice, the establishment critics argued, was both proper and ennobling—a way of atoning for a wicked past unique to that time and place. In a paper called "Brotherhood in the Bear," which he read before a scandalized South Central Modern Language Association, Bradford challenged the canon of criticism on "The Bear," beginning with a gratuitous jab at the critical community in general and his audience in particular: "I am convinced that 'The Bear' has often been admired only for the wrong reasons, valued only because the critic found in the discussion of it a convenient platform for the ventilation of his favorite social and political obsessions."

In case you don't recognize the later Bradford in that passage, consider his commentary on the wisdom and virtue of Ike McCaslin's decision to renounce his patrimony and declare himself absolved from further responsibility:

> Ike confuses brotherhood with the abstract conception of an anonymous equality, or, rather, he imagines that the one presupposes the other. . . . [T]here is nothing further from the social ideals of doctrinaire egalitarianism than the structure of the family unit, and for Faulkner the patriarchal/matriarchal family is the archetype of all natural society. A brother is one whose place is defined by either his dependence upon or his responsibility for another. Cain's question, "Am I my brother's keeper?" is implicitly egalitarian. It posits the "communal anonymity of brotherhood."

As a New Critic, Bradford goes on to prove his reading with evidence from the entire text of *Go Down, Moses*, rather than from a selective reading of "The Bear." This more inclusive reading reveals the long-term consequences of Ike McCaslin's decision and his own reaction to those developments. In "Delta Autumn," the last segment of the novel, Ike McCaslin is a bitter old man—uncle to all the county, father to none—who has watched the world he cherished and the sensibilities he endorsed fall to pieces. His own kin—black and white alike—are living in an amoral society in which exploitation is commonplace and even the sacred rules of the wilderness have been violated.

This reading, written by a graduate student, shattered the previous consensus and reopened debate on "The Bear" and *Go Down, Moses*. It was the first rifle crack from a new combatant in the field, and it struck the literary establishment right between the eyes. Soon the article found its way into anthologies, and old-line critics were crying out in anger and despair. Faulkner was no longer a head mounted on the wall of Malcolm Cowley. Like Hector, his body was being fought for by his own people. First Bradford and Cleanth Brooks, then a whole host of critics joined the battle.

ONE MORE EXAMPLE SHOULD SUFFICE, an essay on "Barn Burning"—one of Faulkner's masterpieces and the story the author himself chose as the first selection in his volume of *Collected Short Stories*. "Barn Burning" has as its principal character the child of a sharecropper—who is faced with a moral dilemma the resolution of which provides the action for the narrative. In the climax of the story this small boy, named Sarty Snopes, must decide whether to allow his father, Ab, to burn down the barn of a rich landowner, or to betray his own flesh and blood by warning the enemy. It is a choice that would tax the moral conscience of a first-century saint.

Faulkner presents the alternatives in perfect balance, then allows the boy to make the pure moral choice, which results tragically in his father's death. The sensibilities of a normal reader would suffice to identify the hero of the novel and its obvious villain. Sarty is loyal but fair-minded, a good son but a better human being. Ab is consumed by malevolent pride, a man who would rather wreak vengeance than provide for his own deprived family.

Yet students of literature throughout the country were reading an entirely different interpretation of the story, one by critic Lionel Trilling, author of *The Liberal Imagination* and chief lion of New York City's literary salons. In the kind of article that gives criticism a bad name, Trilling began his meandering discussion of "Barn Burning" by extolling the virtues of rats, which, he claimed, everyone admires because of their ingenuity and perseverance in the face of malevolent forces out to eradicate them—like the health department. Ab Snopes, Trilling argued, is like a rat, and therefore the hero of the story. For Trilling, it is a tale of betrayal in which a wicked boy, blinded by the munificence of a Southern mansion, squeals on his own father.

I suspect it was that Southern mansion, with its liveried black butler, that blinded Trilling, the New York liberal, to the human nuances of the story and provoked him to side with the rat, while ignoring passages that clearly point to the boy's inner conflict and its painful but just resolution.

Bradford, in answering Trilling, must take the boy's side—in *apparent* opposition to family, to what Faulkner calls in the story "the old fierce pull of blood." At first glance this seems an unlikely confrontation—the Northern liberal defending patriarchy, the Southern conservative taking the side of abstract justice. But the difference of opinion is really over levels of understanding—the superficial *versus* the comprehensive and profound. And Bradford, undistracted by the plight of urban rats, focuses on the entire text, including the aftermath of Ab's death, in which the boy remembers what was good about his father—"He was brave!"

As Bradford writes:

> The moral life is finally a question of internal choice. Sarty and Ab both look like the victims to the sentimental modern reader. Therefore the release provided by Sarty's race to warn DeSpain is hard for them to acknowledge.
>
> Ab is pride alone, with no humility. He is devoured by pride's corrosive force, he rejects the Providential, denies the primacy of the social bond. In contrast, his son lives with, and out of, the given. Though an independent moral force, all the more splendid in this context, Sarty defines his situation within history and responds to kindness, to beauty, and to whatever good examples he can find, reaching out to what answers best to his essential self. Hence, he does more than withdraw from Snopes. Rather, he sorts out certain parts of his heritage from other elements he cannot use. In the terms Faulkner uses to judge Isaac McCaslin of *Go Down, Moses*, Sarty says, "I'm going to do something about it." This is what makes of his experience, as rendered in this wonderfully made narrative, so appropriate an introduction to Faulkner's collected stories.

Bradford calls Sarty "a supporter of the larger family that is community and a protector of right order" and, in this later essay, contrasts the boy with the self-deluding abstractionist Ike McCaslin, thereby linking "Barn Burning" with the larger body of Faulkner's work. Thus the essay, which submits to the inviolability of the text, also reaches out to embrace other texts, thereby shedding much-needed light on the whole of Faulkner's work.

I would like to suggest that it was not merely Davidson and the Agrarian tradition that taught Bradford to understand the highly complicated nature of a traditional society—its predictable intricacies and its capacity for unexpected grace. It was also William Faulkner, a writer who lacked a discursive mind and was singularly naive about politics. An analogue of reality is better than a map. The literary artist creates such analogues, and the critic maps them for the reader. If the analogue is rich and evocative, then the map must be complicated in order to be true and useful.

It was in the mapping of such complexities in the works of Faulkner, I suspect, that Mel Bradford developed his own paradigm of the normative society—a society both fair and hierarchical, though with a shoulder-shrugging accommodation to radical imperfection. You see this society mirrored in the prose of both Faulkner and Bradford—a language whose diction and syntax intimidate the readers of Dr. Seuss and Ernest Hemingway alike.

The world of Hemingway—a remarkably fine writer—is one you can see and hear and touch. Its discrete realities are strung together by coordinate conjunctions. Its adjectives are as concrete as its nouns. In such a world, subordination and abstraction are absent, mirroring its lack of hierarchical values, its essential agnosticism. Any universal principle whose spaceship crashed on that planet would die of starvation.

But Faulkner's prose—and Bradford's—is full of subordinate clauses, which embody precisely and fully a world crowded with competing virtues and values, which must be sorted out and put in their proper places, each one more or less important than another. Such subordination implies the old theological truth that sin is the deliberate choice of the lesser of two goods. Such a prose is never, by definition, mindlessly egalitarian.

As for all those abstract nouns and adjectives, by their very nature they imply the existence of a reality that transcends what can be seen and touched and heard. Such words immediately signal a level of belief unavailable in the works of many other writers—and they also demand more attention and more exercise of conscience from the reader. Richard Weaver once wrote that Milton's prose was heroic and demanded an heroic reader. The same could be said of William Faulkner's and Mel Bradford's.

IN THIS OVERSIMPLIFIED VIEW of Bradford's literary criticism, I have tried to touch on those elements that influenced his later political commentary. Some of them are obvious: the careful attention to the rhetoric of the text, its diction and syntax, a special angle of vision on the historical and social milieu in which texts like the Constitution were written, a shrewd awareness of the audience that a man like Thomas Jefferson intended to address in writing the Declaration, and the ability to worry a single word into new and startling clarity. These are the weapons of the New Critic—with extra ammunition provided by Donald Davidson and Bradford's own imaginative journey into Faulkner's Yoknapatawpha County.

For anyone who views Mel Bradford's literary criticism as mere prelude to the more important work of political and social commentary, let me offer a cautionary word. Literary works always outlast political regimes, probably because every social order contains within it the genetic code that mandates old age and death, while the greatest literature always celebrates what is perennially and immitigably true. Our current attempt to enshrine equality and freedom as political absolutes will surely finish us. We are now in the midst of a civil war in which the opposing sides are not identifiable by region or party or even family. Sworn enemies live under the same rooftop and pass the cream across the breakfast table. And successive terms of George Bush and Bill Clinton and George II may have brought us to the point where discussions of the U.S. Constitution are irrelevant.

But William Faulkner will surely survive all this predictable decay, and so will those who have understood and written about the lasting virtues of his work. I can imagine a time in the distant future, perhaps 200 years from now, when a university professor will assign his graduate students not only the novels of Faulkner, but also, as a matter of course, the standard commentary by the great literary critic Melvin E. Bradford. I can imagine this professor saying to his class, in an effort to put a face on the subject, that the great Bradford was reputed to be a large man—over three hundred pounds; that in the winter he wore a cowboy hat and an Inverness cape; that he was perpetually late to class; that he believed passionately in the integrity of history and language; that he never compromised nor retreated—not once—even in the guise of prudence; that he was generous to his enemies; that his jokes were most often at his own expense; that he vastly underestimated the value of his achievement; that he was a kind and forgiving friend; that he died much too young; and that—as a small footnote to his scholarly career—he also wrote essays about a now-defunct nation called the United States of America.

# Bradford's Argument on "Continuing Revolution"

**M**EL BRADFORD ALWAYS INSISTED—contrary to one of his mentors, Richard Weaver—that the argument from circumstance was superior to the argument from definition. To use a religious analogy, he believed that truth was only knowable through its imperfect incarnation, that as finite beings we could only understand God the Father through God the Son. Or to put it in philosophical terms, he was more a Thomist than a Neoplatonist.

With this temperament—this way of looking at the world—Bradford not only distrusted abstractions like "equality," but questioned their essential integrity when used as absolutes in the political realm. For this reason alone—and quite apart from the grim resonances it had for a latter-day Southerner—Bradford could only see the Gettysburg Address as either a rhetorical parlor trick or else a dangerous exercise in blasphemy—someone pretending to be God the Father for theatrical effect, or someone who really *believed* he was God the Father. He saw in the biblical cast of phrases like "four score and seven years ago" or "our fathers" an attempt on Lincoln's part to cloak himself in the divine mantle of scriptural authority—to speak with the voice of God.

To such a charge, Lincoln's press agent might well reply, "Such a phrase was just Abe's way of catching the crowd's attention—a trope to wake up Grandma." Or, "Everybody talked like that when they made political speeches. People in the 19th century didn't take you seriously unless you sounded like a preacher." There's a good deal of truth in such statements, but you can't have it both ways. Either you trivialize the language of political discourse and say that, like a campaign promise, it is only good until sundown; or else you say that Lincoln's address is an eloquent and profound definition of the meaning of the American experience. If you choose the latter, then you have to deal with Bradford.

He was perfectly willing to take Lincoln seriously, not as a political philosopher but as a rhetor—a skillful and self-conscious crafter of language, less than Aristotle but more than Jimmy Carter. If you make this assumption, then you must be willing to submit to all its corollaries and implications. At this point, Lincoln is on his own, with none of the exemptions generally accorded to everyday discourse. Or, to put it more precisely—the

Gettysburg Address is on its own. It can no longer rock along on the beauty of its own cadences or cuddle up in the warm blanket of some vague piety. It must grow up and take the GRE.

Thus Bradford finds in the address the prescription for a society based on unattainable abstractions like "equality"—and therefore a people whose expectations are doomed to remain unsatisfied, a Union forever in a state of becoming. He believes Lincoln invented this Union, at least for the popular imagination, and that his ideological construct is like a computer virus, always overwriting the concrete data of everyday experience.

AT FIRST GLANCE, such a proposition seems extravagant, at best academic muttering that has little relevance to the real world, like the Kinsey Report. In fact, there is some evidence that what Bradford says can be proved in the discourse of realpolitik, where Lincoln's "new nation," reborn every Friday afternoon, thrives like a sunflower.

Consider the fact that George H.W. Bush—a New England rich boy with a middle-management soul—spoke throughout his cautious and unremarkable presidency of "America's continuing revolution." And what can we suppose he thought he meant by such a phrase, tossed off as casually and as confidently as a call for world peace? And why is it more respectable these days to commend the "continuing American revolution" than it is to endorse Mom and apple pie? Momhood is currently a dangerous idea to embrace, thanks to the feminists, and all pie, the health police tell us, is bad for the heart. Mr. Lincoln's Union spends tens of millions of dollars annually to prevent women from becoming moms, and poor Mrs. Smith is now compelled to put warning labels on her apple pies. Yet George Bush can talk about the "continuing American revolution" without a word of criticism from either the *Washington Post* or *National Review*.

Revolution? Against what? Against the current political regime, our representative form of government? Of course, George Bush doesn't mean anything so radical or so brave, nor do any of the hundreds of other politicians and journalists who enunciate this phrase carefully, soberly—as if they coined it. Somehow we are all revolutionaries together, and we are all revolting against the order we have created—so no one has cause to be upset. (It's like the old New Deal argument against taking the national debt too seriously: We owe it only to ourselves.)

Bradford tells us that the "American revolution continues" because, as Lincoln suggested in the Gettysburg Address, its goal is nothing less than perfection. This goal, he says, is a "millennialist impulse"—one that contradicts the "sensible inertia" built into the history of the nation by its Founding

Fathers. He characterizes Lincoln's vision in the address as one that labors to "abolish time, repeal contingency." He characterizes it as "this gnostic aggression against Being."

Here he is using Eric Voegelin's analysis of modern ideology to place the millennialist movement, and by implication Lincoln and those "secular puritans" who follow him. He goes on to say:

> Millennialism can mean no other thing today—and always moves
> from an ontological reaction against the distance separating,
> by definition, creation and Maker; moves into either a "pulling
> up" or a "pulling down." With it we worship ourselves; falsify,
> and then forget our birthright. Variety, structure, measure, and
> any form of differentiated order are likewise millennialism's en-
> emies—the original bill of things as written for our tenure in this
> place of test and trial.

There is something almost suicidal in Bradford's own rhetoric here. Invoking Voegelin incurs risk enough from certain quarters, but Voegelin is at least intellectually respectable. A phrase like "this place of test and trial" is not merely religious, but derives from a specific Protestant heritage, echoes the language of the two Great Awakenings, and is found in a number of hardshell Baptist hymns Bradford probably heard and sang in his youth.

IN USING SUCH LANGUAGE, he knew the risks and chose to accept them. By implication, he was calling Lincoln a heretic and blaming him and his followers for the secularization of American society that has resulted in the breakdown of order and the redefinition of morality in our own time. It was no surprise to him that, by the 1960's, Christians were engaged in fierce theological quarrels over issues; or that, by the 1980's, mainline churches were beginning to look with fine impartiality on all forms of sexual behavior, including adultery and fornication, and to ordain lesbians—in almost every case, responding to an external egalitarian rhetoric that challenged the validity of Scripture and impugned the fairness of the biblical God.

It is important to understand that Bradford is not talking here about mere opposition to slavery—or, for that matter, to racial segregation, or to equal pay for equal work. In this essay, as in others on Lincoln, the substance of those issues is beyond his chosen purview. He is talking about the nature of the rhetoric and dialectic that Lincoln and others have used in support of their political goals. To suggest that he is motivated by racism or that this essay is an oblique defense of slavery is to resort to logical fallacies. His motives are irrelevant, and his argument is no more a defense of slavery than it is a defense of John Calvin. *Argumentum ad hominem* and *non sequitur*, as popular as they are in current political discourse, are still dishonest ways to respond to legitimate scholarly debate.

# Mel Bradford, Old Indian Fighters, and the NEH

**I**N POLITICS, THE DEAD CAN NEVER REST IN PEACE. The survivors fight over the bodies, the way the Achaeans and Trojans fought over the body of Hector. Mel Bradford died ten years ago [in 1993], and those of us who knew him best are finally reconciled to his death. However, when his detractors insist on exhuming his memory in order to kick him one more time, we find it difficult to remain silent. Thus, this reply to an article David Frum wrote recently for *National Review Online*.

In his commentary, Mr. Frum briefly discusses the attempt on the part of Mel's friends to see him appointed chairman of the National Endowment for the Humanities. The year was 1981. Mel and I were colleagues at the University of Dallas. I was his closest friend. At the time all this happened, Mr. Frum was a Yale undergraduate, hunched over one of the tables down at Mory's, humming the Whiffenpoof Song. So his article is clearly based on the campfire tales of old neocon Indian fighters.

He writes:

> But as the paleos themselves tell the story, the quarrel that erupted into view that day in 1986 began as a squabble over jobs and perks in the Reagan Administration—from the perception that, as [Sam] Francis later put it, neoconservatives had arranged matters so that "their team should get the rewards of office and of patronage and that the older team of the older Right receive virtually nothing."
>
> A quick reality check here: It is not in fact true that the ambitions of the paleos fell victim to neocon plots. Paleo Grievance Number 1 is the case of Mel Bradford, a gifted professor at the University of Dallas, now dead. Bradford had hoped to be appointed chairman of the National Endowment for the Humanities, but lost out to William Bennett. Unfortunately for him, Bradford came to the government hiring window with certain disadvantages: He had worked on the George Wallace campaign in 1968, and he had published an essay that could plausibly be read to liken Abraham Lincoln to Hitler.

First, for what it's worth, the Wallace connection was never a big issue. In a 1981 *New York Times* story, Irvin Molotsky reported that the neoconservatives' "criticism of Professor Bradford includes his support in 1972 of the Presidential candidacy of former Gov. George C. Wallace and his disapproval of Lincoln, which they view as especially inappropriate given Lincoln's role as the nation's first Republican President." So it was the neocons themselves who brought up the Wallace issue in the *Times*. And that's the last we heard of it.

In fact, we were surprised that they had missed the juiciest part of the story: Mel had been Dallas County chairman of George Wallace's American Party in 1968—a potentially more damaging involvement than his 1972 role in the Dallas County Democratic Party (which liberal columnist Ron Calhoun would later say Bradford had single-handedly destroyed).

When the neocons dropped the Wallace strategy, we knew it had failed. Perhaps they understood the degree to which Reagan's victory had depended on Wallace Democrats, who might be provoked to intervene on Bradford's behalf. And perhaps the neocon field officers decided not to press the theme of other-party affiliation because, according to our sources in North Carolina, Bill Bennett, Bradford's rival, had voted in the Democratic primary in 1980. To cover Bennett in this matter, a prominent supporter, a former Nixon cabinet member, had written a letter stating that Bennett had backed Reagan all the way. If our sources were correct, he hadn't even voted for Reagan in the GOP primary; and revelation of that fact would have exposed the former cabinet member's gracious fib.

Whatever the reason, the opposition never really tried to hang Wallace around Bradford's neck; and if any of those old Indian fighters remember differently, I believe they are mistaken.

THE SECOND CHARGE—the comparison of Abraham Lincoln to Hitler—is a bit more complicated than Mr. Frum leads us to believe. Harry Jaffa, in one of his several debates with Bradford, praised Lincoln for believing in higher law. When Mel showed me Jaffa's article, I remarked that belief in higher law was not conclusive evidence of virtue, that Hitler had expressed the same belief in *Mein Kampf*. Bradford, in replying to Jaffa, made the point in a footnote.

In reporting what happened next, I choose to omit the names of those involved, though I remember them well. Instead, I will use obvious pseudonyms to avoid the kind of ritual denials that would force me to name my Washington sources, several of whom are prominent in the conservative movement and still do business with the neocons.

The head of the Office of Presidential Personnel at the time was a

California car dealer who, when the word "Lincoln" was mentioned, probably thought first of the automobile. Certainly he was ill equipped to follow the kind of complex and meticulous argument found in Bradford's reply to Jaffa. A man I will call "The Great Manipulator," a supporter of Bennett, took advantage of this intellectual paucity.

According to our sources, instead of saying that Bradford had compared Lincoln to Hitler, as Mr. Frum suggests, the Great Manipulator told the Car Salesman that Bradford had compared Hitler to Lincoln. "You see, this man admires Hitler. He even compares him to Lincoln." At some point in this conversation, we were told, the word "antisemitism" was used. The Car Salesman's pulse quickened. He read the footnote. By George, Bradford did admire Hitler.

The injustice of this slander, which came late in the game, finally broke Bradford's will to continue. I remember standing with him on the balcony of UD's Braniff Building a few minutes after we had received an account of this latest attack. For a moment, he stared out at the mesquite trees surrounding the campus, then shook his head.

"I'm through. If they want it bad enough to do something like this, then let them have it."

This wasn't the first time the Car Salesman had misread Bradford's work. Earlier in the process, he had summoned Bradford to the Old Executive Office Building and waved the professor's 15-page bibliography under his nose.

"The trouble is, you've published too much. Too many targets. Take this thing you wrote about homosexuals."

Bradford said he had written nothing about homosexuals.

"What's this, then?"

The Car Salesman ran his forefinger down the lengthy list of items, one page after another, until he found the item he was looking for. Then he passed the bibliography across the desk and jabbed at a line.

"There."

The listing was an article on Bishop Richard Corbet[t]'s "The Fairies Farewell"—a light 17th-century lyric about the loss of belief in the supernatural.

Bradford burst out laughing—a tactical error.

The Car Salesman was indignant.

Bradford attempted to placate him by explaining that the poem was not about homosexuals, but about literal fairies, the kind that fly around on gossamer wings and do good deeds—e.g., the tooth fairy. It was like trying to explain trigonometry to a cat.

After this incident, we wondered if the Great Manipulator had put the notion about homosexuals into the Car Salesman's head or if the Car Salesman had thought of it all by himself. One thing was apparent: With the Car Salesman in charge, Bennett's considerably shorter bibliography was an asset rather than a liability.

**Mr. Frum writes further of Bradford**: "Bradford could never accept that it was his own writings that had doomed him. As Oscar Wilde observed, 'Misfortunes one can endure. They come from outside, they are accidents. But to suffer for one's own faults—ah! There is the sting of life.' Easier to blame others and pity oneself."

When and where did Mel Bradford blame others and express self-pity? How about one example? He was appalled at the battle tactics his opponents had used, but he knew he had spent most of his adult life providing them with ammunition. Indeed, he understood better than anyone the liabilities his political opinions incurred—the academic appointments he was denied, the department chairmanship he had lost years earlier, the journals in which he could never publish, the conferences he was never invited to attend. (The University of Dallas trustees even delayed his promotion to full professor for a year because of his politics.) None of this surprised him.

Many years earlier—as a Vanderbilt graduate student—he had consciously made the choice that led inevitably to the succession of professional catastrophes that plagued his life. He had chosen to stand with the losing side, knowing full well what it had cost his intellectual mentors in the way of honors, academic advancement, and cold cash.

He did not, as others did, switch sides after the Reagan victory in 1980. In fact, he had supported Reagan in 1976.

Nor did he hold a grudge, as Mr. Frum suggests. In fact, when Bill Bennett was mentioned as a candidate to succeed Terrel Bell as secretary of education, Mel was contacted to see if he would speak out against his former rival. He replied that he thought Bennett would be a good choice for the job.

It was typical of his generous nature; but the response exasperated many of his friends, who, in this instance, wanted to see less of Jesus and more of Grendel. He had a magnanimous heart where adversaries and detractors were concerned, whether in intellectual debate, partisan politics, or campus quarrels. He forgave trespasses quicker than any man I've ever known.

So I find it singularly unfair that—ten years after Bradford's death—Mr. Frum, who never knew him, would turn him into a neocon caricature in order to make points in a current dispute. Indeed, I wonder if Mr. Frum really believes what he wrote on *National Review Online*. In a 1989 *Wall*

*Street Journal* article, "Cultural Clash on the Right," he tells a somewhat different story:

> [I]t is true that bad feeling between loyalists who trace their conservatism back to 1984 and beyond . . . and those who arrived at their conservatism later has festered ever since the great internal fight over the proposed 1980 [*sic*] nomination of M.E. Bradford . . . to the chairmanship of the National Endowment for the Humanities. Lobbying by Edwin Feulner, president of the Heritage Foundation, William F. Buckley, Jr. and Irving Kristol persuaded the Reagan transition team to nominate William Bennett instead.

So which was it? Did Bradford's political activism and anti-Lincoln sentiments cause his downfall, or was it the persuasive powers of Messrs. Feulner, Buckley, and Kristol? The clever answer to that question is "a little bit of both." However, the more you think about it, the more that explanation fails to convince. If Bradford's acts and opinions alone brought him down, then why credit persuasion? And if persuasion turned the tide, then couldn't one reasonably blame the persuaders, as Sam Francis did?

Besides, I find "persuaded" too benign a word to describe what Bradford's opponents did to defeat him. Here are just a few examples, most of them reported to us by friends inside the Beltway.

Neocons enlisted the support of a University of Dallas colleague who furnished them with passages, violently wrenched from Mel's writings, which the Great Manipulator passed around the Old Executive Office Building. The collection was entitled "Quotes From Chairman Mel"—an arch allusion to a volume of quotes by that old paleo Mao Tse-tung. By an extraordinary coincidence, the colleague who supplied this information ended up working for Bennett at the National Endowment for the Humanities.

Bennett's partisans called the UD English Department and pumped the secretary for negative gossip about Bradford. She refused to give them anything—in large part because there was nothing to give. But they called her again and again, day after day, until she finally began hanging up on them.

According to our sources, the Great Manipulator padded up and down the halls of the Old Executive Office Building, telling everyone from the Vice President to the janitor that Bradford had a meager bibliography and that most of the items were from obscure Southern journals. In fact, Bradford's bibliography was almost as long as the Mississippi River—and included publications from all over the country. One of those obscure Southern journals was *The Sewanee Review*, considered by many to be the most prestigious literary quarterly in the English language. Another was *The Southern Review*, which routinely published works by Pulitzer Prize winners.

The Great Manipulator repeatedly warned the Car Salesman that Bradford would be rejected by the Senate in a nasty floor fight, thereby embarrassing the new President. Aware of this ploy, Bradford's Washington supporters, including the late Sen. John East, visited a number of offices and compiled a dossier of letters signed by, according to someone involved, at least 32 senators, pledging their support to Bradford—Democrats as well as Republicans. These letters were sent to the Office of Presidential Personnel and placed in Bradford's folder. A few days later, they were gone. (Washington insiders called it "stripping the files.") Bradford's supporters told us that the likely culprit was Sneaky Sal, who was an ally of the Great Manipulator and worked in the Old Executive Office Building. Undaunted, Bradford's people went around to all of the offices and again obtained signed letters. A few days later, Sneaky Sal apparently struck again. The second batch of letters disappeared. So a third time, Bradford's supporters made the rounds of senatorial offices and gathered signed pledges of support.

In the end, such tactics prevailed. Since Mel had been vulnerable because of his publications—Antifederalist, pro-Southern, anti-Lincoln—perhaps an honest, straightforward opposition would have won the day for the neocons, as Mr. Frum, in his latest version, suggests it did. But they just weren't willing to take that chance. Hence the "gutter tactics," "hardball," "persuasion,"— whatever Mr. Frum wants to call it.

In 1981, a Washington supporter suggested that we do the same kind of hatchet job on Bennett—who, to our knowledge, had behaved well throughout the struggle and had never engaged in Bradford-bashing. Mel vetoed the idea. In the end, he agreed with Will Rogers, who said, "I'd rather be the man who bought the Brooklyn Bridge than the man who sold it." I can't help but wonder if Mr. Frum and all those old Indian fighters could possibly understand such a remark.

TWELVE YEARS AFTER THE NEH SQUABBLE, Mel Bradford died in a South Texas hospital during an emergency operation to repair a severely damaged heart. Alarmingly overweight, he had suffered a coronary while attending a conservative conference. When I heard he had been hospitalized, I called him. The surgery was scheduled for the next morning. His voice was strong, and he was in good spirits. We talked for about ten minutes. Both of us knew this might be our last conversation. (Earlier that day I had taken a dark suit to the cleaners.)

Then, just before we hung up, he said to me, "If I go out tomorrow, I'll go without any bitterness in my heart. I'm at peace with everybody."

He was not necessarily talking about the Great Manipulator or those who had participated in the various machinations to block his nomination. However, if they were on his mind that night, I'm sure he meant to include them in this blanket absolution. When you're about to die, you can't be bothered with irrelevant matters like the National Endowment for the Humanities.

But what about those of us who are left behind? How should we respond to these renewed attacks? The Christians among us have it on the Highest Authority that we are to forgive our enemies. Whether or not we have the duty (or even the right) to forgive the enemies of our friends is a more complicated question. If a friend is maligned or patronized when he is no longer present to defend himself, perhaps we should turn the other cheek. But then it isn't our cheek that's been slapped, is it?

I'm surprised that this matter has surfaced again. No one has anything to gain by keeping the quarrel alive. The neocons have all the power and visibility and resources they yearned for in 1981. The paleos have been marginalized to the point where their opinions, given voice by a shrinking number of publications, are depicted as scandalous by the left and by such people as Mr. Frum.

The neocons are too busy running the world to tilt with Mel Bradford.

The paleos, in the Era of Political Correctness, risk calumny every time they open their mouths, particularly in defense of the dead.

Besides, what we're really debating here is not substance but form, what is considered "proper" as opposed to what is intellectually true. Simply put, the neocons did things we were taught not to do. Apparently they were taught differently. Today, folks call that "diversity."

At this late date, the neocons' best rhetorical ploy is not to rewrite history but to say, "So what? We won, you lost"—precisely what William Tecumseh Sherman might have told Southern civilians whose farms he ordered burned and whose family members he ordered randomly shot. (It was Sherman who said, "The only good Indian is a dead Indian.")

That kind of response would silence us, since we would be left with no common ground on which to pursue the debate. But let's hear no more of noble Indian fighters and paleo self-pity. We could say a lot more on those subjects. And we will, if sufficiently provoked.

# Harry Jaffa and the Historical Imagination

IN THE 1970'S, Mel Bradford and I were teaching at the University of Dallas, which offered a doctoral program in politics and literature. Students took courses in both disciplines. It was a well-designed curriculum and produced some first-rate scholars.

Bradford had long been interested in political theory, but the program probably encouraged him to read more extensively in this area and to write articles and (eventually) books on the subject. In fact, the time arrived when he had published more commentary on political matters than the entire politics department. His articles on Abraham Lincoln—only four—caused the greatest stir, since, in them, he explicated texts in a way that revealed a Lincoln incompatible with the iconic figure on the penny and five-dollar bill.

When Bradford had become, as he ironically put it, "unbearably distinguished," the head of the politics department arranged a formal debate on the subject of Lincoln and slavery: established scholar Harry Jaffa *versus* upstart Mel Bradford. Mel and I suspected that the true purpose of the occasion was to humiliate him in front of the UD student body and send him yelping into the bushes, tail between his legs.

I don't remember who kicked off the debate; but once under way, it took an unexpected turn. What was supposed to be a Jaffa-dominated exchange became, instead, a Bradford-dominated history lesson. Jaffa would offer abstractions about slavery in the South, and Bradford would correct him by citing primary historical sources (tax records, census reports, studies of wills filed in county courthouses)—evidence unknown to the faculty of Claremont. The audience might well have concluded that Bradford had read everything published on the subject, while Jaffa had read little more than the Lincoln-Douglas debates and the Declaration of Independence.

Jaffa, unfazed by this barrage of erudition, continued to counter facts with generalities. He apparently agreed with fellow Straussian Henry Ford, who once said, "History is bunk." I am sure Jaffa's admirers believed he won the debate that night. I doubt that anyone else in that huge crowd thought so.

The dynamic of the exchange between Bradford and Jaffa exposed for that audience the tendency of Straussians to dismiss any attention to the full historical context of a political document as "historicism," a form of relativism. Societies are transient; principles are eternal. It is dangerous to tie a document such as the Declaration of Independence to the time in which it was written. You might be snatched up by the Spirit of the Age and swallowed whole.

Yet, if we are to understand texts, history—composed of the particularities of time and place—is essential, if only to clothe bare-bones abstractions with flesh and blood. Like God, abstract truth is best understood when incarnate. Facts worry principles into shape, kneading them like biscuit dough. If principles are true, their substance remains unchanged.

More to the point, people who ignore history while finding Truth in political documents presume that they can transcend their own temporal and cultural limitations. It is bad enough to believe that past political texts were written not for the people of that age but for the gods. It is even worse to presume that you are one of those gods. When Archimedes said, "Give me a fulcrum and a place to stand, and I will move the whole world," he knew he would never have to make good on his boast. Straussians, however, believe they have found such a place, where they can transcend the limitations of time and culture to do what Archimedes could only dream of doing.

Thomas Hoving, former director of the Metropolitan Museum of Art, tells of passing the museum's Tang horse daily and viewing it with growing suspicion. Acquired in the 19th century as an authentic piece from the Tang dynasty (A.D. 618-906), the horse—to Hoving's educated eye—began to look more and more Victorian. On a hunch, he had it tested and found that, sure enough, it was a 19th-century fake.

The piece had fooled earlier experts because they were prisoners of their Victorian sensibilities, unable to see their own unique age in the lines of the counterfeit horse. Because he was trained to do so, Hoving could see both the genuine Tang elements and the Victorian overlay.

WILL SCHOLARS IN THE LATE 21ST CENTURY be able to see the late 20th-century bias in the godlike pronouncements of Jaffa and his disciples? Surely they will. Too many believe that all Dead White Males of consequence anticipated Francis Fukuyama in advocating some form of liberal democracy—the best Greek philosophers and historians, Shakespeare, even Machiavelli. Thus, the Ashbrook Center describes Leo Paul de Alvarez's argument in *The Machiavellian Enterprise* as follows: "As the 'first political philosopher to turn to the many instead of the few as the basis of rule,' claims de Alvarez, Machiavelli sought to replace the domination of the Christian Rome with a civil, secular, and egalitarian state."

This Fukuyavellian imposition of the Straussian political paradigm on the works of earlier writers is nothing less than a war on the past, with the ultimate goal to reduce it to rubble, plow it under, and sow salt on it. Yet, like the past, a text has an integrity all its own, a unique identity derived in large measure from the denotation of words, their connotations, and their historical context. If you are not attentive to these elements, a key word can undergo significant transmutation right before your uncomprehending eyes. Take, for example, the poem "Lapis Lazuli," by William Butler Yeats, which begins:

> I have heard that hysterical women say
> They are sick of the palette and fiddle-bow.
> Of poets that are always gay.

You can readily imagine what a current student at Brown University would make of these lines in a term paper entitled "Yeats and Female Homophobia." The poem deserves to be read in its original language rather than in the debased rhetoric of contemporary sexual politics, and that older language can only be recovered by adopting an historical perspective toward the text—easy enough to do with a poem this recent; not so easy, perhaps, in 100 years.

The typical Straussian refuses to submit to the formidable complexities of the past. After all, it is comfortable and self-serving to hear your own beliefs echoed in the voice of Shakespeare. So you treat the Bard as if he were living next door to you, mowing his lawn on weekends, fighting rush-hour traffic, listening to the Dixie Chicks.

Sometimes, however, you run across language that runs contrary to your Fukuyavellian thesis—and in the most embarrassing places. Take Harry Jaffa's problem with the rhetoric of Abraham Lincoln, who, he argues, refounded America as a nation informed by the principle of equality. Jaffa believes Lincoln hoped to create an egalitarian society in which blacks and whites would live together without prejudice. Lincoln's words tell a different story. Here is an excerpt from his debate with Stephen Douglas, held at Ottawa, Illinois, on August 21, 1858:

> I have no purpose to introduce political and social equality
> between the white and the black races. There is a physical dif-
> ference between the two, which in my judgment will probably
> forever forbid their living together upon the footing of perfect
> equality, and inasmuch as it becomes a necessity that there must
> be a difference, I, as well as Judge Douglas, am in favor of the
> race to which I belong having the superior position. I have never
> said anything to the contrary, but I hold that, notwithstanding all
> this, there is no reason in the world why the negro is not entitled

to all the natural rights enumerated in the Declaration of Independence, the right to life, liberty and the pursuit of happiness. [Loud cheers.]

I hold that he is as much entitled to these as the white man. I agree with Judge Douglas he is not my equal in many respects—certainly not in color, perhaps not in moral or intellectual endowment.

In the same speech, Lincoln reassured the crowd that Southerners would not use force to impose blacks on Illinois, which had earlier outlawed their very presence: "There is no danger," he said, "that the people of Kentucky will shoulder their muskets, and, with a young nigger stuck on every bayonet, march into Illinois and force them upon us."

As for Jaffa's egalitarian dream, Lincoln undercut such an idea in his 1857 speech on the *Dred Scott* case. Here, he came out in favor of shipping blacks off to Africa to prevent miscegenation. ("I have said that the separation of the races is the only perfect preventive of amalgamation.") He admits that "colonization" (an Orwellian term) will be a daunting task, but that the Power of Positive Thinking can work to overcome the obstacles: "Such separation, if ever effected at all, must be effected by colonization; and no political party, as such, is now doing anything directly for colonization. Party operations at present only favor or retard colonization incidentally. The enterprise is a difficult one; but 'where there is a will there is a way'; and what colonization needs most is a hearty will."

**So how does Jaffa deal with these statements?** He does what Straussians too often do when the text they have brought to obedience school turns on them and bares its fangs: They find hidden meaning in the work ("secret writing") or simply stand it on its head. The author seems to be saying one thing but is actually saying another. Passages that appear to be straightforward are, instead, ironic, and only the explicator can read the coded message tucked between the lines. Machiavelli was really a moderate democrat. When Mark Antony says, "This was the noblest Roman of them all," he doesn't mean a word of it. In a similar circumvention of the obvious, Jaffa says Lincoln made these remarks only because such rhetoric was necessary to be elected in racist Illinois. When Joe Sobran took Lincoln's statements about race at face value, Jaffa reproved him for not taking history into account: "To understand this however requires some historical imagination—putting oneself in the place of someone in an earlier age—something Sobran seems unable to do."

For a scholar with Straussian contempt for history, Jaffa has his nerve. It is not that he fails to make use of historical facts while creating his fairy tale. In his work, facts are more numerous than the sands of the desert. He recites names, dates, and events as readily as a bright third grader recites the multiplication tables. But his imagination is by no means historical. It refuses to submit to history. It is predatory. It possesses the past, driving out its true spirit, reconfiguring its soul.

Almost anyone can imagine that Lincoln might adapt his campaign rhetoric to the prejudices of those whose vote he was seeking. However, no one with a submissive historical imagination could attribute to a mid-19th-century politician the kind of egalitarian sensibilities that Jaffa has attributed to Abraham Lincoln, particularly given Lincoln's comments on the subject of equality and his careful delineation of its limits. The real Lincoln, as opposed to Jaffa's 20th-century Lincoln, would never have been so moonstruck as to believe in the 1850's that he could actually implement such an anachronistic plan.

Also, if Lincoln lied about his racial views, can we not, through the exercise of our historical imaginations, conclude that he also lied about his opposition to slavery? After all, to run against Stephen Douglas, he had to oppose its extension. Douglas had authored the Kansas-Nebraska Act, which overrode the Missouri Compromise and allowed slavery to expand. Had Lincoln not taken the opposite position, he would have had no significant issue to differentiate himself from the popular incumbent senator.

Frederick Douglass—Abraham Lincoln's contemporary and, therefore, a man who, in evaluating the Great Emancipator, had no need for an historical imagination—said at the dedication of a memorial to the fallen president:

> He was preeminently the white man's President, entirely devoted to the welfare of white men. He was ready and willing at any time during the first years of his administration to deny, postpone, and sacrifice the rights of humanity in the colored people to promote the welfare of the white people in this country. . . . He was ready to execute all the supposed guarantees of the United States Constitution in favor of the slave system anywhere inside the slave states. He was willing to pursue, recapture, and send back the fugitive slave to his master, and to suppress a slave rising for liberty, though his guilty master were already in arms against the Government.

Would it not be a proper exercise of the historical imagination to accept

Douglass's evaluation and admit that Lincoln harbored the prejudices of 19th-century white men from Illinois? Why not grant him a special insight into the injustice of plantation life, but stop short of turning him into a civil-rights leader, marching on Selma? The answer from Claremont is likely to be charges of bigotry, racism, and neoconfederacy.

YEARS AFTER THE LAST JAFFA-BRADFORD DEBATE, I dropped by the Free Congress Foundation in Washington to see Mike Schwartz, whom I had taught at the University of Dallas and who was then working with Paul Weyrich. On our way to Mike's office, we came into a room where Harry Jaffa was seated on a sofa, talking to a young woman. As we passed through, I heard her ask him, "But why would Bradford say such a thing?"

"Because," Jaffa replied, "he believes in slavery."

Shocked, I stopped.

"Why Harry, I never heard him say anything like that."

"That's because you don't know him as well as I do," he said with a smile. "If you were to get him behind closed doors and give him a drink or two, he'd tell you the same thing."

Mike burst out laughing, remembering that I was Mel Bradford's closest friend and that I knew precisely what he thought about slavery, which he once called in print the worst tragedy in our nation's history.

Was Jaffa simply lying? I don't think so. Straussians don't have to lie. They have the power to transform the written word into the image of their heart's desire. I presume they can do the same thing with people—remove them from their context, explicate them, transform them into what they really ought to be, as opposed to what they merely are. Jaffa knew in his heart that Bradford believed in slavery because whatever Bradford did tell him (behind closed doors after a couple of drinks) was something like secret writing, a sly way of saying one thing and meaning another. In the Straussian paradigm, Bradford had to have a whip in his hand, so Jaffa placed it there, just as he placed the "I Have a Dream" speech in the head of Abraham Lincoln.

# Outgrowing the Past:
# Eminent Domain Down South

**W**HEN THE U.S. SUPREME COURT ruled in the case of *Kelo* v. *City of New London*, a chill wind blew across the South. The Court upheld the decision of the city fathers of New London, Connecticut, to grant a private development corporation the right to condemn a middle-income residential neighborhood; evict the property owners; and construct a marina, high-rise office buildings, and upscale residential housing.

Thoughtful Southerners found *Kelo* particularly disturbing because, in their region, the developer is king—more admired and accommodated than football players or country-music singers. To pig-eyed mayors and councilmen, he is Moses, sent by the gods of getting-and-spending to lead the region out of Egypt. No candidate for local office has ever been elected by saying, "I don't want this place to grow. And if the bigwigs at General Motors try to move their headquarters and production plants down here, they'll do it over my dead body." Big is better. Small is embarrassing.

Megacities such as Atlanta and Memphis and Dallas aren't the only places where this ideology prevails. You can find it in the most out-of-the-way rural town. Take, for example, Blackville, South Carolina. According to the U.S. Census Bureau, in the year 2000, Blackville had a population of 2,973. The Census Bureau estimated the 2004 population at 2,935, a loss of 38 people, or 1.3 percent. However, a website maintained by Blackville realtors insists—against all evidence and reason—that the population is 5,149. It isn't a lie so much as a fond hope.

If you drive through the heart of that town, you will see a weather-ravaged building with a sign that urges tourists to stop and visit "Three Flags Over Blackville." You can be certain that the Devil is sitting inside, leaning back in his swivel chair, picking his teeth.

Over in the next county lies a town buried under coils of blackberry vines, kudzu, pine needles, fallen trees, rotten branches, oaks, and innumerable varieties of weeds. If you go there—and few people are allowed behind the high fences—you can see the remains of curbs, some wide places that used to be driveways, and one or two small bridges. The rest of the town exists only in memory. Today, it is called the Savannah River Nuclear Plant. Once it was called Ellenton.

IN 1951, the U.S. government, using its powers of eminent domain, condemned Ellenton and at least four other communities that lay along the Savannah River—Dunbarton, Meyers Mill, Hawthorne, and Robbins. President Truman announced that the action was taken in the interest of national defense. The word spread quickly: The feds intended to build a plant to manufacture heavy water for use in a hydrogen bomb. The government could have chosen a thousand other sites, but this was a town the politicians were willing to waste.

The residents were stunned, but they were too patriotic, too committed to the Cold War, to protest.

Most of the families lived on working farms. A few ran businesses: "the Long Store," so named because of its shape; Brinkley's grocery; and the Blue Goose, a tavern where, for generations, the men had congregated to forget quarrels with their wives, squalling children, and the boll weevil. Most Ellentonians regarded the condemnation as cataclysmic.

Administration spokesmen and South Carolina politicians maintained that, far from being a tragedy, the "taking" was actually the best thing that had ever happened to Ellenton. People would be paid handsomely for the land. They would move to nearby cities. They would get better jobs. It was the same pitch the city of New London made to Susette Kelo.

*Newsweek* parroted this argument in a brief article on the subject. The reporter and a photographer swooped into town, located the village idiot (every town has one) and his female counterpart, posed them in front of an abandoned farmhouse, and presented them to the nation as Ellenton gentry. Readers could see at a glance that these vacant-faced trolls would be much better off in Spartanburg or Greenville, working in a textile mill, making enough money to keep them in Moon Pies for the rest of their days.

The federal appraiser offered $20 per acre for the land and varying amounts for the buildings, some of which were good, sturdy farmhouses, several of which were antebellum showplaces. A case in point: For their spacious, five-bedroom clapboard farmhouse, the Dunbar family was offered $5,000. Combined with 800 acres of farmland—a good portion of it covered with timber almost ready to harvest—they received $21,000, just enough to build a three-bedroom, two-bath house in nearby Barnwell and for Otis Dunbar to buy his wife a half-carat diamond ring, a long-postponed engagement present. It was small compensation for land originally given to William Dunbar by a grateful King James II and farmed by Dunbar descendants until the federal government drove them off.

For decades after they left, the town lived on in the imagination of the dispossessed, lit by memory. But as the years passed, the lights went out one by one, as the older folks died. Today children who, 50 years ago, were snatched out of one world and plopped into another have grown old and forgetful. They have lost touch with one another and consequently with their shared past.

SOME ANECDOTES SURVIVE to commemorate that small, irretrievable world. Here are a few.

One late fall evening, long, long ago, three of their great-grandfathers came back from a hunting trip, ready for a hot meal. To warm themselves as they rode along on horseback, they had passed a jug of whiskey back and forth. When they reached the first house, servants told them that children from all three families had contracted bronchitis and that the women were congregated in one house to share the responsibilities of administering aspirin, reading stories, and applying mustard plasters. When the men came to the house much too late, the women and children had gone to bed. Only one gaslight burned feebly in a downstairs parlor. Full of spirits, they rode their horses up the steps and into the hallway.

The host dismounted and walked unsteadily into the dining room, where he found a bare table. He peered into the kitchen and saw two pots boiling on the stove. Both contained mustard plasters. Starved, the three tethered their horses on the hall tree, sat down at the kitchen table, and ate the mustard plasters.

No one could have made up that story, and it could never have survived the years in New York or Chicago or even Greenville. Southern literature has its origins in places like Ellenton. In just such a small town, William Faulkner sat on a bench and listened carefully as old-timers swapped tales.

Hollywood, terrified of rural America, typically depicts its inhabitants as cruel and insensitive to the suffering of others. Even in the worst of times, people in Ellenton took care of those who needed help, in part because, in a small town, the needy were so easy to identify. Sometimes it happened quite by accident.

Miss Mary Bush decided that she could no longer carry logs to the house from the woodpile, so she went into the field where her husband, Major, was working with several of the hands and called him aside. She told him she needed a boy to tote wood for her—not a child, but not a grown-up either. He thought for a minute and then said, "I know just the boy. That fellow that's living with the Ashleys. I'll send somebody to fetch him right now."

An hour or so later, Henry Todd showed up, the trace of a smile on his face. He was around 16 at the time, and he had a strong back. However, when you looked into his dull eyes, you could see he was "slow." But he worked hard, and he seemed pleased to be there. So instead of returning him to the Ashleys, with their permission the Bushes put him in a back room of the huge house, and he stayed with the family for some 60 years.

Everyone in Ellenton knew the Ashleys had been "hiding" him, though no one could say how he got there or precisely when he came. The talk was that they weren't hiding him *from* somebody but *for* somebody, a family that didn't want to acknowledge the existence of a retarded member, people with a public reputation to maintain. The Bushes may have extracted the truth from the Ashleys. Or they may have gained crucial knowledge from the boy himself, who was a moron, but not an idiot.

Whatever the means, at some point they learned that Todd was only his middle name. His last name—which his mortified family would not allow him to use—was Lincoln. According to what the Bushes found out, he was the unacknowledged son of Robert Todd Lincoln. Robert was the only child of Abraham Lincoln who lived to adulthood. So Henry Todd was the 16th president's grandson.

After he had lived with the Bushes a while, they made contact with a member of the Lincoln family—Mary Lincoln Beckwith, who was then living at Robert Todd Lincoln's estate house, Hildene, located in Vermont. Mary Beckwith acknowledged the family connection and from time to time contributed money toward Henry Todd's keep.

When he reached adulthood, he grew a beard, and his resemblance to his grandfather was striking. He was not tall, but he had the same dark hair, a long, brooding face, and sunken cheeks. People in Ellenton noted the resemblance.

No one called him "Henry," but always "Henry Todd." "Hey Henry Todd, how are you?" "Fine, how are you?" He said little more than that, perhaps because he couldn't articulate complicated ideas.

Indeed, he never grew up. When one of the Bushes would return from town, a middle-aged Henry Todd would run out to the car to see if they had brought him ice cream. When they hadn't, he would sit down in the middle of the driveway and weep uncontrollably.

When the federal government ordered them to leave Ellenton, the whole family moved to Walterboro—including Henry Todd. There they bought a restaurant and a motel, and Henry Todd did a little work for his keep; but by then he had grown old. Up in his 70's, he walked to town one day, perhaps to get some ice cream, and, in his usual daze, stepped in front of an automobile and was killed instantly.

**Thomas Dunbar,** who served as magistrate in Ellenton during antebellum times, appointed one of his slaves as his bailiff. Since the slave was illiterate, Judge Dunbar would read him the upcoming docket the night before, and the slave would memorize it and call out the names and cases flawlessly the next day.

During Reconstruction, Republicans saw to it that blacks took over many state and municipal offices in South Carolina. For Ellenton, the predominantly black legislature appointed Judge Dunbar's bailiff, now a freeman, as magistrate. The new judge immediately appointed his former master as *his* bailiff, and the two served in those roles for a decade, as if nothing much had changed.

A magistrate's court hears cases involving petty theft, simple assault, criminal domestic violence, public intoxication, and any other misdemeanor that carries a penalty of up to 30 days. Such arrangements could not have occurred in a full-blown city, North or South, since they depended not only on an infinitely subtle bond between two men of different races who knew and trusted each other, but on wholehearted acceptance by the entire community, both white and black. That acceptance could only have come about because people knew precisely with whom they were dealing.

The idea that a C is "a gentleman's grade" has been much misconstrued. Most academics believe it is a hangover from an earlier age when the stupid or lazy sons of landowners were given C's instead of F's because of who they were. The men of Ellenton knew better. Gentlemen got C's on purpose, to show they weren't bedazzled by the honors of this world. Tom Dunbar, namesake of the antebellum judge, was a brilliant scholar at the Citadel. He knew the answers to all questions, but he purposely answered only 7 of 10, to show he didn't care.

This attitude dates back to the Renaissance, and was part of the character of great courtiers, such as Sir Philip Sidney, who wrote *Astrophel and Stella*, one of the great Elizabethan sonnet sequences; defeated all comers at jousting; and was a world-class diplomat. He did it all with a studied carelessness called *sprezzatura*.

One fall semester, a young Dunbar made the dean's list at the Citadel. When the family gathered at Christmas time, several of the older men took him outside and, with angry faces, explained the rules to him. As a matter of propriety, Dunbars didn't make the dean's list. It never happened again.

**For many years,** the all-male Ellenton Agricultural Club had convened once a month at its own two-story wooden clubhouse, where members ate barbecued pork, hash, rice, slaw, peas, light bread, and pickles. (The menu was prescribed by the club's constitution.) At these meetings, held every fourth Saturday, attendees heard a 30-minute speech on farming. If the speaker ran over the allotted time, chairs would scrape the floor, and members would begin clearing their throats.

Eminent domain signaled the end of farming for most Ellentonians. Yet they couldn't completely surrender a way of life they had known for generations. So to maintain some sense of continuity with their past, members voted to move the clubhouse to Barnwell, where many of them intended to settle. They also moved Ethel, the black woman who prepared the barbecue, and provided her and her family with a place to live and an adequate income.

In Barnwell, they continued to hold monthly meetings, listen to talks on agriculture, and eat barbecued pork, hash, rice, slaw, peas, light bread, and pickles. No one ever discovered a penumbra in the constitution that justified serving something new, like Lobster Newberg on rusks. In an ever-changing world, constitutions ought to mean what they say.

Out of respect for the long dead—and because it's difficult to break an old habit—the club still meets every fourth Saturday in Barnwell.

UNLIKE ATLANTA or New London or Blackville, Ellenton never tried to grow. It was content to let nature take care of the population. If, at the end of a year, more citizens were born than died, the population increased slightly. If more folks died than were born, the population decreased slightly. A few people moved away, and a few moved in. The last thing the town worried about was importing industry and growing to the size of Babylon, whose citizens—as Aristotle noted—didn't know they had been conquered for three full days.

Then industry came to Ellenton unbidden, and the town ceased to exist. On former Dunbar land, the nuclear reactor, which today looks as stark and majestic as one of the pyramids, is no longer in operation. It stands like a tombstone over the dead and anonymous dreams of an almost-extinct people.

As an exercise of its sovereignty, the government insisted on moving all the graves that lay inside the condemned area. However, at least one remained and remains to this day—that of William Dunbar, who died in 1735. Though ordered to do so by government officials, his descendants refused to reveal the location of his remains. Today, he lies there in the shade of bearded oaks, blanketed by tall weeds and snarled vines, a lone holdout against America's proud and irresistible impulse to outgrow her own britches.

As his descendants were leaving Ellenton, trailers and trucks piled with sleigh beds, high-backed sofas, winged chairs, pianos, wood stoves, and all the detritus left behind by vanished generations, someone attached a square piece of wood to the town-limits sign. On it he scrawled this message: "It is hard to understand why our town must be destroyed to make a bomb that will destroy someone else's town that they love as much as we love ours. But we feel that they picked not just the best spot in the US, but in the world."

America—dressed in a three-piece suit, driving a fishtail Cadillac—flashed past that homemade sign without so much as a glance, rushing headlong toward empire and the wars that empire inevitably breeds. In our time, everything happens so fast. It took the Roman Empire centuries to fall to pieces. It took the British Empire decades. If we try hard enough, we can probably accomplish the same thing over a Labor Day weekend. We are certainly doing our damnedest.

This is happening in part because we have forgotten that towns like Ellenton—once scattered across the American landscape like so many stars—provided our people with a paradigm of truth, virtue, and beauty, insofar as such things can exist in a fallen world. The particularities of such communities are more difficult to preserve than the whooping crane or spotted owl—plowing with mules, hand-drawn wells, ten-row movie houses, dressing up to shop in the city, wooden churches, gas lamps, playing Go-In-and-Out-the-Window and Sling-the-Biscuit, hog-killing time, family cemeteries. Only the dead could possibly remember these things.

As for the quick—at least those of us who understand what has been lost—we mustn't take our decline and fall too seriously. We're not the first civilization to destroy itself in a fit of pride, nor will we be the last. To counterbalance the perennial recurrence of human catastrophe, we have it on the best authority that the Church will triumph, come what may, and that the Lamb will feed us, and lead us to the living fountains of waters: and God will wipe away all our tears.

# Speech at the Confederate Memorial, Arlington Cemetery

THIS MONUMENT, erected to the soldiers of the Confederacy on confiscated property, is singularly appropriate: classical in its lines, carved with a Latin allusion to Cato, situated in the midst of the infinitely patient dead. Jefferson Davis and the people over whom he presided modeled their conduct after the traditions of the Roman republic, which included a strong sense of piety toward family, country, and the gods as well as a commitment to the idea of political freedom.

Cato was a defender of that republic and a vocal opponent of Caesar; he feared the kind of "union" that Caesar was proposing, one built on the principles of central control and rigid conformity, both maintained by force of arms. When Cato, a stoic, was defeated on the field of battle and saw that Caesar was destined to rule, he took his own life. Jefferson Davis, a Christian, lived out his days as an object of national vilification. Both, according to their lights, were good losers; and though neither is well regarded in our own time, that fact is more a measure of modern society than of these two men, who fought so long and so magnificently to preserve the integrity of the past.

As for the dead, they are the same in any age, whether symmetrically arrayed, as in this national cemetery, or scattered like random stars in the darkness of country churchyards. They keep their own counsel. They remain obligingly uncritical. They manage a prudent silence on such questions as states' rights, slavery, the playing of Dixie, and the flying of the Confederate flag.

Renewal of the anti-Southern madness of the 1850's is a relatively new phenomenon. The monument standing behind me, completed in 1914, was dedicated by President Woodrow Wilson, son of a Confederate soldier who nevertheless became governor of New Jersey and later chief executive of the entire nation. Everyone of importance attended the dedicatory ceremonies. No swarm of protesters shouted slogans or waved signs. The president didn't even have to visit Andersonville by way of partial atonement for his sins. And all this during a period when many ex-slaves and veterans of the Grand Army of the Republic were still alive.

Curious, isn't it, how ideological and unforgiving official Washington has become since then. For example, no one until quite recently assumed that

271

the flying of the Confederate battle flag or the playing of "Dixie" had anything to do with slavery. For the past several decades we've been content to amend our lives and to commemorate quietly the heroism and sacrifice of men we never knew, even as bent and wizened figures dressed in faded gray.

So why is it suddenly Standard Operating Procedure to strike our nationless flag and to ban our unpretentious little song? After all, it is not as if in "Dixie" we had claimed that the Lord was on our side, trampling out the grapes of wrath, and that our enemies were marching in the army of the Devil. Our song merely says that we like it back home, even if there's nothing to eat there but buckwheat cakes and Injun batter.

Of course we all know some of the reasons why this startling animosity has surfaced. It's because of a renewed interest in the subject of slavery. But the ultimate cause, I would suggest, is ignorance, an ignorance profound and endemic to the age. No one now remembers the complexities of the world which produced such a tragic conflict as the War Between the States, and as a consequence everyone is free to falsify the past with relative impunity. For only conscience need restrict us, now that people who lived in that world are safely consigned to the earth.

Thus with ideologues writing our textbooks and our history lessons too often taught by the ill-educated and lazy, our citizens (both North and South) don't learn enough historical fact to make responsible judgments concerning the past. Facts are like bones: They give the rest of the body something to hang on. Without our bones we could all be poured into molds as easily as cookie dough, while our frantic eyes floated on the top like raisins. We resist the thought; and so does Clio, the Muse of History, who resents being baked and packaged by an academic establishment that is the intellectual equivalent of the National Biscuit Company.

**AMONG THOSE FACTS WE HAVE FORGOTTEN AS A NATION**, the ones most crucial, are those concerning the origin and practice of slavery in America and the method by which it was finally abolished. Once remembered, these truths—which are complicated and painful—reveal the implausibility of associating these dead or the flag they fought under with an exclusive devotion to slavery.

First, we need to recall how slavery was first brought to these shores and who initially profited from it. New Englanders—and particularly those from Massachusetts—were the first "Americans" who made huge sums of money through slave trading. In fact, in the year the U.S. Constitution was adopted, the chief slave-trading states were Rhode Island, New York, and Pennsylvania.

Southerners were among those who, at the Constitutional Convention, supported a clause abolishing the slave trade; but delegates from Massachusetts, Connecticut, New York, and Pennsylvania were likewise among those who successfully lobbied to extend the trade for another 20 years after ratification.

Yet as late as 1858 a New York ship landed over 400 illegal slaves on the coast of Georgia, and in 1861 Abraham Lincoln was forced to admit to Congress that "five vessels, being fitted for the slave trade, have been seized and condemned." He was talking about Northern ships.

Even after the slave trade the complexity does not end; for the Great Secret, which many historians have kept as well as Rumpelstiltskin kept the secret of his name, is the degree to which the "peculiar institution" was not peculiar to the South. In point of fact, all of the Northern colonies practiced slavery at one time or another, and several of them entered the Union as slaveholding states. John Hancock, who so ostentatiously signed the Declaration of Independence with its affirmation of equality, was often seen in the streets of Boston with four liveried slaves in front of his coach and four behind, trumpets blowing to signal the master's arrivals and departures.

And Benjamin Franklin, who represented Pennsylvania at the Constitutional Convention, was attended in his declining years by a slave boy named Bob, bought with Franklin's money, but technically owned by his son-in-law so that Poor Richard might continue to enjoy the political support of Philadelphia Quakers. Of the remaining delegates from Pennsylvania virtually half owned slaves, including the distinguished James Wilson. Indeed the delegations of other Northern states also contained slaveholders, and apparently most looked with favor or equanimity on the institution.

Seventy-five years later, after secession, five Union states still permitted legalized slavery; and in others, blacks born under slavery were still held in bondage for life. These slaves were not freed until the passage of the 13th Amendment, some time after the slaves in the South had been emancipated by executive fiat. Thus American slavery began and ended in the North.

But what of the Confederate soldiers, whose decency and political propriety are now being called into question? Their leader, Robert E. Lee, voluntarily freed the slaves under his control, saying that the institution was a moral and political evil. He looked forward to a time when, in his words, "the mild and melting influence of Christianity" would eliminate the problem.

By contrast, U.S. Grant was content to keep the slaves under his control until forced by law to surrender them. And his Commander in Chief, Abraham Lincoln—later to be called the Great Emancipator—helped to settle his father-in-law's estate by selling the Todd slaves down the river.

Of course the idea that the North was fighting primarily to abolish slavery came after almost two years of bone-shattering, blood-spilling conflict, upon the issuance of the Emancipation Proclamation. Only two years earlier Lincoln had written: "Do the people of the South really entertain fears that a Republican administration would, directly or indirectly, interfere with their slaves? If they do, I wish to assure you that there is no cause for such fears." And later, in his First Inaugural Address, he said: "I declare that I have no intention, directly or indirectly, to interfere with slavery in the states where it exists." Still later he would repeat the sentiment, saying that if he could perpetuate the Union by perpetuating slavery he would do so.

Why, then, the Emancipation Proclamation? The matter will be debated until the archangel Gabriel declares the question moot, though Lincoln himself said he deemed it "a fit measure for suppressing said rebellion," suggesting that his motives were strategic. But one thing is certain: the proclamation itself did not say or do what most Americans think.

In the first place, it did not free *all* the slaves—not those in the five slave-holding Union states, and not even all the slaves in those states that seceded. Indeed, so morally ambiguous is the document that under certain conditions no slaves would have been freed by it.

What the Emancipation Proclamation said was essentially this: that no Union slaves were affected; that slaves were freed only in those states which had seceded; that certain parishes and counties in Louisiana and Virginia, those held by Northern forces, were excepted from the terms; and that if the seceding states returned to the Union before a certain date, they would be allowed to keep their slaves.

The irony of Lincoln's move was not lost on Lord Palmerston, Queen Victoria's highly civilized prime minister, who pointed out that Lincoln undertook to abolish slavery where he was without power to do so, while protecting it where he had power to destroy it.

I HAVE RECALLED THESE FACTS neither to reassign our substantial guilt to others nor to suggest that, like characters in a comedy, we are all miraculously innocent in the end. Southerners, to be sure, have sinned deeply— and one thing we have always believed in is the reality of sin. In our better moments we dwell on our own transgressions and leave those of others to the disposition of a Higher Authority. In general we have no illusions about the state of our sorry souls; and for this reason it is unlikely that we will ever start a Society for the Prevention of Cruelty to Southerners.

But it doesn't hurt to remind others as well that history is not a "closet drama" exposing the mass appetites of greedy capitalists and sacrificial proletarians, of noble Yankees and depraved Rebels. History is, instead, an account of men and women with names and faces, people at least as complicated as we know ourselves to be, and—in some ages—perhaps even more so. We need to ask ourselves not only *what* these dead were but *who* they were and, to many of us, still are. And it helps to come to places like this, to read names, to ask ourselves questions, and to imagine answers.

We move among these graves in an admiration that is only slightly diminished by the years, asking ourselves what made them willing to fling away their lives in a moment's exchange or sudden skirmish. We go home, take down the books, and study photographs to determine if these men, dead more than a century now, look anything like the boys we see leaning out of car windows or playing frantic guitars, their hair dyed purple. But while there's a superficial resemblance, there's something missing in this latest bunch—a set of the jaw, a glint of the eye.

One of the Confederate soldiers in the book looks like a movie idol— blond, blue-eyed, a square jaw and a straight nose. Called the "Gallant Pelham" by those who wrote of him, he was a member of the horse artillery, and when the two armies were locked in a stalemate, exacting heavy casualties, or when the Union forces were getting the better of the exchange, he would charge out along between the lines completely exposed, dragging his Parrott gun behind him—and while shells burst all around him, he would direct his cannon at the enemy and turn the tide of battle.

No one could believe it when he survived the first such encounter, and he did it again and again, cited for valor almost every time he went into battle. Then one day, when the nearby infantry was beginning to falter, and with nothing better to do, he grabbed a horse, and with sword extended he rode at the head of the rallying line. The last thing he saw was the dark, round eye of a cannon.

Some of the photographs of soldiers were taken on the field after bloody conflict. One shows five Confederate soldiers sprawled on both sides of a rail fence, lying in a newly mown field. At first glance they appear to be resting after a long morning of work. But the more you look at them the more you realize that no one could possibly rest propped at such angles, their legs splayed like the legs of broken dolls.

Many of the boys in such photographs are unbearably young, little more than children. Yet most of them went to war willingly, certain of their duty. Toward the end, when Lee's army was all but defeated, the general was stopped by a small, frail private who asked him wistfully if the men would have to go back into battle soon, having just sustained heavy casualties. Lee looked at the boy for a long moment and then replied in an even voice that, yes, they would indeed have to move to the front again—and immediately. Then the general turned to his duties, and the private prepared to carry out his commander's orders. The soldier was Lee's own son Robert. He was barely 17.

Given names, faces, histories like these, it is difficult to say they were no more than arrogant defenders of a cruel economic system.

Of course, those who have rewritten the past to deprive these dead of their reputation have done so according to a kind of rigorous moral impulsion that is not itself malicious. Yet such historians are too close to the issues of their own day to measure the worth of those who lived in another time with another view of such imperatives as courage and duty and honor. To understand these older virtues—which have fallen into disuse—one must take a long view of history and see these Confederate soldiers in their proper setting, among their true comrades.

LET ME SUGGEST to those who denigrate the past that they fly over this national cemetery, as I have recently done, and see the enormous spectacle of these dead—*all of them*—those who fell on the Fields of Flanders and at the Argonne Forest, on Anzio Beach and the top of Pork Chop Hill, and in the jungles of Southeast Asia—as well as at First Manassas, Shiloh, Chancellorsville, Spotsylvania, Franklin, and Petersburg.

From a great height this place looks like a gigantic green scroll covered in precise calligraphy with thousands and thousands of white, oblong words—or, rather, with one word written in perfect symmetry thousands and thousands of times. Whatever that cryptic word is, it is equally the name for all who are buried here—North, South, East, West—all who wait patiently, silently with one another, eternal brothers freed forever from the indignity of politics and the impurity of time.

# Her Name Was Lady: A Story

**H**ER NAME WAS LADY, and she was an old, old woman when I was a boy. She had been born a slave and remembered the day federal officers rode into the quarters where she lived and read the Emancipation Proclamation. She recalled standing there, her mother holding her hand tightly, while the "Yankee boss" read the words to the assembled crowd of blacks and whites.

"I wasn't stud'in' freedom," she said. After the officers rode out and left them all to fend for themselves, she continued to work for the McCain family, just as her parents and grandparents had done, doing the same housework, living about the same kind of life. This was in Virginia before the turn of the century.

I must have been about ten years old when she told me the story. My nurse, whose name was Belle, had come by to pay her respects to Lady and sing duets with her—"sad Jesus songs," as I called them.

"Tell P.J. about when you saw him."

"I mos' forgot it all." "Tell him," Belle insisted. "Who did you see?" I asked. "I saw Robert E. Lee," she said. Now that interested me! I had already read a life of Lee, a tattered book my father had owned when he was a boy, so I knew he was a formidable figure. I also knew he had been a saint as well as a great warrior. The book also said he had freed his slaves long before the War.

"What did he look like?" I said. "Did he have a white beard?"

"He looked just like he do in pictures," she said. "He looked fine."

"Where did you see him?" I asked, a skeptic even at the age of ten. I knew all about Santa Claus. She said she had seen Lee in Richmond, riding down the street on his "dandy" horse, while all the people stood on the sidewalk and waved.

"He holt the reins like this," she said, making a fist of her knotty old hands, "and he kicked the horse's sides with his spurs, and that horse he rare back on his legs, and he paw the air. And the Gin'ral, he take off his hat, and he wave it. He wave it to the young ladies, and then he wave it to me."

"Did he say anything?" I said. "Did he speak to you?"

"Oh, yes. He stop his horse in front of me, and he smile, and he say 'Hello Lady.'"

"That's how I got my name," she said. "Mama called me Nanalee, but after the Gin'ral called me 'Lady,' so did my Mama and my Daddy and my

277

sisters and my brother and all the rest."

That night I told the story to my father, who, for a change, seemed interested in what I had to say. That weekend we drove over to the McCain's house, and the whole family had our picture taken with Lady. She must have been forewarned, because when we got there, she had on a gray dress and a black straw hat that perched on top of her head like a bird's nest.

A few days ago, while going through a box of photographs, I found that snapshot, taken in 1956. I'm the only one left now. My father dropped dead of a stroke a few years later, and my mother died of cancer in her late 60's. Buz McCain was killed in an automobile accident when he was 80, and his wife, always frail, died a year later. As a matter of fact, all of my parents' friends are dead now, with one exception, a doctor who at 92 still practices a little medicine.

AS FOR ME, I'M GETTING OLD TOO. I have only 20 teeth left, and I can barely see my own face in the mirror. Lately I find myself remembering things that happened 50 years ago and forgetting where I went and what I did yesterday. They say it happens to everybody, a trick time plays to ease us out of this world.

Yet when I look at that photograph, I can't help thinking how young we are as a people. Robert E. Lee's father was a Revolutionary general, and I knew a slave who talked with Marse Robert himself, was even named by him. And as late as 1956 we still had that sense of continuity—black and white, old and young, seated together under an oak tree to commemorate the figure of General Lee, cutting a caper with his horse, even as the shadows gathered around him.

Today—when the forces of change are rewriting history to justify the Second American Revolution, the one that will separate and destroy us as a people—I can look at that picture and remember that Southerners (most Southerners) once understood each other and shared the same vision of the past. And as I search those long-dead faces, I find it hard to forgive the New Breed of Americans—Yankee and Southern alike—who, out of envy and intellectual hatred, have lied about our region and set race against race, generation against generation.

# About the Author

THOMAS HILDITCH LANDESS was born in 1931 in Sarasota, Florida. He finished high school at Deerfield Academy, and upon graduating from Vanderbilt University four years later, he enlisted in the Army, returning to Vanderbilt for graduate work after his time in the service. He completed a master's degree and most of the doctorate before deciding that he should "try out" teaching, which he first did at Converse College in South Carolina. Years later, his experiment successful, he completed his Ph.D. in two summers at the University of South Carolina while serving as academic dean at the University of Dallas, where he continued to teach for some time before retiring. After an interlude of several years of living at the beach in South Carolina, writing and speaking in several states and on numerous occasions, Tom was appointed to the U.S. Department of Education by President Reagan. Ten years and a dramatic change in the nature of the administration in Washington prompted Tom's return to South Carolina, where he lived and worked until his death in early 2012. He was married for over 50 years and predeceased his wife, three children, and a grandson.

www.ingramcontent.com/pod-product-compliance
Lightning Source LLC
Chambersburg PA
CBHW030410100426
42812CB00028B/2897/J